KV-628-122

DISPOSED OF
BY LIBRARY
HOUSE OF LORDS

# LONDON DISPOSSESSED

# London Dispossessed

## Literature and Social Space in the Early Modern City

John Twyning

First published in Great Britain 1998 by
**MACMILLAN PRESS LTD**
Houndmills, Basingstoke, Hampshire RG21 6XS and London
Companies and representatives throughout the world

This book is published in Macmillan's *Language, Discourse,
Society* series
Editors: Stephen Heath, Colin MacCabe and Denise Riley

A catalogue record for this book is available from the British Library.

ISBN 0–333–62270–7

 First published in the United States of America 1998 by
**ST. MARTIN'S PRESS, INC.,**
Scholarly and Reference Division,
175 Fifth Avenue, New York, N.Y. 10010

ISBN 0–312–17652–X

Library of Congress Cataloging-in-Publication Data
Twyning, John, 1952–
London dispossessed : literature and social space in the early
modern city / John Twyning.
p. cm.
Includes bibliographical references (p.      ) and index.
ISBN 0–312–17652–X
1. English literature—Early modern, 1500–1700—History and
criticism.   2. Literature and society—England—London–
–History—17th century.   3. English literature—England—London–
–History and criticism.   4. Dekker, Thomas, ca. 1572–1632–
–Knowledge—England—London.   5. City and town life in literature.
6. Cities and towns in literature.   7. London (England)—In
literature.   I. Title.
PR8476.T95  1997
820.9'32421—dc21                                          97–18288
                                                                CIP

© John Twyning 1998

All rights reserved. No reproduction, copy or transmission of this publication may be made
without written permission.

No paragraph of this publication may be reproduced, copied or transmitted save with
written permission or in accordance with the provisions of the Copyright, Designs and
Patents Act 1988, or under the terms of any licence permitting limited copying issued by
the Copyright Licensing Agency, 90 Tottenham Court Road, London W1P 9HE.

Any person who does any unauthorised act in relation to this publication may be liable to
criminal prosecution and civil claims for damages.

The author has asserted his right to be identified as the author of this work in accordance
with the Copyright, Designs and Patents Act 1988.

This book is printed on paper suitable for recycling and made from fully managed and
sustained forest sources.

10   9   8   7   6   5   4   3   2   1
07   06   05   04   03   02   01   00   99   98

Printed and bound in Great Britain by Antony Rowe Ltd, Chippenham, Wiltshire

For my mother and the memory of my father

# Contents

# Acknowledgements

I am indebted to Peter Womack, for his wonderful sense of play, Sarah Beckwith, for her intelligence and inspiration, Joad Raymond, for his friendship and acumen, and to Colin MacCabe, who is a gentleman. My gratitude goes to Curt Breight, who generously offered his insights into Elizabethan military matters which have enriched this project. Thanks, too, to Lynn Harper, who read the entire manuscript and provided many comments and suggestions; and to Charmian Hearne and Keith Povey, both working for Macmillan. My thanks also go to Roger Sales and Kate McLuskie, who gave me invaluable help both within and without their institutional roles. Special thanks are due to Eric Clarke and Jim Seitz. Looking back, there seems to have been many chilly hours and minutes of uncertainty in the writing of this book so I would like to thank and acknowledge those with whom I have conversed and communed: Trevor Wadlow, Andrew West, Laura Scott, Tony Gash, Tim Marshall, Norma Campbell, Janet Harnden, Ian Archer, Annabel Patterson, John Waters, Maura Nolan, Ethan Knapp, Patricia Naylor, Thomas Ferraro, Carolyn Steedman, Annette Seitz, Valerie Krips, Nancy Atkinson, Nick Coles, Genelle Gertz-Robinson, Andrew Wood, Elayne Tobin, Mark Douglas, and Peggy Knapp. For giving me succour and encouragement, I thank my siblings Frank, Mark, Jane, Tom, and Laura. Finally, 'according to my bond', I owe a special debt to Nikki Twyning.

JOHN TWYNING

# Abbreviations

Bowers    *The Dramatic Works of Thomas Dekker*, ed. Fredson Bowers, 4 vols (Cambridge, 1953–61).

Bullen    *The Works of Thomas Middleton*, ed. A. H. Bullen, 8 vols (London, 1885–6).

Grosart    *The Non-Dramatic Works of Thomas Dekker*, ed. A. B. Grosart, 5 vols (London, 1885, reissued New York, 1963).

Hall    Thomas Hall, *The Loathsomnesse of Long Haire: or A Treatise Wherein you have the Question stated, many Arguments against it produc'd, and most materiall Arguments for it repelled and answer'd, with the concurrent judgement of Divines both old and new against it* (London, 1653).

Pendry    *Thomas Dekker, Selected Writings*, ed. E. D. Pendry, The Stratford-Upon-Avon Library no. 4 (London, 1967).

**Robbins**    Thomas Dekker, ***A Knight's Conjuring 1607; A Critical Edition***, **ed. Larry M. Robbins (The Hague, 1974).**

Wilson    *The Plague Pamphlets of Thomas Dekker*, ed. F. P. Wilson (Oxford, 1925).

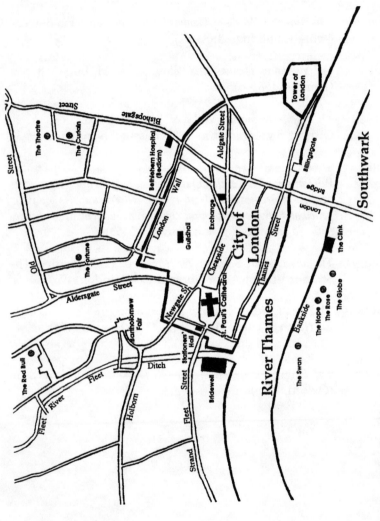

*Source:* Ian Archer, *The Pursuit of Stability.*

# Introduction: 'Our Scene is London'

> Our scene is London, 'cause we would make it known,
> No country's mirth is better than our own.
> No clime breeds better matter, for your whore,
> Bawd, squire, imposter, many persons more,
> Whose manners, now called humours, feed the stage...[1]

By 1600 London's population was 200 000, more than double what it had been a century earlier. It nearly doubled again in the first half of the seventeenth century.[2] This was an extraordinary rate of growth, and was due to many factors. According to Beier and Finlay:

> London's massive growth in the sixteenth and seventeenth centuries took place mainly because of two developments which encouraged migration: first, the centralization in London of the nation's political and economic life ... and secondly, upheavals in the provincial economies, including ... agrarian changes and urban crises... .[3]

When the Crown and its Court took up permanent residence at Westminster it contributed greatly to the metropolitanization of London. There was a 'huge increase in legal business' in the sixteenth and seventeenth centuries which, along with parliamentary meetings, and the vastly expanded land market, brought large numbers of the aristocracy to London; 'a minimum of 750 upper-class young men were coming each year to be apprenticed and to frequent the Inns of Court'.[4] But not everyone who arrived in early modern London was so well-heeled, yet 'almost everyone was a migrant'.[5] Some were foreign, or 'alien', workers (Flemish, Irish, French Huguenots, and so on) who, like many home-grown 'prentices, were seeking better rates for their labour; some came hopefully, with few shillings, not just to visit the queen but to make their fortune; a number were demobbed servicemen (soldiers and sailors from the state's excursions abroad); but the vast majority were ordinary workers turfed off the land by Acts of Enclosure and unscrupulous landlords. My point here is that the vast majority of

1

those who made London were in some way dispossessed from
their livelihood and/or their family, but always from the society
and culture which had provided them with their identity. But the
milieu in which they were to find new lives and identities was far
from stable and, as we shall see, their arrival created the very
dynamic conditions of that instability. All these demographic
factors, and their multi-faceted effects, had an enormous impact on
making London and underpin almost everything in this book.

In Henry VIII's day, if you had the means, the easiest way to get
from the City of London to Westminster was by boat along the
river Thames. By the Elizabethan period, the Strand was becoming
a much more viable highway. Many fancy houses sprang up along
this thoroughfare, marking the incursions which the aristocracy
were making upon London's geographic and social landscape.
Nearing the city's western Liberties, the Strand took you to the Inns
of Court adjacent to Fleet Street, named after the Fleet River which
ran into the Thames at this point. At the boggy mouth of the Fleet
was one of the sprawling shanty towns in which many of London's
less fortunate immigrants had to live. The smell of urban poverty
must have wafted up the nose of many a lawyer at this time. Still, a
quick step through Ludgate and you were in the City of London
proper, and right in front of you was its famous landmark, that
which could be seen for miles around, St Paul's Cathedral. By the
early seventeenth century, the ever-growing links and tensions
between Court and City had become embedded in urban topography, and the new city types, like the gallant, the 'prentice, the
vagrant, occupied London's new and intermediate spaces.[6] From
the bookstalls around St Paul's, via Bridewell (once the Savoy
Palace, now a place of punishment), to the fashion shops in
Piccadilly, the latest places appeared to characterize life in early
modern London. Highways into London (and all roads, it seems,
led to London) brought large numbers every day; those evicted or
impoverished seeking employment; those seeking office and political connections at Court, in law or administration; and those
seeking entertainment or a new life and place in the city. But the
growth and significance of London was more than the tale of two
cities (City and Westminster) and the space in between. Located at
the southern threshold of London Bridge was Southwark, a place
which gathered many of those who came, willingly or otherwise,
from Kent, Surrey, and Sussex. Southwark boasted the oldest and
newest attractions of the city; its theatres and the brothels.

Logistically hard to reach by the various institutions of control
(law, civic administration, and government), such places often fell
beyond the grasp if not the reach of Court and City, and the attempts by both to close them down met with limited success. The
people of Southwark have always, it seems, been fond of taking
Liberties. In early modern London, Bankside, the south side, was
synonymous with both strumpet and stage. Such juxtapositions of
old and new tend to link and spatialize traditional and modern cultural forms, and thus serve as a synecdoche for that which made
the metropolis and that which changed it. And in that making and
changing London played host to a wide range of dispossessions.

By the early seventeenth century London had not only 'outgrown
its traditional guild structures' but also outstripped or over-stressed
nearly all its institutional, customary, legal, and administrative
practices.[7] Because of this it was at once in a state of flux and in the
continuous process of reinventing itself. No one can deny that this
new space, this *Troynovant*, created the opportunity, energy, and resources, for some to improve their lot, to 'make it' one way or
another. On its way to the political and cultural dominance of
English and British life, London has been framed by the idea that
expansion, development, and success go hand in hand. But in this
excursion I seek to explore the casualties of growth and change, to
chart the limits and failures of the policies which attempted to
harness, contain, or direct the bandwagon of growth.

If nothing else, a city is a monument to the accumulation of cultural resources; it is a place where society takes stock. As a principle of social organization the poverty–wealth axis is, arguably, the
most basic form of dispossession; and one which is all too easily
naturalized. Yet all real reform eventually has to address and
redress this principle. In the city, because of their proximity,
poverty and wealth exist with a particular poignancy; cheek-by-
jowl they operate through an antagonistic dependence upon each
other. In essence, politics is about the organization, definition, and
distribution of society's resources in relation to its people. Most
policies, then, through a combination of coercion and consent seek
to gloss or enforce, and/or naturalize the predominant way in
which society creates its wealth and the forms of exploitation which
accompany it. Usually the class which controls the major economic
resources gets to define the culture which it dominates through
legal, social and moral categories. In this respect early modern
London became an arena where such cultural conflict was played

out with considerable intensity. Between 1500 and 1700, the dates which Beier and Finlay use to bracket 'the making of the metropolis', London changed from being the place where the ambitions of the Tudor and Stuart Court took root, flourished, and fell, from being a city dominated by the post-feudal policies of an absolutist monarchy, into the great pioneering flagship of capitalistic enterprise and the heart of the empire. It was a revolutionary act of dispossession. When Charles I abandoned London in January 1642 his political dethronement began; only to be completed when the new owners dragged him back there to be executed seven years later. Much was, and still is, at stake in the tenure of London.

While the forces which shape this grand narrative of London's expropriation – endlessly celebrated in the Whig (and Protestant) accounts of history – provide the larger highways in this book, my excursion into the city, midway between 1500 and 1700, is a much more local venture. 'Maybe its because I'm a Londoner' that I wanted a view of London which corresponded to the way in which people experienced and understood life in the city. Yet, at the same time, I wanted to remain sensitive to the larger forces which shape the lives of those who cannot always see them. No city-dweller can inhabit the whole city even though the impact of that whole may be felt by her or him. In a sense, to live in a city is to occupy a locale (social, topographical, imaginary) which is distinct from, yet integrated with, all the other locales which make it up. An overview of London, as if seen from a historical balloon, would be no more complete than a view from the street. Such a perspective would render people into mere landscape, render experience into structural abstractions; and this, too, would be an act of dispossession. What I offer, then, is a highly partial and local view, but because of its special focus it is able to provide insights into the shape of London as a whole. This perspective depends upon charting the ways in which those in London inhabited the city and the way in which the city inhabited them. For Jonathan Raban, the city performs a special function in this regard;

> The city ...[can] effectively break down many of the conventional distinctions between dream life and real life; the city inside the head can be transformed, with the aid of the technology of style, into the city on the streets ... The city as a form is uniquely prone to erode that boundary between the province of the imagination and the province of fact.[8]

Including drama, much of the writing in early modern London appeared to aid and abet that erosion. London, as place and ethos, necessarily and continuously kept inventing and reinventing itself, and the demand for literature kept pace with the city's expansion and development. By the end of the sixteenth century hundreds of booksellers could be found in the streets, byways, and alleys around St Paul's Cathedral. All kinds of literature, popular and elite, was bought and sold there; pamphlets for entertainment, edification, and explanation, many of them articulating the strains and excitement of the new urban milieu. Quintessentially operating in the space 'between dream life and real life' stood the theatre – an institution which grew and flourished during the stand-off between Court and City. For those migrants who crossed the city's threshold, and passed the great playhouses as they did so, all London must have seemed a stage, though not always one full of boundless opportunities. Roles in the city, especially if you were poor, might be just as circumscribed and tragic as those on the stage. In his excellent study of *The Market and the Theater in Anglo-American Thought*, Jean-Christophe Agnew explores the way in which players on the stage, 'artificial persons', agitated and expressed the impact London's commercial ethos and trading practices had on the people who lived there.[9] Accordingly, 'the new drama showed, as no other genre could, how precarious social identity was, how vulnerable to unexpected disruptions and disclosure it was, and therefore how deeply theatrical it was.'[10] It was the protean quality of both market and theatre, as Agnew argues, which deeply distressed many of the city's Puritans because they upset the relationship between representation and that which is represented; what you see is never quite what you get. A fundamental principle of theatre is that a character on the stage, the dramatis persona, is not and cannot be precisely that which s/he is supposed to denote.[11] A good deal of Puritan energy went into the impossible attempt to obliterate that gap, to make themselves and others into 'solid' citizens. For all that, many of those who had arrived in London already knew about the precariousness of social identity, often, ironically enough, through bitter experience. In effect, they had already traded places. Whatever the state of the feudal nexus in rural England in the sixteenth and seventeenth centuries, agrarian life structured identity in very different ways from that in the city. In the countryside a person's identity is much more compounded by external factors such as place, custom, occupation, family, and, of course, class. While I recognize the constraints and effects of the cash nexus, city life seems more atomistic and allows for a certain anonymity. In the city it is both more possible and necessary to function through your appearence. Not surprisingly trust and doubt are two major themes which receive enormous attention in this period. Forced migration from country to city, where the complexion of identity is much different, was a trauma for each and every person, as well as for the culture as a whole. Small wonder, then, that so much Elizabethan and Jacobean drama is concerned with a change, or decline, in the old way of doing things, along with a concern for what will replace them. Most Londoners had to find new ways to pay their debts, both old and new; and in so doing they often had to become very different people.

Literature and the city are radically dissimilar forms, and the dificulties of writing about the connections between the two was something I ran into many times during the writing of this book. Despite all kinds of strategies, writing remains tenaciously linear and sequential whereas the city never ceases to function upon a number of intersecting spatial planes, streets, and places. Like most people coming to a city, I had to find my way around, I needed a route and a guide. It is for these reasons, as much as those given above, that I have set out this particular path. As he often claimed in his literature, Thomas Dekker will be our 'guide' to London; though by no means exclusively. Although Dekker's writing forms the immediate point of access to the city, the examination and analysis of what Raban calls the 'urban technology of style' as it applies to early modern London largely organizes my book. I hope to show how literature enacted the connection between the rhetoric of place through the materiality of the imagination, and how it became a medium for understanding the city. Dekker's early drama (pre-1600) was imbued with a sense of post-feudal romanticism and nostalgia somewhere outside the city; at least, in the imagination. *Old Fortunatas* (1599), for example, is a story about a beggar who, upon an encounter with Fortune, chooses wealth instead of wisdom and goes on his travels with a magic purse. Maybe this fantasy appealed to the many who began their journey to the city, often in doubtful financial shape, hoping for something better while still lamenting the past. As the Elizabethan period faded, theatre audiences and pamphlet readers changed their taste. Now, the scene was London: and from the late 1590s onwards, writers increasingly dramatized the stresses of metropolitan life and its new cast of characters, including prostitutes, pimps, huxters, cheaters, gamesters, gulls, gallants, rogues, and the city itself.

In many respects Dekker was the quintessential urban writer of his period. He worked in all the city's primary genres: city-drama, plague pamphlets, jest books, pageants, satires, underworld writing and canting literature.[12] His topicality and vivid urban description in all these genres, his 'slices of metropolitan life', have made him beloved of historians and yet denigrated by literary critics. Yet it is the troubled relationship between these disciplines which has impeded our access to the value of Dekker's writing. For the more he is perceived as 'Un Peintre De La Vie Londonienne', as a colourful chronicler of the city, then the more he becomes simply a transparent observer separated from the very stuff of his writing through the categories of realism, empiricism, or 'vraisemblance'.[13] Undoubtedly he was an acute observer of the city, but it was a way of seeing which performed and required active interpretation. It was as much the work of the brain as of the eye, and it therefore occupied that most fluid province between imagination and fact. Certain urban literature has the ability, as Raymond Williams argues, to work through the 'perceptions of relations between persons and things', which, in turn, is a conscious way of seeing and showing.[14] Thus the 'city is shown as at once social fact and a human landscape', and, according to Williams, 'what is dramatized in it is a very complex structure of feeling.'[15] It is precisely this analysis of urban narrative which fits Dekker like a Jermyn Street glove.

More than most, Thomas Dekker was a collaborative writer: he wrote plays with, Middleton, Jonson, Webster, Massinger, Ford, Rowley, Chettle, Heywood, Wilson, Drayton, Day, Haughton, Hathway, Munday, Smith, Wilkins, and Mynshull.[16] Sometimes, through the office of the impresario Henslowe, he was paired with others to write certain plays. In Massinger's The Virgin Martyr (1620), for example, he was drafted in to write the picaresque scenes, giving the play a bit of (much needed) colour. Later, in 1621, Dekker teamed up with Ford and Rowley on The Witch of Edmonton, a highly topical play, which has, at times, an almost journalistic quality. Based on the execution of Elizabeth Sawyer in a small town ten miles north of London, the play's success probably depended upon its reaching the stage while public interest was at its height. His pamphlets reveal a similar sense of collaboration, even though, technically, he was the sole author. Dekker was deeply impressed by the prose stylistics of Nashe (especially), Harman, and Greene, and he often borrowed heavily from them in his non-dramatic writing. He was, then, a particularly porous, plastic and receptive writer of a kind which embarrasses more modern conceptions of authorship. For this reason I have refrained from attempting to distinguish Dekker's lines from those of, say, Middleton, or anyone else. Apart from the impossibility of such a task, I prefer to accept the unique quality of collaborative dialogue, of creative borrowing, and the dynamics of intertextual action; all of which, I know, are anathema to our laws and understanding of copyright – under which, of course, *this book* operates. I have not tried to give an account of the whole of Dekker's *oeuvre* in the literary critical sense, rather I offer an expedition and tour of the cultural space and place which made him as a writer.

In *The Wonderfull yeare* (1603), for example, Dekker sets up the kind of intricate relationship between the city, writing, imagination, and fact, upon which Williams and Raban have commented:

A stiffe and freezing horror sucks up the rivers of my blood: my haire stands an ende with the panting of my braines: mine eye balls are ready to start out, being beaten with the billowes of my teares: out of my weeping pen does the inck mournefully and more bitterly than gall drop on the palefac'd paper, even when I do but thinke how the bowels of my sicke Country have bene torne, *Apollo* therefore and you bewitching silver-tongued Muses, get you gone, Invocate none of your names: Sorrow & Truth, sit you on each side of me, whilst I am delivered of this deadly burden: prompt me that I may utter ruthfull and passionate condolement: arme my trembling hand, that it may boldly rip up and Anatomize the vicerous body of this *Anthropophagized* plague: lend me Art (without any counterfeit shadowing) to paint and delineate to the life the whole story of this mortall and pestiferous battaile, & you the ghosts of those more (by many) then 40 000. that with the virulent poison of infection have bene driven out of your earthly dwellings: you desolate hand-wringing widowes, that beate your bosomes over your departing husbands: you wofully distracted mothers that with disheveled haire falne into swounds, whilst you lye kissing the insensible cold/lips of your breathlesse Infants: you out-cast and downe-troden Orphanes, that shall many a yeare hence remember more freshly to mourne, when your mourning garments shall look olde and be for gotten; And you the *Genij* of all those emptyed families, whose habitations are now among the *Antipodes*: Ioyne all your hands together, and with your bodies cast a ring about me: let me behold your ghastly vizages, that my paper may receive their true pictures: *Eccho* forth your grones through the hollow truncke of my pen, and raine down your gummy teares into mine incke, that even marble bosomes may be shaken with terrour, and hearts of Adamant melt into compassion. (Grosart, vol. i, pp. 36–7)

For all its length, significantly, this paragraph is a single sentence. Both plague and narrative run on in the city until stopped by death. Meanwhile, the equipment and inspiration of disease and writing commingle through the writer's conceit and metaphors, thereby substantiating the plague. More than just a description of the plague's effects, Dekker's overtly melodramatic language integrates horror and bathos, anguish and pathos, while articulating a genuine sense of fear. Despite claims to the contrary, in the excessive use of figurative language, he strikes a tone of outrageously affected tragedy. It is, after all, a deeply ironic way of seeing. With London savagely hit by plague in that year, Dekker's darkly comic view captures the complex experience many felt every day, and he makes this structure of feeling an integral and indispensable part of the city's human landscape. Although the writer-narrator appears to claim a certain verisimilitude (in mockery he eschews the bewitchment of his Muse in favour of an empirical 'Truth'), the delineations of life and the whole story are at once intensely personal and extraordinarily panoramic. This was Dekker's 'technology of style'. He begins the sentence by writing a particular view of the plague's effects via his own terrified body. Though this seems like a visceral and immediate reaction to the carnage, the writer upsets the script by which he appears as an objective observer. With a sense of literary play, writer and instrument are conjoined: he becomes the 'stiffe' pen, with blood and tears as ink, which will write the horror of the plague. Later he melds the 'ghastly vizages', which he beheld, into a vision of London as a vast and tragic game of 'ring-around-the-roses' with the writer in the middle.[17] Drawing upon an oral folk tradition which encapsulates the trauma of the plague, the writer, as witness and recorder, appears to be ostracized by the very community in which he is ineluctably located. As London's bereft are implored to join hands and dance in a ring around him we realize how integrated the writer is within the city and its dispossessed inhabitants. In this account there is no escaping the plague: no one can exist outside the circle of society. When they 'all fall down' his function as narrator dies with them. Such a particular scene is far from idiosyncratic: people, plague, city, and literature, all merge into a pandemic drama. Though Dekker makes a drama, as well as some money, out of the crisis, his writing fully retains a sense of the calamity which threatens the city and what is at stake in its interpretation. Finally, he makes an impassioned appeal to those who, for moral and political reasons, deem the plague God's punishment for a sinful city. Perhaps, also, the writer was even trying the impossible, a petition to God himself.[18]

Chapter 1 is an excursion into two infamous institutions of the city: Bedlam, the first asylum; and Bridewell, the first workhouse. Our starting point will be two plays written between 1604 and 1605: *The Honest Whore, parts I and II.* The first was a Dekker and Middleton collaboration, though the sequel was written solely by Dekker. Both plays deal with a number of issues concerning social and political disenfranchisement which culminate in their final scenes being set directly inside the institutions. What was at stake in such a staging? By unpacking the cultural and historical forces which shaped those institutions, I explore the way in which the writers meticulously reconstruct a drama of social space as a densely critical theatrical medium. Riven with the ideological struggles between the Court and the City, Bedlam and Bridewell are seen as interstitial sites which display and embody the frustration of conflicting authorities. Located between these political forces, neither play resolves the tension between them. Instead we get a detailed picture of the consequences of such conflict. Both plays allow the dialogue of the institution's inmates to enter into a dynamic relationship with their surroundings, and with various forms of official power. Those incarcerated, those dispossessed of their wits and liberty, not only provide an expression for the real conditions of their existence but enact a discriminating gloss on the play's denouements.

Certain critical trends in the early modern period have tendentiously authorized a crypto-royalist agenda. This happens when the theatre is deemed to re-enact the abstract, totalizing, and circumscriptive function of power, especially royal power. I would argue that such a view is unable to address the *theatrical* texture or social dimensions of metropolitan drama – not least because it was a drama forged through its multi-faceted dependence upon the many locations of power which constituted the city. The theatrical reconstruction of London's infamous institutions, exploited by Dekker and Middleton, deliberately creates a setting for the scrimmage of authority, in all its various forms, including that between the ambitions of the Crown–Court system and a burgeoning civic oligarchy. The ensuing struggle inevitably impinged upon, and recast, those within its scope and in its institutions. Perhaps more than any other example of popular city drama, Dekker and Middleton's *The Honest Whore, part I* is simultaneously an exclamation and critique of the claims of civic power and the ethos of the City. It is here that the writers' ambivalent relationship to the City, and its administration, is most complexly articulated. Both Dekker and Middleton were arguably city-orientated writers, capable of valorizing the city's values while denigrating those of the Court. For all that, their writing is never an expression of the static oppositions of Court and City through which London's literary history has often been told. Though remaining vigilantly suspicious of the Court, they show and express concern about the hegemonizing strategies of the City's government, especially those which involved political dogma and moral coercion. It was this uneasy relationship with the character of the City's governors which, when combined with a flair for the mischievous, led them to cast Bellafront, the eponymous 'whore' of the play, as both central character and elliptical reflector through which the City could perceive itself and its values.

On a more theatrical level, I explore the way in which Dekker and Middleton run the gamut of the social and cultural meanings of 'mad'. As the leitmotiv of *The Honest Whore, part I*, madness symbolized the stress of metropolitan life. Along with its often manic conflict with tameness, or 'patience', madness, as a theatrical trope, encodes infra-class and inter-class antagonism, urban stress, social dislocation and courtly emblems, as well as the genuinely, and somewhat anarchically, insane. Not only are the scenes staged so precisely in Bedlam unique within the canon of English drama, but they encourage us to read out into a metropolitan culture's preoccupation with madness. This strategy is enhanced by the many juxtapositions of madness and their various and different forms of social comprehension, and by the neat dramatic ploy of concluding the play within a madhouse. In seeking to produce a culturally textured account of both parts of *The Honest Whore*, one which weaves together historical narrative, social analysis, and textual/dramatic criticism, it is necessary to avoid certain strictures. One is the sense of elite literary history which disqualifies the work of 'minor' writers while paying lip service to the blandishments of 'cultural criticism'. Another, is turning the city into a text, as if it were an epic poem or even a pamphlet. This is especially important, as I argue for a deep connection between writing and city space. The sense of place must not be erased nor lose its function as inhabited space. Reducing the city into mere rhetoric would dissipate the sense of what Raymond Williams calls 'structures of feeling' or 'structures of experience' which makes dynamic 'meanings and values as they are actively lived and felt'.[19] Too easily, it seems, London disappears into the wholly semiotic, and agency evaporates under the mesmeric glare of displays of power. As artefacts of the developing metropolis, Bedlam and Bridewell's faults bear all the strains and pains of the city's growth. As such, these institutions denied the authorities easy acts of social containment, or recoupment of power, which is why Dekker and Middleton found in them a vital stage for voices of conflict and contention.

Perhaps no other figure characterized the unvarnished principles of trade which lay behind the city's ethos more than the prostitute. Certainly no character on the London stage revealed a more telling image of the changing city to itself than did the so-called 'whore'. In short, and often in literature, prostitution appeared as a synecdoche for the strains of sub/urban development. A key factor in the 'making of the metropolis' was the enormous growth of unofficial and unregulated modes of production which operated in and about the 'Liberties' of London. Chapter 2 explores the full implications and consequences of the *place* and *practice* of prostitution in London. Dekker's extensive writing on prostitution, including *The Honest Whore, part II*, brings into play the means for locating the social and psychic economies in which the prostitute needs to be understood. To provide an adequate critical disposition on prostitution, one which remains sensitive to its complex social implications, I have tried to hold in balance the metaphoric, metonymical, and material aspects of the business, each of which shapes our understanding in different ways. Without attention to that balance such a study could, as often happens, lapse into a prurient empiricism. Worse, perhaps, the material fact of prostitution as a real business might evaporate into a textual ether. Once this happens prostitution is likely to be relegated to the margins of the main cultural story instead of being perceived as developing within it. As usual, prostitution then becomes seen through the eyes of those culturally dominant, of those who deem it a 'problem' for authority rather than a symptom of it.

According to Mary Douglas, 'ideas about separating, purifying, demarcating and punishing transgressions have as their main function to impose system on an inherently untidy experience'.[20] Drawing upon the implications of this broad concept, I explore the way in which topographic delineation of suburb and City came to occupy a range of socially specific class and gender definitions within the sprawling metropolis and the way it was experienced. This does not simply mean structuring an opposition between prostitute and citizen (though that was an important element). More important, I think, is the way in which the strategies of taxonomy came to inhabit the psycho-social make-up of certain men of the City. Much of Dekker's 'plague pamphlets', written during the periods when the theatres were closed, engaged the desire to demarcate and transcribe (hence the effect of *'vraisemblance'*) the 'inherently untidy experience' of metropolitan life. Canting dictionaries, detailing the so-called language of the city's underworld, were among the first books to order words in this way. Such literature of categorization was very popular because it echoed the experience and perception of organizing the city. Robert Darnton argues:

> Exclusion and inclusion belonged to the same process of boundary drawing, a process that took place in men's minds as well as on the streets. But the boundaries acquired their force by being acted out.[21]

By reading Dekker's 'underworld literature' through the patterns of cultural anxieties and psychic fears we gain a greater understanding of what was at stake in the disciplinary and punitive practices aimed at prostitutes in early modern London. The legal and social injunctions directed towards the disenfranchised had profound effects on metropolitan identity. Masculine anxiety about sexual security reached almost epidemic proportions – can you think of a Jacobean play without some reference or allusion to cuckoldry? From jokes about bumps on the forehead to the grand tragedies like *Othello*, no woman, 'in men's minds', could really be deemed 'safe'. Prostitution both exploited, and was exploited by, these anxieties. In much of the literature and drama of this period, prostitutes were put on display, initially for titillation, only to be later viciously satirized.

In summary, literature reveals how the narrative and material dimensions of metropolitan space and the concepts of gender and class are intricately connected. Based on a denizen of London, Mary Frith, Dekker and Middleton's Moll Cutpurse (who is the 'roaring girl' in the play of that title) actually charts the city in a dramatically complex way. Her ability to combine gender ambiguity with the rich tradition of rollicking lower-class energy make her both a charismatic and symbolic figure of London's culture. She exposes the fraudulence of those who call women 'whores', while her role-play opens up the discursive and practical implications of prostitution. Significantly, prostitution became the root metaphor, in Marxist terms, for both the abstraction of commodity, the labour process, and pure exchange value – 'Gold ... thou common whore of mankind'.[22] Prostitution's capacity to encode the raw liquidity of commercial relations enabled it to become a resource for the displacement of all kinds of anxieties associated with trade. This desire for displacement was especially active with certain city-men who saw the need to obscure their relationship with the very modes of production in which they were engaged. Figures like Moll and Jonson's Ursula in *Bartholomew Fair* are fantastic examples of the embodiment of those anxieties; both topographically, in the sense of either the city's underbelly or its suburbs ('outskirts'), and in their ability to incorporate symbolically newly-urban plebeian energy through the dwindling forms of popular folk culture.

In Stephen Greenblatt's seminal study of our period, *Renaissance Self-Fashioning: From More to Shakespeare*, he states that 'great art is an extraordinarily sensitive register of the complex struggles and harmonies of culture'.[23] Who in the academic trade could disagree with that? My concern is with the unwritten elitism which tags that statement. For, as Stallybrass and White demonstrate, the elitism which gave rise to the notion of 'great art', Literature, depended upon the categoric distinction between that category and the popular.[24] This seems ironic given the recent impetus for critics of early modern literature to recontextualize the text. But it is precisely the fact that Dekker's writing cannot, in this sense, be removed from its context which provides the resistance for any adoption of his work into the annals of belletristic refinement. Even his most contemporary popular writing, his drama, is often considered flawed or second-rate when examined through the grid of dramatic rules which came to be applied ever more precisely after Jonson. Moreover, Dekker's scurrilous 'booke-trade' literature remains, for the most part, excluded from the canon which necessarily needs to expunge such works for its own definition. Emerging from my study of prostitution and Dekker is the hypothesis that 'fashioning', a key concept in the acquisition of metropolitan culture, had a particularly harsh connotation for the city's dispossessed. And it is the wider drama of city fashion(ing) which marshals the topic of dress codes and the body politic in Chapter 3. Using Dekker's *The Guls Horne-booke* as a literary and social anchor, I find fashion and its commentaries a vital and 'sensitive register of the various struggles and harmonies' of metropolitan culture. To analyse fashion in this way, I lean on Bakhtin's insight into the bodily economy of representation which depicted the tense struggle between the classical body and the grotesque body. In addition, I enlist the suggestive principles of Stallybrass and White's contention;

that cultural categories of high and low, social and aesthetic ... are never entirely separable ... The high/low opposition in each of our four symbolic domains – psychic forms, the human body, geographical space and social order – is a fundamental basis to mechanisms of ordering and sense-making in European cultures.[25]

The topographies of body and city are mutually interactive via the categories of high and low. Many of the city fashions, the ruff, the doublet, the peascod belly, and so on, can be read through mechanisms of ordering social and bodily relations. My point of departure from Stallybrass and White can be found in the constraints of the structuring a high–low dichotomy, which, in terms of early modern London, cannot account for the stylistic rivalry for the category 'high' within the competition of defining the ruling classes: the most striking example of this being manifest in the fashion aesthetics of 'roundhead' and 'cavalier', styles already becoming polarized in Dekker's time. As the seventeenth century wore on, these antagonistic styles provided the outfits for one of the bloodiest fashion shows in English history.

Socio-economic tensions, class contention, individual ambition and competition, can all be encoded within the language of fashion. If fashion was the urban language *par excellence*, then St Paul's, the city's unofficial centre of cultural exchange, was the supreme place for proclamation and argument. It was here that the newly fashioned came to be made. Seeking urbanity and social tenure were the gulls and gallants who strutted their hour between the columns, while all around them, seeking a more mundane living, were the 'russet-coated' vagrants and huxters who were also fashioning a different, but no less characteristic, form of urban identity. Writing about this same place, 'Paul's Walk', the heart of the publishing trade in London (or England for that matter), came the professional writer, men like Thomas Dekker, who, like those he lampooned, was also attempting to re-fashion himself within the city.

Dekker has been described inaccurately as a 'puritan playwright'.[26] Yet Gasper's more recent epithets 'religious-political' and 'militant Protestant', are considerably more valuable.[27] This stress on Dekker's place in the Protestant tradition seems both timely and appropriate considering past assumptions. According to George R. Price:

> [Dekker] gave to religion a lifelong reverence and loyalty. Neither his plays nor his tracts give any evidence of a mind troubled about doctrinal points, about Catholicism's claim to authority, or about the inroads of scientific and philosophical skepticism on dogma.[28]

It's not just that this is wrong, but how could it be written by Dekker's literary biographer? How can this view be squared with critics like Gasper? Was there something/anything about Dekker's writing which gave the appearence of being so untroubled? Perhaps the English protestant tradition, in which Dekker is firmly located, is continually trying to iron out its history? Chapter 4 provides an extensive excursion into not just the realm of the troubled mind but also into Dekker's tense religious world. The topographization of Hell through the tropes and rhetoric of the city provided Dekker, and other writers, with the means to comprehend the role, function, and practice of writing in metropolitan society. It was both a serious and irreverent business, with literary and physical survival at stake. If religion, as Terry Eagleton says, 'is probably the most purely ideological of the various institutions of civil society', then Hell, in the early seventeenth century, yielded itself as the most brilliantly refined form of imaginative terror.[29] The subjection induced by this terrorization, and its effects in writing, is unflaggingly explored in a recent book by John Stachniewski; whose project, in part, is to counterbalance the view which finds that 'the brighter side of protestantism has attracted a disproportionate attention' (a view evidently registered in Price's blandishments above).[30] But while this corrective is valuable, and pertinent to our understanding the forces which shaped Dekker's writing, it sometimes appears to bear the kind of strategic closed-circuitry with which post-Foucaultian criticism of early modern texts has become all too familiar. In my view

Dekker's literature is a complex engagement with the 'mind forg'd manacles' of Calvinistic theology, Puritan morality, and the social strait-jacketing which such totalizing world views tend to demand. Even without focusing on topics such as Hell, any discussion of early modern London or Dekker requires an engagement with the elusive terms 'Puritan' and 'Puritanism'. To define either term adequately would necessitate another study; and that, to be sure, would have to settle for an expansive rather than a precise meaning. However, the attempt should not be abandoned, even if difficulties are confronted. With these partialities recognized, my comprehension and use of Puritanism is guided by Douglas's formulation which explains the impulse to thematize 'untidy experience' through ideas of purification. Furthermore, I once again invoke Williams' concept of 'structures of feeling' as a way towards grasping the relationship between mind and world. In spite and because of this relationship, Puritans both needed and were suspicious of the imagination. Although I recognize Christopher Hill's spectrum of those who constituted the Puritans as 'those who wanted reform from within the Church' to 'any opponents of the policies pursued by hierarchy and Court', my use of 'Puritan' is broadly social.[31] Hill clearly relates that the 'word had no narrowly religious connotation'.[32] In this spirit, then, and leaving aside the specific question as to who was and was not a Puritan, Puritanism can be viewed as a 'structure of feeling', tied to and produced by the politics of the period, whose practice was to organize an internal sense of purity, either individually through the 'master principle discipline' *or as a group within a group* or society (significantly Puritans were not, strictly speaking, separatists).[33] At the 'heart of Puritan experience' was 'an extremely exalted view of ... unity', motivated by the drive for purity within.[34] As Collinson says, 'the Puritans were those whose lives were strung between the contrary principles of inclusion and exclusion.'[35] This paradox produced structures of violent disruption and containment at a multiplicity of levels: social, theological, institutional. It also underscored certain psychopathic behaviour, manifest in Puritanism's principle creative force, the vigilant inquisition and hunting down of every thought and deed which might sully it.[36] With savage perspicacity, John Manningham indicated that, 'A puritaine is such a one as loves God with all his soule, but hates his neighbour with all his heart' (1602).[37] Such a formulation powered both the positive energy of Puritanism, what history has kindly called 'social reform', as well as the excessive, even cruel, disciplinary apparatus which still inhabits us. If we expand Collinson's notion that 'Puritanism has to do with process, not state', and that process was connected to a pattern of psychic and social behaviour, then his concept of 'The Puritan Character' is best seen as one who embodies characteristics of Puritanism.[38] For it is a simple social truth that a Puritan can never be completely unsullied, merely one in the attempted process of purification. Thus 'Puritan' is always an ascribed rather than assumed name. Hill makes this clear: it was a 'political nickname', and a general term of abuse directed at others.[39] It follows from what I have been saying that to call someone a Puritan is an act which contains within it the very principles of Puritanism that it is attempting to attribute to others. Being over-precise, or excessively vigilant, about defining a Puritan would leave oneself open to the same charge. Everyone, including those who attempted an official definition, can in some sense point to a Puritan but rarely does anyone admit to being one. This is why Dekker's writing can be said to contain Puritan tendencies, while he is not a Puritan.

Hell, of course, was the ultimate crucible of purification, and much was at stake in its definition. Because Hell was the focus of so many cultural forces, its reflection in the city enabled an eccentric and viable critique and elaboration of both. This necessarily had to be oblique because of political and Church injunctions against any direct meddling with religious affairs by secular writers. In the Hell of their writing, writers like Dekker and Nashe found enormous scope for giving vent to social anger and frustration. Although Dekker is often caricatured as a writer offering a mutedly harmonious view of the world, he found in the discordant images of Hell a vision of his own neglect and an indictment of society in general. *Dekker his Dreame*, for example, contains some lavish resentment of the years he spent in a debtors' prison. Even so, in its urban relocation of gothic aesthetics Hell appears as a ferociously comic state. Dekker encourages the realms of Hell and the city to interact, and the devil's arrival in London was the comic mainspring of more than just Dekker's *If This Be Not a Good Play, the Devil Is In It* (1611). That the devil found himself, in London, out of his league in wickedness, is a joke which registered and encouraged his demise as a principle for the 'old religion'. If, as Price believes, Dekker was untroubled by 'Catholicism's claim to authority', then why did he target it with such assiduity?

For Dekker Hell was a canvas upon which he painted the ultimate dystopic realm. Although he has often been seen as a kindly idealistic author, 'gentle-hearted' and 'honest' (this tone of Dekker criticism was set long ago by Hazlitt), he appears, in my account, as a writer of dystopic fiction.[40] Writing in this way is quite radical: it enables us to see the city as an ill-place, allowing plague and social concerns to overlap into social critique. Yet those dystopic descriptions also contained, albeit tacitly, images of Utopia, of *Troia-Nova Triumphans* (his mayoral pageant for John Swinerton), of a new Jerusalem. Dekker's sentimentality is a facade. In his writing about the city he reveals a deep mistrust of all forms of authority, including a rejection of despair because that too is a form of quiescence which eventually endorses the status quo. And now, our scene is London.

# 1

# Bedlam and Bridewell in the *Honest Whore* Plays

The walls of confinement actually enclose the negative of that moral city which the bourgeois conscience began to dream in the seventeenth century; a moral city for those who sought, from the start, to avoid it, a city where right reigns only by virtue of a force without appeal – a sort of sovereignty of good, in which intimidation alone prevails and the only recompense of virtue (to this degree its own reward) is to escape punishment.[1]

## I 'FFOR WANTE OF EXECUCON OF GOOD LAWES & BY NECKLIGENTE GOVERNEMENTE'[2]: PROBLEMS FOR THE ADMINISTRATION OF BEDLAM AND BRIDEWELL

Following Elizabeth I's death, Dekker responded quickly to the growing fashion for staging the dynamics of city life in the *Honest Whore* plays (1604–5). It was a fascination which also marked Shakespeare's only full-scale intervention into the contemporary milieu of the metropolis; into what the Duke in *Measure for Measure* calls 'The nature of our people,/Our city's institutions, and the terms/For common justice' (I.i.9–11). With Middleton, Dekker began to chart the same tense relationship between people and government by throwing into relief certain institutions which characterized that tension. One such place was Bedlam, England's first asylum for the insane. At the beginning of the seventeenth century this hospital, with its thirty or so inmates, had become symptomatic of the many changes which wrought London during this period.[3] By staging the asylum so meticulously in *The Honest Whore, part I* the writers theatricalized the social vision and governmental forces which constituted it. Obviously, it was a popular play because a year later Dekker returned to the Fortune theatre with a sequel, *The Honest Whore, part II*. In this play Bedlam was replaced with the infamous Bridewell, the first workhouse or 'house of correction'. Though quite small operations, they both represented the dark side of the city's social and political profile. What emerges from Dekker and Middleton's dramatic remaking of Bedlam and Bridewell is a multi-faceted exploration of the nature of authority in the city as those institutions were used by competing factions and interests for the purpose of defining social values and morality along with all manner of new urban identities. The place and practices of such institutions, and their histories, became the battleground for social and political space in early modern London.

Bedlam, or the Bethlehem hospital to give its full name, was founded as a monastery in the thirteenth century when London was a mere fraction of the size it had become by the early seventeenth century. Gradually developing specialized treatment for the insane, it became increasingly overwhelmed by the forces of metropolitan expansion and cultural change.[4] Ironically, perhaps, the very stresses which characterized that change, as we shall see, were often inflected by madness. In 1603 John Stow published his comprehensive testimony *A Survey of London*, which formed part of a new urban literature whose impetus was drawn from the desire to interpret the city for its citizenry.[5] The *Survey* was unabashed in its defence of the City's 'greatnesse', and refocused opinion on the validity of the City's claim, against the Crown, for controlling Bedlam. Though locatable within the Crown's post-Reformation land-grab of Catholic and monastic lands, Bedlam's history was assiduously reconstructed by Stow to accommodate a decidedly civic viewpoint. Founded by a 'worthy citizen', according to Stow, Bedlam was part of a long dispute between the Crown and the City dating back to at least the fourteenth century. Over the years London's City Fathers sought to purchase institutional control in the name of social justice. The cash-strapped Crown often took the money but attempted, usually successfully, to hold on to its powers of influence and patronage. Bedlam's exhaustive and diligent biographer, E. D. O'Donoghue, reports an agreement between Henry VIII and the City which encapsulates these factional stresses:

And the king further granted that the said mayor, commonalty, and citizens and their successors should be masters and governors of the house or hospital called Bethlem, and should have the order, rule, and government of the hospital and of the people

there, and should have full authority to cause the revenues of the
lands and possessions of the hospital to be employed for the
benefit of the poor people there, according to the true meaning of
the foundation, or otherwise, as it should please the king.[6]

More than just social etiquette, the phrase 'as it should please the
king' revealed deep political tensions. It certainly did please the
king, and later the queen, to regard the appointment of Bedlam's
chief administrators and beneficiaries as being within his or her
purview.[7] This agreement reveals the way in which the City Fathers
and the Crown were making demands and exercising rights over
the government of Bedlam.[8] In its increasing competition with the
Crown, the City vauntingly presented itself as the moral custodian
of the community through its self-appointed ability to weigh the
rights of the poor on behalf of the people. The Crown, meanwhile,
sanctioned its governmental claim through the long arm of its
patronage, and through tradition and custom. What emerged from
this, and similar agreements, was a joint authority producing
considerable administrative tension and disunity in institutional
government. Those incarcerated became ensnared in the power
brokerage between various metropolitan factions. Dekker and
Middleton weave this reconstruction of Bedlam's conflictual history
into *The Honest Whore, part I* and expose what was at stake in the
process of controlling the insane. Governing the mad in Bedlam
defined key social terms: not just 'mad' and 'sane' but the fundamental and changing concepts of freedom and liberty, or what
could be considered rational and irrational.

Bridewell was much more an immediate response to the political,
social, and urban settlements which governed the metropolitanization of London after the Reformation. Conceived in the latter half
of the sixteenth century to embrace the very strains of urban expansion which had overburdened Bedlam, Bridewell was constructed through the practice and rhetoric of social reform which
characterized the mid-sixteenth century. Drawing upon the
master–apprentice structure of the guild workshop, the original
vision of Bridewell – at least of those who advocated its inception –
was that every vagrant should come under the master's tutelage
and learn to be a productive member of the city's community.
Bridewell was launched with what the City authorities presented as
the laudable aim of alleviating its so-called annoyances (vagrancy,
poverty, and unemployment) which were symptomatic of the

underlying problems of Tudor and Stuart society. A City petition to the Crown stressed that 'this house being obtained to the City, it was employed for the correction and punishment of idle vagrant people and dissolute, and for setting them to work, that they might in an honest way take pains to get their own livelihood.'⁹ To flatter and calm London's working citizenry, Bridewell's history was often written with City bias, with a sense of a glorious social rescue rather than the restoration of hitherto neglected ancient rights. Dekker reinforced this view, again drawn from Stowe, as he opens the Bridewell scene in *The Honest Whore, part II* with an interchange between the monarch and the institute's keeper. As they outline Bridewell's history, we learn that it was once a fine palace where visiting princes stayed and where 'Acts of State' were performed. As the tale unfolds, we become aware that the affirmation of the City's rights and charitable aims are being written against the background of courtly dilapidation: 'Thus Fortune can tosse the World, a Princes Court/Is thus a prison now' (V.ii.15–16).¹⁰ In spite of this symbolic upending of monarchical power, Dekker's account still manages to gloss the account of Bridewell's transfer: 'that Duke dead, his Sonne/(That famous Prince) gave free possession/Of this his Palace, to the Cittizens ... to [be] an Hospitall' (V.ii.7–12). In fact, the palace 'Belonging to a Duke of Savoy' was a dilapidated eyesore located in an unsavoury swamp next to the Fleet river. The place had fallen into such disrepair that the Crown happily sold it to the City in 1553. Once they 'tooke possession' of Bridewell, the City Fathers proceeded to turn the old palace into what was arguably the first workhouse in Europe.

Bridewell became part of the City's attempt to deal with vagrancy, unemployment, and other itinerant inhabitants of the metropolis.¹¹ Its more underlying or insidious purpose was to redefine poverty and the poor, and to (re)locate physically and culturally those considered less socially viable. At the same time it sought to recast the nature and meaning of work. In the late sixteenth-century London's Recorder, William Fleetwood, worked tirelessly rounding up and punishing vagrants by whipping and/or branding. Fleetwood's biographer says that 'the endeavour was then made to establish a settlement for every man, and prevent him from wandering from it to other parts of the kingdom.'¹² Fleetwood became obsessed with the origins of the so-called 'masterless men', and continuously tried to discover whence they came. In terms that demonstrate his view that vagrants were merely social detritus, he says 'the residue for the most part were from Wales, Salop, Cestre, Somerset, Bowkingham, Oxford and Essex ...'.[13] What made the consequences of poverty so unacceptable, and such a potent threat, for Fleetwood and men like him was his conception that vagrants were socially unlocatable, outside the edifying effect of work, and thus beyond the reach of the law and socialization. Viewed in this way, as they still are today, the poor are deemed to remain 'deliberately out of work' by their own volition.[14]

Supported by the men who ruled the City, such attacks on rootlessness were regarded as a valuable street-cleaning exercise. After one particularly savage campaign, Fleetwood proudly reported that 'I found not one roog stirring' on London's streets.[15] The City's offensive against the 'multitude of ydell people' proceeded along a number of fronts.[16] Under the guise of giving the inmates a trade, many prisoners were put to work at menial or arduous tasks. Enforcement of cheap labour was most graphically demonstrated by Bridewell's infamous giant treadmill. Built to grind corn, it was operated by its male inmates to the point of exhaustion. Alongside these practices, Bridewell operated as a penal institution. According to Dekker's 'Master' of Bridewell, 'The sturdy Beggar, and the lazy Lowne,/Gets here hard hands, or lac'd Correction./The Vagabond growes stay'd, and learns to 'bey,/The Drone is beaten well, and sent away' (*The Honest Whore, part II*, V.ii.37–40). Such punishments were among the most savage moments of Renaissance fashioning: 'As iron, on the Anvill are they laid, /Not to take blowes alone, but to be made /And fashioned to some Charitable use' (V.ii.45–53). With a large measure of unintentional irony, Pendry notes that 'whipping was certainly an important cause of Bridewell's degeneration, since it obscured the good intentions of the scheme.'[17] This comment, unfortunately, obscures the institution's punitive teleology. Certainly by the late sixteenth century, Bridewell's main intention, its *raison d'être*, was precisely its purposive whipping.[18] The authorities tried to flog wholesome laws out of what they were determined to see as the city's degeneration. Ironically, the only appeal against this open manifesto of social violence was an institution run by the City's social rivals, the Court of the Star Chamber (itself no stranger to violent punishment). Evidence of Bridewell's torture was often heard there: the case of a prostitute beaten 'to the great danger of her life' was all too familiar.[19] Antipathy between the Crown–Court and the City provided what little brake there was on Bridewell's practices. Political prejudice had a limited effect. Star

Chamber only poked its nose in when someone, usually a woman, died or nearly died from the brutal excesses of punishment.[20] Such authorized violence was exacerbated by the fact that the City condoned 'arrest and corporal punishment without trial.'[21] Habeas corpus, or other protective rights, did not apply to the city's masterless women or men.[22] Yet for many the idea of whipping as a form of social therapy, or 'correction', was ethically bankrupt. By those who opposed official policy, it was held to be indiscriminate, vindictive, and ineffective, rather than a credible remedy for the city's social problems.[23] Dekker's Duke proffers the official view that the apparent control of disorder is also that which structures order: accordingly, 'wholsom'st Lawes spring from worst abuse' (*The Honest Whore, part II*, V.ii.54). As the play proceeds, however, we see how often 'worst abuse' springs from the facetious imperatives of 'wholesom'st Lawes.'[24] As the century turned, the image of a hapless social victim, disenfranchised, writhing under the lash of authority, increasingly emblematized the failure of such institutions. Frustrated by the poor results which followed from the practice of 'purposive whipping', the city authorities often responded by pursuing more vigorously the policies which had failed.

In many ways Bridewell was a distinctly City response to vagrancy and roguery. By contrast, Elizabethan government (especially the Crown) used conscription as a strategy for dealing with the expanding undesirable sectors of society – the unemployed, the poor, and the criminal. Both the size of armies and the frequency of their deployment increased during the early modern period, with particularly high levies of troops during the latter years of Elizabeth's reign.[25] According to Cruickshank, 'conscripts formed by far the largest group' in these armies; and 'the levy of masterless men was an expedient resorted to by the government when it was necessary to raise troops quickly.'[26] In spite of this apparent sense of reluctance, the government seemed to find itself 'resorting' to this 'expedient' with increasing regularity as the numbers of vagrants multiplied – especially in London where much of the impressment was conducted.[27] Military campaigns abroad, J. R. Hale argues, were 'actually ... provoked' by governments, for a 'wide expression of reasons' all related to domestic politics.[28] In effect they 'diverted men from making trouble at home': they 'rid a country of social dross'; and 'acted as a stimulating tonic to a lethargic body politic'.[29] Such callous language only reflects the cynicism with which Elizabethan government dealt with the disenfranchised. As Hale reveals 'a foreign war calmed, by diverting, civil passions and gave governments the excuse to pack off the unproductive elements in society – rogues, vagabonds and paupers – to be slaughtered.'[30] Through its cultural emphasis on a martial ethos, it is not surprising that the armigerous class used the battlefield to rid society of its problems in this manner. A conscripted soldier's lot was one neither chosen nor happy. They could, as Falstaff frankly tells us, die or beg: 'I have led my ragamuffins where they are peppered. There's not three of my hundred-and-fifty left alive, and they are for the town's end, to beg during life.'[31] And this was the fate of many who begged in London: to be dragged off to become 'food for powder', or be returned, often crippled, to the streets.[32] For the aristocracy who formed the Crown–Court system of government 'there was a novel emphasis on the use of war as a purgative or laxative to evacuate criminals from the body politic.'[33] But for the class which Hale calls the 'urban social elite', the City Fathers, there was 'an in-built pacificity ... [they] defined themselves as the sector that did *not* fight.'[34] In early modern London the social, political, and ideological, distinction between the 'urban elite' and the ruling aristocracy was drawn around control of those living on the city's streets who got caught between the discipline of the institution or the killing fields of European battlefields.

The social and historical contradictions upon which both Bedlam and Bridewell were founded came to a head immediately prior to the production of Dekker and Middleton's plays. Two scandals broke in the early seventeenth century which proved to be nothing less than a crisis in the City's administration. Difficulties developed from a privatization scheme which was concocted and authorized by the Court of Aldermen. Four 'enterprising' contractors were paid £300 for putting, as O'Donoghue reports, 'four hundred poor people to work at new and profitable trades.'[35] Within a few months, rumours were rife throughout the city of widespread administrative corruption. Only eighty people were ever 'accommodated' by this botched scheme. Worse than the shortfall of accommodation was the discovery that the contractors had been involved in criminal behaviour and gross mismanagement, including embezzlement, illegal sub-letting, impropriety, stealing cloth donated to the institution for bedding, and pimping.[36] This gang of four entrepreneurs coerced the incarcerated prostitutes to return to their old trade within the actual institution. For a while, then,

Bridewell operated as a brothel, 'one of the matrons even acted as procuress for the whores in her charge.'[37] Riotous and infamous parties were held there as prostitutes appeared 'flaunted in brave apparel'; as opposed to wearing the customary prisoner's blue gown.[38] The whole incident made a mockery of the values which had invested and maintained the institution. Yet it was a scandal rooted in the conflicting and contradictory ethos of the new metropolis. Masterless men and women were, after all, the raw material of urban expansion, unofficially incorporating the city's spirit of huxterism, even though they often appeared at odds with the City's image of itself as London's legitimate master and the right to self-government.[39] The *Honest Whore* plays, and *Measure for Measure*, capitalize upon the discrepancies and hypocrisies which attend this contradiction. There was, of course, a delicious irony to be exploited: Bridewell, which had been conceived to put people to work and punish 'bawds' and 'whores,' had got its purposes mixed up, or maybe it took them too literally, as it put the city's designated 'whores' back to work.[40] Never one to miss a topical irony, Dekker brought the whole show – one which all London was laughing at – on to the Jacobean stage, and the play joined other voices in London which were critical of the policies which governed the city's unemployed.[41]

But Bridewell was not the only London institution mired in scandal at this time. Profit-seeking and private gain could also be found at Bedlam around the turn of the century.[42] Against a background of squabbles between the Crown and the City, a 'factor ... which adds much confusion to the administrative scene in the sixteenth and early seventeenth centuries', the asylum's government appeared to be riddled with corruption.[43] Mismanagement of Bedlam produced intolerable conditions through systematic abuse of its inmates, as an early seventeenth century report revealed:

> We do fynd divers other defaults in the sayd house in such sorte that it is not fitt for anye man to dwell in wich it was left by the Keeper for that it is so loathsomly and filthely kept not fitt for anye man to come into sayd house.[44]

Whether expropriating funds, depriving prisoners of food, or utilizing the labour of the inmates for personal gain, the keepers of both institutions were exploiting for profit those incarcerated. One contemporary observer noted that a Bridewell inmate 'was wasted to a skeleton and in a state of exhaustion from grinding at the treadmill, a most pitiful sight. There was nothing left of him except skin and bones.'[45] Word on the street was that those who were meant to be custodians of the disenfranchised were the ones to blame, as the writer of *Greevous Grones for the Poore* explains: 'the decay of Hospitality in our Land, whereby many poore soules are deprived of that releefe which they have had heretofore.'[46] Bridewell's clerk, John Howes, targeted the authorities, claiming problems in the workhouse were due to 'certaine abuses in ye governmente of the poore in this present tyme'.[47] Confining distracted people, as Foucault's narrative in *Madness and Civilization* suggests, targeted poverty to a much greater extent than either insanity or deviance.[48] Dekker and Middleton's prison characters – like their real counterparts – were densely coded symbols of social disrepair and were often the tragic consequence of the clash of idealistic or dogmatic social policies. Like the theatre itself, Bedlam and Bridewell were part of an ever more dynamic political tussle between a burgeoning City, its government, and the centralizing valences and ethos of the Tudor and Stuart administration. In Bedlam and Bridewell, the writers found a peculiarly appropriate space in which to set the denouements of their *Honest Whore* tragicomedies, a space which maximized the intersection of the theatre and the institution through the wider dramatic context of the City.

## II STAGING MADNESS: 'YET DO THEY ACT SUCH ANTICKE AND SUCH PRETTY LUNACIES, THAT SPITE OF SORROW THEY WILL MAKE YOU SMILE'

In meticulous detail Dekker exploited London's popular fascination with Bedlam as a theatrical spectacle.[49] Visitors arrived daily at the asylum, sometimes provoking the inmates to perform by whipping, taunting, or plying them with drink.[50] According to MacDonald 'in the greatest age of English drama, the longest running show in London was Bedlam itself.'[51] Is this a matter of vulgar taste, as some critics would have us believe, or is there something more at stake in such a spectacle?[52] Foucault's observation that 'madness and madmen became major figures, in their ambiguity: menace and mockery' able to articulate 'the dizzying unreason of the world, and the feeble ridicule of men' is both compelling and beguiling.[53] In *Madness and Civilization* Foucault tends to romanticize early instances of madness because he feels that they were less tarnished with the exigent structures of a bourgeois rationality.[54] Accordingly, the 'great confinement' of the mad was implemented in order to contain that which was antonymous to reason: unreason.[55] For MacDonald any idealization of madness should be resisted: 'lunatics were not treated with superstitious reverence', he says, 'nor was their privileged legal status the result of a belief that they were goofy sages, ever ready to utter a profundity.'[56] Furthermore, 'Lunatics and fools were living tropes, simultaneously man and beast, social creature and natural ... whereas real madmen were terrifying and disgusting, impossible to control and oblivious to the rules of normal violence.'[57] MacDonald attempts to draw a line of demarcation between 'real madmen' and 'lunatics and fools'. Yet for Foucault madness remains an intense form of theatre, playing on the 'ambiguity of reality and illusion ... which unites and separates truth and appearance.'[58] Put another way, the mad do not just trace the lines between 'mad' and 'tame', happy and sad, or 'blemisht' and pure, but they also, as Neely says, occupy 'the point of intersection between the human, the divine, and the demonic.'[59] However we categorize madness, it *is* theatre, and compelling social theatre at that. Bedlam's visitors were less witnesses and more audience as they came to see a drama which discovered rather than glossed the instability of identity.

In *The Honest Whore, part I* a group of visitors arrive at Bedlam and demand to see the inmates 'act ... anticke and pretty lunacies.' From a variety of madfolk on display, the Keeper offers them a selection of those in whom 'God's image' had become bestial, or 'blemisht and defac'd.' Some, according to the Keeper, are 'like hungry Lions' or 'Fierce as wilde Buls, untamable as flies.' So dangerous and unpredictable are they that 'oftentimes from strangers sides' the madfolk have 'Snatcht rapiers suddenly, and done much harme' (V.ii.158–66).[60] Yet being in such dangerous proximity, flirting with the untamable, was, in part, why the visitors came, as the spectators obviously enjoyed the bathos which characterized the behaviour of the mad. Madness, as the Keeper reveals, was Janus-faced; it appeared at once grotesquely farcical and deeply touching. Madness staged the tense confrontation between the farcical and the pathetic, a truly disarming emotional state. In a dramatic sense, the insane and the fool could and did occupy the same role or function, with neither facet diminishing the significance of the other. Although a multi-faceted perception was undoubtedly possible at a 'real' asylum like Bedlam, the importance which the mad held for the writers could in essence be found in the medium of theatre. Because the city increasingly stressed the quality of role-play as a form of social identity, staging madness was loaded with a particular relevance in this time. In bringing Bedlam to a wider stage the writers sought to harness the elements of satire and disgust and present them there in a way which had not been done before.[61] Madmen especially could combine in the right proportions the ludicrous and the ironic, together with the horrifying spectacle of boundaries being unflaggingly transgressed.

Madness, then, dramatized the indeterminacy of the threshold, of the transition from one cultural space to another. The distracted figure of 'Tom O'Bedlam' became a synecdoche for socio-economic change and agrarian upheaval.[62] 'Tom O'Bedlam men' were, as Beier says, 'arrested as vagabonds.'[63] Many of the multitudes who migrated to London were, in the public mind, as bereft of wits as they were of a livelihood.[64] In *King Lear*, for example, madness encodes nothing less than the complete breakdown of feudal order. As well as Lear's antics, Edgar becomes a madman, the ultimate symbol of social dispossession.[65] Although less an obvious index of rural displacement, Dekker and Middleton's drama still represents madness as a symptom of social abrasion. In *The Honest Whore, part I* all manner of 'mad' behaviour is depicted: from Hippolito's melancholy, through Candido's wife's short temper, to Bellafront's disguise as an inmate of Bedlam. Social conflict is not discrete but interconnected as each character is paired with some other form of aggravatingly maddening behaviour. The Duke's Machiavellian behaviour precipitates Hippolito's discontented actions; Candido is 'A patient man linkt with a waspish shrowe' (I.v.141); and Matheo's selfish disinterestedness ensures Bellafront's 'mad' antics. The play revels in a long-running pun on madness as social anger and as mental instability. One of Bedlam's inmate-workers explains that 'the Courtier is mad at the Cittizen, the Cittizen is madde at the Country man, the shoomaker is mad at the cobler, the cobler at the carman, the punke is mad that the Marchants wife is no whore, the Marchants wife is mad that the puncke is so common a whore' (V.ii.146–50). And the 'whore', we learn in *The Honest Whore, part II*, is mad at the courtier; thereby completing another cycle of stress. Madness, in this sense, seems quintessentially urban, and part of the endless interaction of business which makes up the city and its ethos. For the Sweeper, whatever the 'quantitie of the Moone that got into em', madness appears as a product of caste antagonism and inter-trade rivalry, with its roots in rural upheaval and the beguiling world of the City where an 'abundance' of 'Courtiers, Citizen's sons and heires', and 'Farmers sons' come to lose their money as fast as their wits (*The Honest Whore, part I*, V.ii.125–38). All these are processes which, he senses, are lubricated by the capital's lawyers, who on no account should be admitted to Bedlam: 'for heele make em mad faster than we can recover em' (V.ii.135). Through the knockabout jocularity of the Sweeper, himself a confessed 'mad wag', we see how Bedlam and the City appear to interpenetrate one another. When asked 'are all the mad folkes in *Millan* brought hither?', the Sweeper acutely intones; 'How all, theres a wise question indeede: why if al the mad folkes in *Millan* should come hither, there would not be left ten men in the City' (V.ii.120–3).[66] Although madness could be seen as part and parcel of the anxieties and neuroses of early modern life, it chiefly registered poverty and social disintegration.[67] At the historical juncture when the poor became, in the eyes of the authorities, an overwhelming embarrassment, then 'madness began to rank among the problems of the city'.[68]

Through examining the relationship between comedy and violence in his study of *Elizabethan Grotesque*, Neil Rhodes notes that 'visceral imagery has a peculiar and revolting relevance to Elizabethan London.'[69] In *The Honest Whore, part I* this relevance is graphically displayed in the form of a madman offering his emaciated body for the delectation of his tormentors and the audience: 'for looke you, here be my guts: these are my/ribs, – you may looke through my ribs, – see how my guts/come out – these are my red guttes, my very guts, oh, oh!' (V.ii.234–6). Horror and farce intermingle as they hold revulsion and compassion in a moment of grotesque dramatic tension. Yet the moment also evinces a mixture of pathos and comedy which is simultaneously sympathetic and disaffective. The drama agitates our response in order to elicit an understanding of the mad-poor, and their plight. We cannot shun, or fully objectify, someone so bathetic and comic, especially as the audience have asked for and been given his 'very guts.' 'Grotesque of this kind makes us laugh', says Rhodes, 'but our laughter chokes on an awareness of the scene's actual horror ... the grotesque becomes a penetrating examiner of our concept of what is entertaining, what is festive.'[70] Yet there is little sense here of a fully redemptive festivity of the kind so eloquently elaborated by Bakhtin in *Rabelais and His World*.[71] The social exigencies and ethos of early modern London tended to corrupt grotesque aesthetics, making them more avaricious than exuberant, more horrifically ironic than festive. While the instrumentality of poverty and disease, combined with the increased jostling and intermingling of bodies, provided the very stuff of grotesque, the ethos of self-interest fundamentally diminished the notion of the collective social body. Yet there remains enough visceral violence in Elizabethan grotesque for it to become a vital tool for social analysis and critique. As Rhodes says, 'bodily distortion in the microcosm reflects disharmony in the body politic.'[72] This neatly describes the functional ability of theatrical characters on stage and in the asylum who, when dramatized, can be made to embody the very problems for which they have become the focus.

Madness as a spectacle complicated the relationship between audience and the 'performer.' One of the main purposes in visiting Bedlam was to hear the mad speak 'all manner of languages' (*Northward Hoe*, IV.iii.48). Roy Porter notes, 'visitors to Bedlam [who came] there to enjoy a spectator sport, took pleasure in the uncensored, unbuttoned rantings of the 'collegicians' (as they were called) ...'.[73] Being 'all words' was what the audience unflaggingly demanded. It seems that people came to Bedlam or the theatre to hear the special kind of violence done to language that we could say constitutes the grotesque.[74] Through the appropriate theatrical metaphor, MacDonald observes that the 'behaviour of the insane seemed to observers to be a pantomime of unchecked passion.'[75] In Dekker and Middleton's Bedlam we see that pantomime: we see the mad spending their speech, running riot with language and an unchecked passion which chaotically spills over into farcical arguments and absurd dialogue, drawing into their linguistically disruptive mêlée anyone who comes near. On and off the stage inmates were goaded until they spoke: 'Heele not speake a word/Unlesse hees throughly vext' says Anselmo, and later 'Unlesse you urge em, [they] seldome spend their speech' (*The Honest Whore, part I*, V.ii.246). Having induced a torrent of grotesque language, Anselmo responds somewhat paradoxically: 'Ile whip you if you grow unruly thus' (V.ii.20). As soon as the mad exhibited any kind of (linguistic) anarchy they were 'whipt for their unrulinesse' (V.ii.243). Madness was seen to be tamed: order was extracted from disorder. Paradoxically, the crux of these scenes was depicting the uncontrollable loquacity of those who needed to be controlled and shut up. That troubling paradox, and farcical quality of these anarchic displays, denied any complete sense of closure and often remained to haunt the spectator.

Interpreting madness, as *The Honest Whore, part I* reveals, was also a matter of class distinction. Whereas madness for the lower classes, whether on stage or in Bedlam, appeared as a spectacular theatre of social dislocation and disenfranchisement, for the upper classes mental instability became transcoded into a class emblem. As MacDonald notes, the 'idleness of melancholy aristocrats was seldom viewed as a sign of mental illness; it was instead the very mark of gentility, a cause and not a consequence of melancholy'; to put it another way 'melancholy and gentility became boon companions.'[76] Perhaps for this reason a certain type of mental instability seems symptomatic of the same period that witnessed the rapid development of early modern drama. 'Between 1500 and 1580 there are only three references to melancholy in English plays' according to Vieda Skultans; 'after 1580 references to melancholy suddenly proliferate – so much so that writers have been led to talk of an "epidemic" of melancholy.'[77] She goes on to say that, 'for some time melancholy men were so numerous in London that they constituted a social type, often called the malcontent.'[78] As the contemporary physician Burton said; 'For indeed who is not a fool, melancholy, mad? ... who is not brain-sick?'[79] Burton was not, of course, referring to the commonalty but to England's elite.[80] *The Honest Whore, part I* capitalized on the social trendiness of melancholy, and its equally popular satirization of what was often perceived as aristocratic pretension.[81]

As the play opens we see a high-born woman lying on a hearse surrounded by the usual regal obsequies. A mood of pathos and prophecy seems appropriate as the audience witnesses a state funeral, one which deliberately invokes an image of Elizabeth's very recent death. Far from being a tribute to Elizabeth, though, the drama quickly turns into a dark and bathetic satire on the courtier class' as the apparent 'death' quickly induces madness in Hippolito. Though merely drugged, the royal object of love seems extinct. Hippolito is confronted by the Duke's edgy requiem:

> If to behold
> Those roses withered, that set out her cheekes:
> That paire of starres that gave her body light,
> Darkned and dim for ever: All those rivers
> That fed her veines with warme and crimson streames,

Froxen and dried up: If these be signes of death,
Then is she dead.

(*The Honest Whore, part I*, I.i.22–8)

Such quaint metaphysics and archaic rhetoric have, like the images
they previously idealized, now degenerated into a discourteous
parody of the transcendence which they once bore. The corporeal
clichés and metaphors of courtly romance take on different
meaning as we realize that Elizabeth's blood, once so full of the
power to legitimate courtly politics had, like Infelice's, abruptly
stopped flowing. These 'signes of death' are made brutally immanent for the distraught Hippolito. Like a slap in the face he is
told, 'you see shees dead' (*The Honest Whore, part I*, I.i.17); and later
the Duke says 'Queenes bodies are but trunckes to put in wormes'
(I.i.57). Even thinking about such an image would have been trea-
sonable a couple of years earlier.[82] In his ensuing madness, distraction, and, as the stage directions indicate, 'discontented apparance',
Hippolito appears as a caricature of the melancholic wooers of
power who littered the Elizabethan court.[83] As it reworked aspects
of Elizabethan iconography, many of which had congealed around
a virgin queen who (at least in the imaginary) could be wooed but
never won, the play's leitmotiv of madness highlights the problems
of retextualizing 'Eliza's' semiotic edifice. Yet, as James and others
were aware, Jacobean culture needed to restructure Elizabethan
iconography, so a degree of satirization was both popular and tolerated. Elizabeth was the chief component of a Crown–Court
system which seemed to be disintegrating because of the problems
of an ageing cantankerous queen, and by the growing problems of
metropolitan and national government.

Elizabeth's death twisted the aristocracy's love affair with its
own ennui into a heightened exposition of melancholy. For
Hippolito, Infelice's apparent death produces an ontological crisis
while inducing a complete loss of identity: 'I shall forget my selfe',
he says, beginning an obsession with horrific images of a living
death which precipitate his slide into social dysfunction and mental
instability (*The Honest Whore, part I*, I.i.73). In melancholic decline,
he becomes a parodic tragedian, 'a barbarous Moore', as well as a
permanently, if not terminally, jilted lover: 'Let me but kisse her
pale and bloodlesse lip … Or if not touch her, let me looke on her'
(I.i.37–8 and 40). Parodically capturing the sex–death transgression

which characterized the dark undertones of Jacobean tragic theatre, his cadaverous attention turns Elizabethan poetics of comedy into a ghoulish joke. The convergence of desire and chastity which marked such comedy becomes realized as a tragic obsession in Hippolito's mind – that dead women are nothing if not exquisitely chaste.[84] And here we could turn to Bellafront, whose chastity, as we shall see, becomes the focus of so many issues in the play. Even her father admits that she is a 'Sive' who can 'hold no water' (*The Honest Whore, part II*, I.ii.135). By using this metaphor of a 'leaky vessel' to reveal unchastity, Dekker allows the image to both gently parody and valorize Queen Elizabeth, whose legendary virginity and chastity were symbolized by her miraculous ability to hold a sieve full of water whilst none leaked out.[85] As Bellafront slowly compromises her reconstructed chastity Hippolito becomes increasingly anxious and deranged. By Act IV he has locked himself in his darkened chamber, fearful of the outside world in general and terrified of Bellafront in particular. He fails to grasp that it is Court politics and the ambitions of the monarch which ultimately threaten him. As a result of his deluded state, he sees Bellafront as a 'whore', and therefore the main threat to his integrity. Her mere presence throws him into a misogynistic temper about all living women: 'Purge this infected chamber of that plague,/That runnes upon me thus: Slave thrust her hence .../Hence, guard the chamber: let no more come on' (*The Honest Whore, part I*, IV.i.130–2). Only by idealizing the incorporeal spirit of a high-born woman does he seem able to structure his own looked-for sense of purity by imagining that he is 'on meditations spottles wings' (IV.i.143). In his mind, the safely dead Infelice is figured as a totem by which he seeks to protect himself from self-disintegration. But his elegiac meditations are far from untarnished. Instead they contain a deteriorated, mock-Petrarchan, ramble about truth and death with no legitimate source other than his own self-obsessed solicitude. Bereft of the icon which once endorsed courtly poetics and politics, Hippolito's fractured language idolizes Infelice as it demonizes Bellafront:

> The soule whose bosome lust did never touch,
> Is Gods faire bride, and maidens soules are such:
> The soule that leaving chastities white shore,
> Swims in hot sensuall streames, is the divels whore.

> (*The Honest Whore, part I*, IV.i.178–81)

To protect the purity of his soul, all his filthy lust is projected on to the hapless, and over-loving, Bellafront.[86] Bereft of probity, Hippolito feels that he would be swept away, caught up and carried off in the flow of his own lust; a lust which was the dark side of Elizabethan courtly love.

Hippolito's psychic breakdown produces strong elements of denial and dislocation, whose ensuing effects result in a spectacular obsession and fetishization of death: 'I cannot rest, ile meet it at the next turne,/Ile see how my love lookes' (I.i.69–70). The gaze upon the figure of the chaste noble lady of power and lineage rather pathetically becomes a voyeuristic, necrophilic fantasy. Her body now disrupts and fractures the aristocratic identities it had previously held together. *The Honest Whore, part I* presents courtly love, and the identities which were formed around it, as part of an atrophied state. Elizabeth's death haunted the courtier class as she became integrated into their melancholic fantasies and anxieties about self-identification and identity. Somewhat tauntingly, Dekker had written earlier in his eulogy for Elizabeth, *The Wonderfull yeare:* 'She was the Courtiers treasure, therefore he had cause to mourne ...' (Grosart, vol. I p. 87).

## III  FRUSTRATING INSTITUTIONS

Dekker's Bridewell is full of melodrama: the so-called 'Shee-Devils' from 'Hell', 'Doll target', 'Penelope Whore-hound', 'Mistris Horsleach', and 'Catyryna Bountinall' all curse, spit, swagger, flirt, and generally abuse everyone who comes to see them (*The Honest Whore, part II*, V.ii.253). These prostitutes refuse to be contained by their surroundings. Produced to titillate the audience with a display of unrepentant vice, the play's parade of recidivous 'whores' quickly collapses into farce. The Duke and his courtiers become wholly immersed in the scandalous and bawdy world of Bridewell. Ostensibly just a sideshow, the so-called 'whores' soon overwhelm the main action of the play. With 'their tongues [which] walke more free' they quickly get the better of their former protagonists and clients (*The Honest Whore, part II*, V.ii.261).[87] Eventually the Duke gets caught in the absurd and insulting linguistic centrifuge.[88] It was his own fault because he had, after all, disguised himself to 'make the sceane more Comicall' (V.ii.263). Like the Duke in *Measure for Measure*, of whom he is a parody, he discovers that his authority is threatened more by mockery than outright opposition from the inmates.[89] In spite of himself, he ends up bandying words with the recalcitrant Catherina about the lining of her petticoat:

DUKE     Is't Silke 'tis lined with then?

CAT       Silke? I Silke, Master Slave, you wud bee glad to wipe your nose with the skirt on't: this 'tis to come among a company of Cods-heads that know not how to use a Gentlewoman.

DUKE     Tell her the Duke is here.

I. MASTER   Be modest *Kate*, the Duke is here.

CAT       If the Devill were here, I care not: set forward, yee Rogues, and give attendance according to your places, let Bawds and Whores be sad, for Ile sing and the Devill were a dying.

(V.ii.425–31)

Yet more than Ducal dignity is being plucked of this particular nose. For someone who was meant to be broken and reshaped on Bridewell's anvil, the intractable *'Kate'* remains completely unimpressed by the blandishments of regal authority.[90] Even when attention is drawn to the Duke's presence, she flagrantly disregards him. All the Duke gets for his surveillance is a poke in the eye and the slanderous promise of a 'nose' in her petticoat. His disguise brings unruliness rather than the looked-for order. It appears that Catherina's autonomy takes centre stage rather than the Duke's sovereign presence. Finally, like the madmen in *The Honest Whore, part I*, she can only be removed rather than awed or coerced by the spectre of ducal authority.

Good drama though it was, such a view of saucy 'whores' requires some contextual qualification. According to Leah Lydia Otis, 'Outlawing brothel keeping and prostitution was part of a comprehensive program for strengthening the criminal law undertaken by the secular rulers of the sixteenth century', which amounted to 'the monopolization of criminal justice and its strict enforcement'.[91] In England, however, consolidation of power through monopolization of criminal justice was compromised by the alternative to monarchical power presented by the City of London. The Crown's mid-sixteenth-century drive towards controlling London's brothels for the purpose outlined by Otis became hijacked by the City because it was responsible for the administration of the measures. In *The Honest Whore, part II*, the Duke's attempt to consolidate his authority (judicial, patriarchal, and monarchical) is considerably embarrassed by his efforts to control the city's prostitutes. Because Hippolito cannot resist 'mutton-mungering' the Duke insists that 'on Harlots heads/New Lawes shall fall so heavy ...' (IV.ii.100–1). His compunction to protect what he deems to be the purity of his daughter and her marriage results in savage sanctions against those women who are the objects of his son-in-law's lust. The consequence of this sin-turned-law shifts the burden of culpability on to Bellafront, the scapegoat-prostitute. Mocking such attempts at social purity, Dekker exposes these practices ironically through Bellafront's impeccable honesty. At first the Duke deems it necessary to castigate all prostitutes in a face-saving exercise to clean up courtly appearances: 'Panders and Whores/Are Citty-plagues,' he says, 'which being kept alive/Nothing that lookes like goodnes ere can thrive' (*The Honest Whore, part II*, V.ii.455–7). This allusion to the 1603 proclamation ordering suburban brothels to be pulled down suggests that according to the authorities their eradication was necessary for the good of the body politic. However, it was widely perceived that dismantling brothels and evicting their occupants in order to protect that which 'lookes like goodnes' merely redistributed prostitution throughout the city, and made it less locatable in brothels.[92] The 1603 brothel *blitzkrieg* was a replay of the earlier Crown-inspired raids of the 1540s to close 'officially' London's Bankside brothels. This move to consolidate judicial and administrative power proved to be ineffective and counterproductive. As Dekker was to observe; 'Bawdes, that now sit no longer upon the skirts of the Cittie, but jett up and downe, even in the cloake of the Cittie' (Grosart, vol. II p. 93). In response to such a pandemic 'problem' the Duke fondly imagines his own omnipotence; whereby his 'Graces reach' is required in order 'to cure,/The outward parts, the Suburbes' (IV.ii.91–5). Such a cure would, however, produce worse symptoms than the 'disease'.[93] Echoing Pompey in *Measure for Measure* (II.i.226–40), Carolo suggests that locking up 'all the Whores within the walls, and without the walls' would be like diving into a 'Well unsearchable' (*The Honest Whore, part II*, IV.ii.105–7). Faced with this overwhelming impossibility, the Duke streamlines the judicial process as he becomes the law's sole arbiter, arrogating 'with eye most severe', upon exactly who will

be incarcerated (IV.ii.114). In seeking absolute control the Duke
reveals a judicial brittleness. Such a stance appears as an inflexible
and inadequate form of government for his city.
Variously cryptic, Dekker and Middleton's drama sustains its
critique of absolutist tendencies in those who rule. In *The Honest
Whore, part I*, the Duke comes to Bedlam in order to intercept the
marriage of his daughter to his house rival. Following the tradition
of romantic comedy, it was a marriage which sought to end internecine conflict within the feudal aristocracy; to heal 'the ancient
hates' of 'two houses' (V.ii.378).[94] Unable to command obedience,
the Duke attempts to underscore his authority via scheming,
tricks, disguises, and finally, coercion.[95] He begins by orchestrating
the false funeral of his daughter by drugging her so that she
appears dead, in order to dispose of her suitor (Hippolito). Then
he coerces the doctor who performed this service to befriend
Hippolito merely for the purpose of poisoning him. In justifying
this murder, the Duke insists on an absolutist view of his own
power and image: 'A noble youth he was, but lesser branches/
Hindring the greaters growth, must be lopt off ...' (IV.iv.26–7).
Once this political pruning has been achieved, the Duke realizes
that he then has to rid himself of the dangerous Doctor. Because of
his nefarious duties for the Duke in assisting him to enforce his
will, the Doctor now poses a potential threat to the power he previously supported. But, having been a party to the Duke's designs
and thoughts, the Doctor anticipates that he is likely to share the
fate decreed for Hippolito. He proves to be one betrayal ahead of
the Duke as he seeks protection from the very person he was hired
to kill, informing Hippolito of the Duke's plot to separate him
from Infelice irrevocably. Thus we can see how the Duke's single-
minded schemes are thwarted by his desire for complete control.
His authority appears compromised and his enemy, Hippolito,
strengthened. All the while, his disobedient daughter, once
revived, actively eludes his commands. So much for patriarchy.
When the Duke's attempted assassination of Hippolito fails, the
lovers elope to Bedlam.[96] As the Duke perceives his authority slipping away, he disguises himself as a visitor and follows them to
the asylum to 'worke out some prevention' of the marriage
(V.i.101). Scheming to enforce his singular view of the law, the
Duke, like most of the rulers in the so-called 'disguised Duke
plays', actually creates the conditions for governmental instability.[97] The 'patriarchal principle', rather than being able to 'save the

situation', as Tennenhouse describes, structures its own fragile state. In addition, the 'outbreak of desire' which appears so disruptive to the principles of patriarchal power operates, in this play, as a force for social cohesion outside the purview of the monarch.[98] In demarcating the limits of the Duke's influence, the writers allow us to scrutinize that authority by bringing it into the asylum. Before the Duke can enact his power-play, he becomes ensnared in the intractable and fraught world of Bedlam where the symbolic force of its historical limits, failings, and contradictions, are grounded. The first madman the Duke meets was once a 'very grave and wealthy Cittizen' and ship-owner (V.ii.170). A pro-City view is expressed that trade cannot be safely conducted upon the high seas as he refers to the 'great floud' which resulted in the 'losse at sea' of all his wealth (V.ii.174).[99] It was a tragic loss which resulted in his penury, punishment, social ostracism, and madness. This fallen bourgeois tacitly indicts the Duke's maritime and warlike policies; a criticism with echoes beyond the play. A few months prior to the play's production, probably around the time of its completion in 1604, appeared a re-enactment, and expansion, of an Elizabethan Act for the punishment of 'Rogues, Vagabonds and Sturdie Beggers'. It was part of a gamut of early Jacobean legislation which systematically targeted the underprivileged.[100] Mostly aimed at all kinds of 'fayninge', the Act stated:

> That ... all Sea-faringe men pretending losse of their Shippes or Goods on the Sea, goinge about the Countrie begginge ... shalbe taken and adjudged and deemed as Rogues and Vagabonds and Sturdie Beggers, and shall suffer such Paine and Punishment as in said Acte is in that behalfe appointed ...[101]

Vigilance against so-called faking concentrated judicial, legislative, and social power into the hands of those who decided who was feigning and who was not.[102] Much of Dekker's so-called 'rogue literature', with its exposition of arcane language and endless categorization, is an extended parody of the incessant adjudication upon 'fakes'.[103] Rounding on those who doubt his authenticity, the 'Cittizen'-madman of *The Honest Whore, part I*, implores the Duke to stop the pirates who destroyed him. He presents a farcical and poignant account of his bankrupt state and consequent social downfall.[104] Ripping off the guise of wisdom in folly, through his raving, he implicates and indicts the Duke: 'Alas! there! tis sunke – tis sunck: I am undon, I am undon, you are the dambd Pirates have undone me, – you are bith Lord, you are you are, stop em, you are' (V.ii.224–6). A year prior to these words being spoken, James had issued a proclamation attempting to curb the activities of the 'Warlike ships at sea.'[105] Supported by war with Spain, under Elizabeth, 'the English became known abroad now as a nation of pirates'.[106] Piratical acts continued after her death, flouting the new king's law which sought to stop these attacks. James was encouraged, 'through the manifold and dayly complaints made to his Highnesse, aswell by his owne Subjects', to issue a further Proclamation later that year, though it had little effect.[107] It called for 'the speedier suppressing of all such Piracies and Depradacious crimes, most hatefull to his minde, and scandalous to his peacable government ...'.[108] Trade was clearly being disrupted by the backwash of Tudor martial ambitions on the high seas. The madman's wits and livelihood are both 'undone' by sovereign impotence and the limitation of proclamations to underwrite peacable government.[109]

With his wits gone the way of his wealth, the poor man finally exposes the moral and social bankruptcy which underlies his punishment: 'whip me? what justice is this,/to whip me because Ime a begger? – Alas? I am a poore man ...' (*The Honest Whore, part I*, V.ii.231–2).[110] Clearly, he feels, it is a system which victimizes him exactly because he is a social failure. The unemployed and the deranged were whipped as criminals, and criminalized as they were being whipped. Dekker's madman stands as a supreme symbol of this type of institutional futility.

IV   'A PATIENT MAN'S A PATTERNE FOR A KING':
CHOP OR CHANGE, ADVICE FOR THE TOP

men are congregated into Citties and commonwealthes, for honesty and utilities sake ... men by this nearness of conversation are withdrawn from barbarous feritie and force to a certaine mildnes of manners and to humanity and justice: whereby they are contented to give and take right, to and from their equals and inferiors, and to heare and obey their heades and superiors. Also the doctrine of God is more fitly delivered, and the discipline thereof more aptly to be executed ....[111]

If the Duke in *The Honest Whore, part I* is forced to confront the limits of his authority, then what of the ostensible hero of the play, Candido, a linen-draper and man of the City? In the final scene, Candido is invited by the frustrated Duke to instruct his lack-lustre court in higher principles: 'Come therefore you shall teach our court to shine, So calme a spirit is worth a golden Mine' (V.ii.514–15). An unlikely scenario, perhaps, but in the commercial world outside the play, the City of London certainly was a 'golden mine' and an expanding one at that. Candido's 'calme spirit' is more than a mere sensibility, it stood for moral, social, and political power. Dekker and Middleton scrutinize the authoritarian claims of this 'calm spirit' by dramatizing the stresses of Candido's milieu, his City-based drapers shop. The running irony of the play is that his much-vaunted calm provides the mainspring for all the chaotic comedy around him: his wife wants to make him mad precisely because he is so tame; his apprentices want him to stand up to abusive customers in the shop; and courtiers only come to his shop in order to antagonize him as a class-specific form of amusement. All threats to Candido's authority are met with the stoical virtue of 'patience', which is endorsed by an unyielding rationality. In the face of all attempts to upset him, he tells everyone; 'Nothing can drive me from a patient man' (I.v.238). With a good helping of dramatic irony, we see his patience create so much friction and confusion that he has to be carted off to Bedlam as a madman.

Yet the valences of such dispassionate reason characterized a significantly powerful number of London's civic leaders, and formed the backbone of their political philosophy. *The Honest Whore, part I* explores the impact of these values upon the city which they tried so hard to discipline. Alderman Candido is notably a prestigious member of one of the major companies which formed the backbone of London's elite civic rulers. Perhaps more than Shakespeare's Angelo in *Measure for Measure*, Candido would have been identified as someone imbued with the spirit of the City of London's civic oligarchy, and, of course, its Puritan tendencies. Underpinned by their growing socio-economic power, the Fathers of the City consistently posited themselves as authentic civic rulers. To legitimize themselves they sought a social model which radically refashioned the ethos of civic autonomy; a model viable enough to challenge existing cultural forms. *Patience* was the key. 'Moderate thy mind, and keepe thy selfe content' typified the intensity of self-government as it revealed control of an inner moral sanctum.[112] This combination of centripetal

self-discipline and centrifugal moral behaviour was, of course, politically motivated. Self-disciplinary integrity was translated into a bold
political vision. As exemplar of that vision Candido muses through a
number of legal metaphors on the properties for civic office:

> A happy land,
> Where grave men meet each cause to understand,
> Whose consciences are not cut out in brybes,
> To gull the poore mans right: but in even scales,
> Peize rich and poore, without corruptions veyles.
> Come, wheres my gowne?

(*The Honest Whore, part I*, III i.165–70)

In government, then, London's 'Best fathers of the poore' were also
those who could effectively resist corruption – so the claim goes.[113]
Candido leads a two-pronged attack on what is, by implication, a
decaying Court system; one which can no longer uphold justice in
the common interest. Mayoral pageants did much to construct a
language of civil rights as social justice: 'the Rich and Poore must
lye/In one even Scale' says 'Justice' in *Troia-nova Triumphans*
(Bowers, vol. III, p. 246). After being asked by the Duke 'What
comfort do you finde in being so calme', Candido, whose name
invokes honesty, purity, and candidature, replies with a powerful
speech which hypostasizes the ethico-political spirit of rationality
through the concept of 'patience' (*The Honest Whore, part I*,
V.ii.487–509). Marked by the principles of a Puritan theocracy,
Candido's claims amount to a manifesto. In Gramscian terms, he
attempts to seize intellectual and moral leadership and cultural do-
minion.[114] Considering its reach, Candido's challenge to sovereign
authority is subtle. Drawing upon a language of Christian humility,
Candido does not offer a posture of direct confrontation as he attempts to avoid structuring the forces to which he is opposed (that
is, the monopolizing strategies of sovereign power); a pattern
which has been so comprehensively documented by recent
critics.[115] Criticism of the monarch's place in the divine hierarchy is
made tacitly as Candido suggests a more direct approach to the acquisition of God's law. Candido's claims, while appearing to offer
both criticism and advice, should be considered part of a hegemonic strategy adopted by the City's rulers: 'Patience my Lord' is
both instructive of, and an explanation for, his alternative to

absolutism. As a political philosophy 'Patience' was, ironically, yet another totalizing strategy of cultural control.

By displaying Candido's City politics, Dekker made a significant departure from his earlier City hero-leaders. In *The Shoemakers' Holiday*, Simon Eyre, once he became Mayor, sought to contain the impulses of a festivity and play by accommodating them in his shoemaker's shop.[116] It was a bold political move which both contained the potentially rebellious spirit of the workforce within the bourgeois workshop and brought the king to feast there with all London's apprentices. Eyre's claim for cultural and governmental legitimacy rested on his appropriation and incorporation of festive elements, an important component of carnival. Candido, by contrast, is all Lent. Candido stands for the nascent bourgeoisie who set their face against any cakes-and-ale practices – political or otherwise.[117] For Dekker, the switch to a Candido-style figure indicates a move away from writing which appealed to the nexus of Crown–Court patronage and towards a more professional engagement with the City. It was a move which coincided with his writing partnership with Middleton, who was making his name as a writer for London's civic tradesmen. It would, perhaps, be too much to suggest that Candido is figured as a rightful ruler usurping the Duke.[118] Yet undoubtedly there is a moment of hubris, if not impertinence, in having the newly-cast exemplary virtues of kingship so completely embodied in this paragon of City virtue. 'A Patient man's a Patterne for a King' stands as the portentous last line in (*The Honest Whore, part II*, V.ii.497). Without doubt Candido is the most patient man who ever trod the boards of the early modern stage; and patience was a quality for which neither Tudor nor Stuart monarchs were especially noted.

But Dekker and Middleton were no more City-stooges than other playwrights were propagandist lackeys for the Crown and aristocracy. Candido's values and ethos are not presented without serious qualification. Candido's moralization of patience owes as much to sound business practice as it does to Christian ethics. When faced with class-baiting from his courtier clientele he preaches that 'We are set heere to please all customers' because 'he that means to thrive, with patient eye/Must please the divell, if he come to buy' (*The Honest Whore, part I*, I.v.125–8). The customer has always been right for a long time and, according to Candido, the virtues of the seller are those which underwrite the values of commercial practice. No moral quality whatsoever can necessarily be ascribed to the customer, which is why even the devil could be served without tainting either seller or the transaction itself. Because all trade is potentially troublesome, potentially fraught with dishonesty, 'patience' is needed to erect an impregnable barrier between buyer and seller; hence, 'thy patience, which they finde /A wall of Brasse, no Armour's like the minde…' (*The Honest Whore, part II*, V.ii.493–4). Furthermore, as Wiltenburg has commented, the 'maintenance of mental order was inseparable from the maintenance of social order.'[119] Antagonism between Candido, the trader, and his courtier clientele microcosmically enacted the wider drama of City–Court relationships. It was widely understood that Puritan shopkeepers were being hypocritical when they morally condemned those who wore extravagant clothes and consumed fine goods; not least because they were often the ones who had sold them the stuff in the first place. Clearly the seller needed to be removed from the social transaction in which he was implicated or risk facing the same moral disapprobation levelled at his client. Patience, therefore, separated seller and buyer, and disguised the Puritan's desire for earthly rewards. As Weber made clear, it was this 'development of a rational bourgeois economic life' by way of Christian ascetic principles, which underpinned 'the anti-authoritarian ascetic tendency of Puritanism'; and, 'which was so dangerous to the State.'[120] Although essentially a two-sided act or contract, Candido rationalizes trade as an impermeable transaction: 'He has my ware, I have his money fort,/And thats no Argument I am angry: no,/The best Logitian can not prove me so.' (*The Honest Whore, part I*, I.v.114–16). The irrefutable logic of this notion of trade is pushed to its most absurd extreme when a group of courtiers arrive at his shop and insist on purchasing a pennyworth of lawn from the centre of the cloth, thereby ruining the whole piece. The hole-in-the-cloth becomes a farcical metonym for patient City values as Candido is forced to wear a carpet with a hole cut in the middle for his head because Viola has refused him access to his civic gown.[121] Like his Shakespearean counterpart, Angelo, Candido is a fall-guy; even though Dekker and Middleton enhanced their careers through writing for men like him. The difference, however, is that neither Duke from either of *The Honest Whore* plays finds the space in which to stage the voice of authority which Vincentio does in *Measure for Measure*. Candido is a caricature, even though Dekker and Middleton were, artistically at least, much more pro-city than writers like Shakespeare. By setting such an exemplary Puritan within the impatient medium of the city the writers produced some highly marketable satire. With ironic poignancy, no sooner does Candido find his distinctly civic voice than it is embarrassed through the unconfined voices of those located in Bedlam. Candido's rational account of how he came to be unjustly incarcerated sounds just like all the others babbling in the asylum: he is literally surrounded by bedlam (*The Honest Whore, part I*, V.ii.467–78).[122] Within the mad context of the institution, Candido's voice and the Duke's authority simultaneously dilapidate in the very chaos of which they are the architects. Mocking Candido, as symbol of City government, proved to be as popular as staging the institutions with which he was civically bound. In Dekker's sequel, the agitation of the phlegmatic shopkeeper, and the attempt to drive him from his humour, was once again staged with great gusto. Perhaps it appealed to the audience to see that no one, especially the self-elected Candido, could really escape the anxieties of the times; 'no matter how rigid his Stoicism or profound his trust in Providence.'[123] After the moral explorations of *The Honest Whore, part I*, Dekker's *part II* returns to some of the bawdy folk energy of his earlier work; though now, perhaps, with more satiric than Utopic tendencies. In the more raunchy *The Honest Whore, part II* Dekker humiliates Candido through a carnivalesque idiom; as the ever-temperate linen-draper is forced to his knees in order to toast 'a whores health' whereupon he is immediately arrested for receiving (albeit unknowingly) stolen goods. Once again, Candido's sobriety and pretentious morality is deeply embarrassed by its context within and without the play.[124] The stolen 'lawne' theme was based on the fact that several pieces of cloth had been misappropriated from Bridewell a couple of years earlier. Ultimately, of course, being the butt of the joke did reinforce his sense of identity.[125] Upon being discovered in Bridewell, he phlegmatically notes that his purpose is 'to beare wrong here with patience' (*The Honest Whore, part II*, V.ii.204).[126] Martyrdom fortifies him, and gives him a certain brittle-strong sense of security. Puritanism owed its very identity and existence to rejection, protestation, and even social scorn.

V   'HOLD OUT STILL, WENCH': THE CONTINENT CITY
AND THE HONEST 'WHORE'

Poking fun at Puritan City politicians was not confined to ridiculing Candido in the *Honest Whore* plays. By making Bellafront bear the City virtues of self-control, the writers produce some hard-hitting satire which targeted London's rulers. Bellafront was initially created as a stereotypical 'whore' precisely so she could expose the values of those who castigated her. Dekker typically deployed marginal figures to indict the society which had marginalized and disenfranchised them. In *The Honest Whore, part I* (and to some extent *The Honest Whore, part II*) Bellafront, a fallen women, becomes 'Honest' in order to secure the integrity of the City's values.[127] Bellafront's conversion to 'the honest whore' is depicted as an exemplary process, one designed to tease those Puritan zealots who so passionately detested, and were titillated by, prostitution. Through suffering and trials, Bellafront acquires the kind of moral veracity which would make the ardent Puritan tingle with excitement. She embarrasses the City's elite because it is she who really plays out the consequences of Candido's speech on humility at the end of *The Honest Whore, part I* in a way that Candido, who generates the conditions of his own forbearance, cannot. From the moment Bellafront falls in love with Hippolito, and his instantaneous rejection of that love, Bellafront renounces her former life as a prostitute. As she changes from bad to good, Bellafront's behaviour would be perceived as socially unexpected and theologically impossible. Upon departure from her role as stereotypical 'whore', Bellafront proceeds to parody the path of the typical Puritan.[128] She starts with a strenuous bout of soul-searching and a journey of inner exploration. Precisely because she is a prostitute, Bellafront is able both to ridicule and exemplify the intensity of this inner scrutiny. It is, however, Bellafront's continuous wrestling with her tainted soul which becomes a matter of self-definition for her. As a paradigm of Puritan consciousness, Bellafront reveals how continual self-doubt provides an identity which, though it looks for security, it could never wholly be found. Self-knowledge implies self-deception and could be considered 'less reliable than other forms of knowledge precisely because there was so much incentive to distort and deceive in drawing conclusions about oneself.'[129] According to Theweleit, the move to 'faith in one's feelings' was ineluctably tied to an ontological crisis.[130] Ironically it is Bellafront's initial faith in Hippolito which precipitates her self-doubt and the ensuing search for a sense of her own integrity. As the bearer of moral verisimilitude, Bellafront is tempted, scorned, and chastised in order to strengthen her self-disciplinary resolve; that she might remove 'the foule black spots that stick upon my soule' (*The Honest*

*Whore, part I,* III.iii.12). This self-disciplinary eradication of contamination is further elaborated in *The Honest Whore, part II,* where she
becomes a highly virtuous, long-suffering, 'patient Griselda' as her
moral mettle is thoroughly tested.

Dekker's valorization of Bellafront is less about his sympathy for
prostitutes, or even his mockery of Puritans, and more about exposing the dynamics of city–court contention. Anti-court sentiments sanctify the City, which appears as a realm overwhelmingly
threatened by courtly laxity. The social tensions which underscore
Hippolito's obsessive 'mutton – mungering' – his desire for
Bellafront – endorse the role of the consumer-gallant chasing the
city's merchandise. In telling Hippolito's messenger that she rejects
his advances, the city's values and hers become tied by metaphor:

> Thou to this Lord shalt goe, commend me to him,
> And tell him this, the Towne has held out long,
> Because (within) 'twas rather true, then strong.
> To sell it now were base; Say 'tis no hold
> Built of weake stuffe, to be blowne up with gold.

> (*The Honest Whore, part II,* II.i.241–5)

Only the integrity of an inner purity could withstand such financial
force and moral corrosion. In fending off Hippolito's inducements,
Bellafront's chastity becomes a synecdoche for the City's virtue, its
very autonomy. Conversely her virtue, her honesty, becomes the
'Towne' strength against the corruption of the court. Dekker inverted the common image that the City was full of 'whores' tempt-
ing wealthy and naive young men into a lascivious life as they led
the innocent aristocracy astray (a view often reproduced by critics
and historians). In resisting the besiegement of lusting courtiers,
she is continually entreated by them to 'draw up her Percullis'; but,
for the sake of the 'Towne', she keeps them out (*The Honest Whore,
part II,* II.i.262). Metropolitan conflict is thus mapped onto
Bellafront's body. Her sexuality is later reductively referred to as 'a
waste piece of ground, which is her owne by inheritance', as
Hippolito's sexual aggression towards her becomes increasingly
homologous to the practices of an unscrupulous landlord.
Bellafront's father reveals that 'There's a lord now that goes about,
not to take it cleane from her, but to inclose it to himselfe, and to
joyne it to a piece of his Lordships' (*II,* III.i.4–8). Bellafront seems

about to be assaulted by another aristocratic, semi-legal land-grab; and her rightful, legal, inheritance is depicted as the virtue she has to defend.

Although Bellafront is the eponymous heroine of the play, her 'honesty' does not allow her to escape the limited categories in which she is framed. Her loins are still discursively or materially up for grabs both within and without the play. For this reason it would be difficult to champion her characteristic virtues without endorsing the chastity which was part of the same social and semiotic system which designated her a 'whore'. Neither should she be cast as the self-effacingly chaste rescuer of marital disharmony. According to Richard Horwich, Bellafront follows convention in 'her self-loathing and subsequent desire to reform after hearing a sermon from an honest man' and in 'her conviction that marriage can make her honest and rehabilitate her socially.'[131] Yet in *The Honest Whore, part I* Bellafront's marriage to the sociopathic Matheo is graphically depicted as a prelude to further abuse. Dekker follows this line in *The Honest Whore, part II* when husband Matheo tries to support his gallant lifestyle by pimping off his wife. Horwich's remark that 'in *The Honest Whore*, the state of marriage itself is rehabilitative' is a difficult conclusion to draw from either play.[132] Not only do the 'whore-chasing' Hippolito and the unhappy Infelice remain estranged at the end of *part I*, but in *part II* the marriage of Bellafront and Matheo is presented as a moment of ironic capitulation on her behalf. Even by the post-Elizabethan standards of comedic disunity there does not appear to be a shred of harmony in their nuptials. As Bellafront's father indicates, the man she is about to marry was also the one who had 'beaten thee, kickt thee, trod on thee … pawnd thee … sold thee, made yee leape at a crust…' (*The Honest Whore, part II*, V.ii.464–6). She replies: 'Oh yes, good sir, women shall learne of me,/To love their husbands in greatest misery…' V.ii.468–9). If we fail to take this kind of self-sacrificial 'patient Griselda' stuff with a pinch of salt, then we risk patronizing seventeenth-century audiences. With considerable irony Bellafront points up the fractures that the conventions of comedy-marriages once glossed. This irony is symptomatic of her character's position. For all the problems Bellafront has in being shaped by, and confronting, her context, she still exhibits a remarkable amount of dramatic autonomy through her presence. Unlike many stage prostitutes of the time, she does not simply fade from view to allow the primary action to take centre stage.[133] Uniquely in

early modern drama, Bellafront, the eponymous 'whore', is both
the central character and the hero of the play.


## VI   ORLANDO FRISCOBALDO: 'NOW TO BE AN ACTOR
IN OUR ENSUING COMEDY'

As an embodiment of the city's anti-theatrical forces, the phlegmatic Candido displayed a deep and intense suspicion of any form
of dissimulation, albeit in language, intemperance, dressing-up, or
in trade. For him, all representation was charged with uncertainty
and inauthenticity: in essence, it was a travesty. That everything
might be theatrical produced, as Agnew says, 'a crisis in representation' which could only be solved by eradicating the theatre and
all things theatrical.[134] It was on just such grounds that the Puritan
City Fathers sought to close down the theatres. Hired by the City,
hacks like Gosson and Stubbes always stressed the 'whoredom' and
'wantonness' of the 'strumpet' stage. Not surprisingly, Dekker took
Candido to task over this issue through the very means by which
he despised the theatre.

Candido is thus advised to use theatrical means to restore order
to his household, and, at the same time, (re)instigate spousal hierarchy. With malicious intent, the courtier Lodovico implores the
reluctant Candido to admonish his wife through the device of
acting in a punishing 'Comedy'; one which would humiliate her.
Eventually, Lodovico scolds the reluctant draper through the very
theatrical medium which horrifies him. In goading Candido,
Lodovico demands, 'S'blood cannot you doe as all the world does?
counterfet' (*The Honest Whore, part II*, II.ii.15). When faced with this
taunt, and the prospect of adopting another persona, Candido,
ironically, gets stage fright. 'I cannot doo't' he claims, and, later
more emphatically 'I shall not act it' II.ii.18). Antipathy to the stage
developed when anxieties about the intrinsically theatrical quality
of trade became projected on to the function of play.[135] Candido
expends endless effort in order to contain and quell this very
effect.[136] Even losing his temper would just be too dramatic, for it
would involve losing himself, losing his self-control. He would be
'beside himself', which is something he simply cannot countenance.

Yet the theatrical devices which Candido eschews become the
means by which the play rescues its protagonists, especially from
themselves. Not the Duke's authority, Candido's patience, or

Bellafront's virtue, can fully disguise, gloss, or resolve, all the social conflicts which develop during the play. The comic action staged in Bedlam and Bridewell authorizes drama as the only force to disencumber them from the grip of their own ineffective or rigid convictions. By pretending to be mad Bellafront craftily outmaneuvers the opprobrious Matheo, her future husband. Posing as a 'counterfeit crank' was something about which the City authorities were deeply anxious and those suspected were brought under considerable scrutiny. Theatrical devices save Bellafront again in *part II*. There she is rescued through the dramatic office of her father, Orlando Friscobaldo, who operates through a complex performative arrangement:

> I beseech your Grace (tho your eye be so piercing) as under a poore blue Coate, to cull out an honest Father from an old Servingman: yet good my Lord discover not the plot to any, but only this Gentleman that is now to be an Actor in our ensuing Comedy.   (IV.ii.1–5)

Embodied in the figure of Orlando, theatre appears as a traditionally poor, but honest, retainer. The Duke's tacit approval of Orlando's dramatic devices closely corresponds to the relationship between the Crown–Court and the theatre. London's theatre functioned through a combination of the logistical support which the city provided (location, capital, writers, and audience) and sovereign or courtly patronage and protection. Protection was required if the City Fathers were to be resisted in their efforts to close down the theatres. Although Orlando is licensed by the Duke, crucially he does not act wholly on behalf of the Duke. To some extent, Orlando follows his own agenda: and this means saving his daughter from the three-pronged attack on her virtue; consisting of the Dukes harsh 'New Lawes', Hippolito's 'mutton-mungering', and the profligacy of her newly gallant and socially ambitious husband. The 'ensuing Comedy', as he puts it, finally owes its success to the 'Actor' Orlando's disguises and trickery. Dramatic deception, or feigning, extricates Bellafront from the pressures of three men who are considerably more powerful than her. Orlando's interventions within the play are presented as a drama which privileges itself in relation to the tensions which produced it. For not only does Orlando rescue the hard-pressed Bellafront, but he achieves this via a theatrical act which simultaneously nullifies the charges against the incarcerated Candido and extricates the stymied Duke from the problems created by his own laws. Ironically, both the Duke's authority and his court, as well as Candido's precious dignity, are dependent upon the medium of the theatre itself. For Dekker, theatre could rescue people and embodied authority from the dysfunctional impact of political and moral certitude.

Within the stresses of ideological conflict, Orlando uses the very forms which excited official anxiety in early modern London: disguise, trickery, and counterfeiting. As Horwich says, Orlando 'becomes, in a sense, the author of the action, a force for moral stability as he passes, disguised, through a vicious and apparently chaotic world.'[137] It is precisely because he is steeped in the world in which he operates that he can be so instrumentally effective. Operating between and within the court, City, street, brothel, and Bridewell, he exploits the gaps, fissures, contradictions, and collisions of authority. As Dekker offers the audience their own plebeian hero, he offers them the potential of the theatre itself. Orlando is not merely, as Leggatt says, a 'fairy-godfather', one who can only 'solve the problems of fictional characters.'[138] Rather he is a synecdoche for the function of theatre. As such he is able to deploy the imaginary theatrical world in a way which reveals and indicts social problems outside that realm. Through theatre our eyes are opened to official sleight of hand, the deceitful motives of those in power, the function of class ideology, and the doubtful purpose of the city's institutions both inside and out. Orlando's play within the play, which charts the contours of social tension, raises important questions about theatricality and the City. In presenting the *Honest Whore* plays as an interacting and permeable multilayering of the City, the theatre, and the institution, we are encouraged to see the interstitial qualities of urban space. Metropolitan London functioned through competing power loci; not just the power brokerage between Crown and City, but through the multifarious 'worlds within worlds' which constituted London's society.[139] Teasing out and reading the culture through one strand, albeit absolutism, the bourgeoisie, the Court, Puritanism, or the City Fathers, runs the risk of reproducing and reconstructing the anxieties and perspective of that specific group. Each locus of power will see chaos, decadence, and disorder, in a composite picture of the others. The more a particular faction, through fear or fantasy, seeks to impose its own version of order on the world, particularly when faced with a force powerful enough to challenge it, the more the contest in legitimation will prescribe deleterious attitudes to those less socially enfranchised. The faultlines produced in the various institutional and power clashes of early modern London provided a limited, but sometimes viable, space in which the less privileged could operate. Orlando's success at trickery, for example, stems from his roguish past: 'I scorn to cunny-catch: yet I ha beene Dog at a Cony in my time' (*The Honest Whore, part II*, II.i.226–7). It is, therefore, noticeably his ability to be a 'Dog' which facilitates his acts of social and dramatic intervention more effectively than does his moral or patriarchal roles: 'roguery and theatricality were intertwined'.[140] It was a theatricality which depended upon the intersection of social forces and topographical sites within a new metropolitan space.

# 2

# Prostitution and Dekker

## I  HUSTLING IN SEVENTEENTH-CENTURY LONDON

He has come to the metropolis to sell his labour power ... [he] is free to sell his labour power like a commodity ... To live he can sell his life ...[1]

Evidence of prostitution in any period is likely to be patchy, but recently the work of Ian Archer has considerably expanded our knowledge of brothel activities in early modern London. Archer, whose sources admittedly cover the upper end of the market, has found 'evidence for at least 100 bawdy houses operating in the latter 1570's'[2] Consequently, prostitution could be deemed 'among the most highly organized sectors of criminal activity in London ...'[3] So the overall business of prostitution was likely to have been considerably larger than many of the so-called licit trades in the capital. Prostitution, and the prostitute, figure large in the drama of early modern London. Why? And what was the relationship between the prostitute on the stage and her role on the street or in the brothel? To answer these questions, neither literature nor the examination of the limited historical evidence would be wholly adequate to the task. If we are to take our understanding beyond the clichés – that it is the 'oldest profession', 'love for sale', or that 'whores' are 'wanton women and wayward wives' – then we need to unpack the relationship between social imagination and its material consequences and the way they were lived out in and through metropolitan space.

In Chapter 1 we saw how a prostitute, Bellafront, was made to bear all kinds of social and political stress. As an encoder of cultural tensions the prostitute had few peers. In *The Honest Whore, part II*, a pimp and a bawd, Bots and Madam Horsleech, offer a stark demystification of the city's sex industry:

We want tooles, Gentlemen, to furnish the trade: they weare out day and night, they weare out till no mettle bee left in their

54

backe; wee heare of two or three new Wenches are come up with a Carrier, and your old Goshawke here is flying at them. (III.iii.4–7)

Like perverse artisans, Bots (a bawd) and Horsleech (an ex-soldier) eagerly prepare to prey upon the new immigrants. Prostitution is read through the exploitative metaphors of trade – and trade was after all the City's *raison d'être* – to render people into mere commodity. To acquire their human stock, they go to meet the increasingly popular carriers bringing in their carts up to twenty to thirty passengers at a time into London from the provinces.[4] As many as 500 migrants per month arrived in the city during this period, a number which increased sharply after the turn of the century.

War had a significant impact on prostitution. When Shakespeare's Mistress Overdone claims 'what with war, what with the sweat, what with the gallows, and what with poverty, I am custom-shrunk' we can see how integrated prostitution was with the rest of society, and how adverse social conditions could affect 'trade'.[5] Such problems may have had a deleterious impact upon 'trade' in the short term, but the kind of social disruption which war caused hit the lower class especially hard and provided a climate in which prostitution thrived. While Overdone laments her soldier-clients going off to war, those who departed left their wives at the mercy of pimps and bawds; many of whom were discharged soldiers or deserters.[6] When Ralph is drafted, in *The Shoemakers' Holiday*, his new bride Jane implores the muster captain, 'O let him stay, else I shall be undone' (I.i.144); and implication is clear that to 'be undone' is to be 'overdone', to be faced with poverty or prostitution, especially as your husband was unlikely to return.[7] War ruptured the already fragile lives of the poor and left them further exposed to social and economic uncertainty; for many prostitution was the only option.[8] In effect, war increased the number of women forced to turn to the trade and, periodically at least, increased the number of potential clients in the form of men both in and out of service. Those who had once sold themselves or had been sold were forced to exploit others when faced with the falling value of their own bodies: 'Fish that must needs bite or themselves be bitten' says *The Roaring Girl*'s Moll, as she describes the competitive ethos of the world of the underclass – a world so often romanticized by writers and critics. In reality, London's dynamic underworld consisted of hustlers, huxters, pimps, and panders who preyed upon the likes of 'distressed needlewomen and trade-fallen wives' (*The Roaring Girl*, III.i.93–4). Upon coming to the city, the undercapitalized found themselves free to sell themselves and there they lived in 'appalling conditions of sweated labour'.[9]

Immigration was the huge demographic engine which provided the energy of the new metropolis. In the strains of that expansion, and in the eyes and minds of the authorities, the prostitute and the immigrant were aligned in material, discursive, and topographical ways. It was all too easy to see the landless and dispossessed on the city's threshold as a source of cheap and exploitable labour, or potential cannon fodder, rather than a tragic problem of social dislocation. The 'Country Wench', in Middleton's *Michaelmas Term*, encapsulates the forces of immigration, and the moment of threshold, as she comes to London to sell herself. Michaelmas occurred at the end of the rural wage-labour cycle and was one of London's busiest legal terms for sorting out tenure rights, labour rates, and rents. At this time, the capital experienced a particularly large increase in people seeking farm-work, tenure security, equitable rents, or, failing that, a drastic change of employment in the City. Streets thronged with bewildered and vulnerable people either trying to find a new livelihood or attempting to secure the one they had. For many this provided a traumatic induction into the matrix of the metropolitan economy, both materially and symbolically. These were good times for the likes of Bots and Horsleech, both for acquiring the 'tooles' of their 'trade' and for supplying their well-heeled visiting clients.

A paradigm of rural-to-urban immigration, Middleton's 'Country Wench' has no personal name: she is both ubiquitous and alienated. Like Bellafront, her familial separation intersects with her social dislocation.[10] In this vulnerable state the Country Wench meets the cynical Pander who attempts to seduce and procure her with images of a new City identity. This transformation, he promises, would bring an end to her poverty and secure her 'better advancement' (*Michaelmas Term*, I.ii.4). Pander trots out the hackneyed seductions of the city:

> ... wouldst thou a pretty beautifull-Juicy squall, live in a poore thrumbd house i'th cuntry in such servile-habilements, and may well passe for a gentlewoman i'th Citie, do's not 5 hundred do so thinkst thou, and with worse faces, oh, now in these latter dayes ... (I.ii.4–9)

Middleton's Pander and potential prostitute begin a relationship, built on suspicion, which meets their different needs: he requires the commodity, and she has to escape poverty. But the Country Wench's escape from 'servile-habilements', in Middleton's drama, is quickly translated into social ambition: 'I am in a swone till I bee a gentlewoman, and you know what flesh is mans meate, tell it be drest' (I.ii.57–9). The dynamics of survival, when framed by the cynicism of upward social mobility, underscored the price paid by those more euphemistically called 'the enterprising poor'.[11] Anyone, it seems, seeking a different role could be figured as a prostitute. For many immigrants, then, their bodies became the crudest arena of self-fashioning as they negotiated new urban identities. Non-brothel prostitution constituted the largest portion of the trade in what Haselkorn has described as the 'countless thousands of women peddling their persons, their one marketable commodity'.[12] Prostitution exemplified and metaphorized the immediacy and alienation of labour as a commodity, of the body as a product. 'Bawdes, Panders & Curtizans', says Dekker's narrator in *Lanthorne and Candle-light*, '... these Suburb sinners have no landes to live upon but their legges ...' (Grosart, vol. III, p. 266). Unfixed and unlocatable, prostitutes had no secure form of their own identity, or any perceivable social autonomy. They were often associated with the topographically unstable shanty towns like the infamous Alsatia, situated upon the eastern edge of the City, outside the walls. These suburban areas, with cheap accommodation and a repository of immigrant labour, occupied a crucial place in the imagination and construction of early modern metropolitan London. The 'suburbs of London', wrote James Howell, 'are much larger than the body of the City.'[13]

According to Archer the majority of brothels, some 80 per cent, were located in the suburbs.[14] This location for brothels was due to historical determinants related to the political, social and topographical development of the City. The ancient sites of licensed prostitution, particularly in places like the Bankside in Southwark, were always outside the walls and sometimes beyond the scope of the City; though this area was more 'governable' than we might expect.[15] In Dekker's time, the outskirts of London, the 'Liberties', were still officially less openly harassed or supervised by the authorities, but they were not the locus of anarchy which some critics have observed.[16] The suburbs were ghettos for all kinds of unofficial work; as Ruth Mazzeo Karras argues 'prostitution was a natural outlet for casual unskilled labour ...'[17] With semantic economy, Nashe asks, 'London, what are thy suburbs but licensed stews? Can it be so many brothel-houses of salaried sensuality and six-penny whoredom (the next door to magistrates) should be set up and maintained.'[18] Like Dekker's juicy phrase about 'suburb sinners', Nashe's disapproval functions to excommunicate the suburbs from London proper. Yet descriptions like Nashe's disclosed the uncontained flow of extra-mural commercial activity which the cash nexus brought to human relations. This dynamic was characteristic of the new metropolis: Agnew indicates 'that in the early seventeenth century, a new extraterritorial zone of production and exchange sprang up outside London's ancient marketplaces and thus out of reach of their juridical, ceremonial, and talismatic protections – and restrictions.'[19] The making of the suburbs had a material, discursive, and imaginative impact on the City proper.[20] In the period which witnessed the 'important transformation in the character of the metropolis with a change in emphasis from the municipality to the suburbs', the figure which characterized the suburbs, the prostitute, became something of an icon, or axis, around which the meaning of trade, and the culture's attitude to it, got defined.[21]

Cultural visibility and economic importance found expression in extraordinary ways. At the very heart of Jonson's *Bartholomew Fair*, for example, we find Ursula, a 'Bawd' whose presence, rather like the suburbs themselves, appears larger than the mere confines of her characterological configuration; 'The body o' the fair', as Quarlous says, is also the 'Mother o' the bawds' (II.v.69). From a place of monstrous growth, Ursula lambastes those who come to sample her wares:

> Aye, aye, gamesters, mock a plain plump soft wench o' the suburbs, do, because she's juicy and wholesome: you must ha' your thin pinch'd ware, pent up i' the compass of a dog-collar(or 'twill not do) (II.v.77–80)

Ursula encodes the massive expansion of the suburbs which had fundamentally altered the equilibrium of the metropolitan socio-economic infrastructure. She mocks the 'sippers o' the city', as she embodies the economic vigour and good value of illicit suburban trade. Commercial activity in the extraterritorial zones presented a competitive challenge to the sub-optimal modes and practices of official trade in the City. Whatever else prostitution is, it is a trade, a transaction of services for money; and all trade, in effect, could be linked to women in the city. Even 'the New Exchange', says Karen Newman, 'was immediately a place of both erotic and economic exchange.'[22] In the sexual and semiotic economies of London's commerce, ideas associated with the voracity of trade moved to the 'skirts' of the City. Prostitution and trade were synonymous: Dekker's *The Deade Terme* simply states that the 'setting up of a whore-house is now as common as the setting up of a trade: yea, and it goes under that name' (Grosart, vol. IV, p. 58). The city's so-called 'shoppes ... of the world', were situated alongside the economically vulnerable small-trader. Mysogynistic images encouraged the idea that prostitutes were an egregious function of the cash/trade nexus. In Dekker and Webster's *Northward Hoe*, Doll, a prostitute, considers the degrading process of selling herself. Speaking of her exploitation, she notes, with rueful acuity, that 'a woman is a man's stampe, we are not currant till we passe from one man to another' (I.ii.82–3). Doll cynically reviews the world where she can only acquire value by becoming a prime vector of exchange. Self-exploitation offers her a double-bind because she then merely fulfils the cultural preconceptions of her supposedly innate promiscuity. On the one hand she exploits the cliché that there is something intrinsically promiscuous about the nature of trade itself, while on the other she exploits the fact that she is exploitable. Whatever else is happening here, it should not be confused with sexual autonomy or economic liberation.

This underlying promiscuity of trade consistently haunted the minds of many men in the city. Francis Lenton's version of a Sempster Shopkeeper is ostensibly descriptive but reveals its anxieties through its prurience:

[She] Is a feminine creature furnished with the finest ware ... She is very neatly spruced up and placed in the frontispiece of her shop, of purpose (by her curious habit) to allure some custom, which still increaseth and decreaseth as her beauty is in the full, or in the wane. She hath a pretty faculty in presenting herself to the view of passengers ... where they are rapt into a bargain by her beauty ... In her trade ... if you cannot bargain for her ruffs in her shop, she will fit you with choice at your chamber, so you will pay her well for her pains ....[23]

Lenton perceives the woman shopkeeper as far more for sale than her wares.[24] Trade is sexualized and that which is sexual is traded. It is precisely because of this that Candido attempted to circumscribe the act of trading, separating himself from the promiscuity which Lenton perceives as underwriting such transactions. It was a common perception; as the author of *Hic Mulier* attests, 'Women have nothing ... to divide themselves from the inticing shewes or mooving Images which do furnish most shops in the City.'[25] All commercial intercourse in the city became caught up in this semiotic traffic between prostitution and trade. Both Laxton and Goshawk, two men-about-town in *The Roaring Girl*, share this reductive perspective. In a meticulously directed shop scene (II.i), one designed to capture the sexualized arena of the shop as the new private threshold of urban interchange, the three shopkeepers' wives take up their ambiguously designated social-sexual space in the front of their respective shops. Like the prostitutes who stood on the threshold of brothels to attract business, in the front of the shop the shopkeepers wives and daughters occupied a similarly hybrid realm between public space, the street, and the increasingly demarcated and privatized interior of commercial activity in the city. Sexual and social liaison, coupled with shop-talk innuendo, forms the mainspring of this comedy. Goshawk sarcastically comments on the nature of early modern London's enterprise culture as he refers to Mistress Gallipot's tobacco retailing; 'tis many a good woman's fortune, when her husband turns bankrupt, to begin with pipes and set up again' (II.i.10–11). With a sexually degrading *double entendre*, his remark commodifies her and makes the economic power of the purchaser part of a fantasy about his sexual power. At the same time his class-specific jibe serves to emasculate her husband's socio-sexual status. Not to be outswaggered in the investment of sex-trade innuendo, Laxton insists that 'the raising of the woman is the lifting up of the man's head at all times: if one flourish, t'other will bud as fast ...' (II.i.13–15). Cuckoldry, the stock-in-trade of Renaissance playwrights, appears as the root metaphor of commercial activity, and, more specifically in *The Roaring Girl*, of the ensuing comedy between the shopkeepers, their wives, and the gallants.[26]

This continual mixing of sexual and commercial energy, at a discursive, practical and dramatic level, made those whose civic integrity depended upon trade highly anxious. Assessing the rights and values of trade, and the identities attached to them, was of crucial importance in a changing civic arena. When Middleton's 'Country Wench' 'becomes courtesan', she acutely asks 'doe not al Trades live by their ware, and yet cald honest Livers?' (*Michaelmas Term*, IV.ii.10–12). It was a question many found hard to answer. Precisely who could be called 'honest Livers' was a question by those with social and political power, and figured through urban topography.[27] In the character writing of the period the prostitute was continually constructed as the devalued opposite of the respectable trader.

Less-official business in the city was often considered to be the province of women, partly because their access to the guild organization was heavily restricted, and partly because they were likely to be less capitalized. Donald Lupton describes London's ever more scrutinized 'Fisherwomen', street-traders, who 'carry their shops on their heads ... They are free in all places and pay nothing for shop-rent ... If they drink out their whole stock, it's but a pawning a petticoat in Long Lane, or themselves in Turnbull Street, for to set up again.'[28] Clearly it was not only James who became anxious about women who wore 'wide-brimmed hats', the specialist headgear of the street-trader.[29] This type of trading within the official bounds of the City excites and troubles Lupton because the Fisherwomen exhibit, for him, a toxic mixture of sexual, social and spacial fluidity. For Lupton, being 'free in all places' was a form of sexual corruption which mocked as it contaminated the official 'Freedom of the City'; the ritual which inaugurated City identity proper.[30] Women free-traders flouted the conventions and strictures of male-dominated commerce in the City; no doubt their prices were lower as well! Lupton's literary gaze is driven by the impulse to control and taxonomize such activities. It was a view which became an increasingly significant part of the principles governing and defining urban identity. Prostitution was positioned as a crucial site of unregulated forces which, through their exclusion, sought to anchor the idea of citizenship for certain men in London. Pander, in Middleton's *Michaelmas Term*, offers the Country Wench an ironic version of urban identity, one which savagely mocked the legitimation of citizen-subjectivity:

> Women nere rise, but when they fall,
> Let a man breake, hee's gone, blowen up,
> A woman's breaking sets her up,

Virginitie is no Citie-Trade,
You're out a'th Freedome, when you're a mayde ...

(I.ii.42–46)

Never one to doubt the deleterious relationship between commerce and sex, Middleton traces the manner by which a woman's ruptured sexual integrity was perceived as the very hall-mark of her commercial value. Within this realm women were construed as essentially low, suburban, bodily, disintegrated, and non-citizens. If men break, they simply cease to exist; women can only exist if they are broken. Having the Freedom, being a citizen, gave men access to a place of imagined social security.[31] To achieve this, integrity and masculinity were forcefully, and topographically, aligned in contradistinction to the indicted prostitute. 'Honest Livers' were those men who could claim, and had the power to claim, to be able to distinguish those who were not.

## II CITIZENS AND THE SUBURBS

Suburban expansion was often posited as a parasitic growth upon the 'body of the City', a canker which could drain the City of its spirit and resources. One contemporary observer noted with alarm, 'I believe there will be no City left shortly, for it will all run out at the gates to the suburbs'.[32] There was a common misperception that the suburbs expanded from the outflow of the City rather than through rural migration; a view which was predicated upon socioeconomic polarization and antagonism. City virtue being privileged in the face of suburban vice underscored much of the popular pamphlet industry of the late sixteenth and early seventeenth centuries. What could be worse, Dekker wonders in the chapter of *Lanthorne and Candle-light* entitled 'The Infection of the Suburbs', than 'the plague which a Whore-house layes upon a Citty?' (Grosart, vol. III, p. 265). Dekker provided topical literature full of terrifying fantasies whereby the City and citizen were matched against the horror of suburban incursion: 'How happy therefore were Citties if they had no Suburbs', he writes, 'sithence they serve but as caves, where monsters are/bred up to devowre the Citties themselves?' (Grosart, vol. III, p. 267).[33] According to Manley, Dekker simply presents a contemporary view; 'Dekker and others achieve much of their descriptive force by pitting the personal fears and perplexities of Englishmen against London's size and complexity.'[34] Furthermore, 'they attempt to mystify London, to present it as an alien realm honeycombed with shadowy sub-communities.'[35] Yet paradoxically, Dekker's literature also owed its artistic and cultural potency to its ability to de-mystify, or translate, that alien realm. His hyperbolic descriptions ostensibly threw the light of a scrutinizing 'Lanthorne' upon the menacing monsters of London's underworld. Vivid topographical portraiture and sharp social characterization provided a self-perpetuating resource for the newly professional writer. Dekker always promised 'more strange Villanies' with every pamphlet, and advertised 'dayly to fight so common, so bolde, so strange, and so dangerous an enemy' (Grosart, vol. III, p. 181). And the enemy was as morally lax as it was peripheral: 'the skirts of London were pitifully pared off' by the 'poverty and sluttishness' of the 'sinfully polluted suburbs' (Grosart, vol. III, p. 181).

Dekker's self-acknowledged readership appeared to consist of 'Gentlemen, Lawyers, Merchants, Citizens, Farmers, Masters of Households, and all sorts of servants' (Grosart, vol. III, p. 305). The literature, which was 'delightful for all men to reade', targeted a wide metropolitan readership; a constituency not confined by class, institutional, civic, or political, affiliations (Grosart, vol. III, p. 305). Expositional writing could simply appeal to all the anxious men in the city. Buying a pamphlet enabled each man to feel like a discrete personal citadel operating 'in defence of Law, Justice, Order, Ceremony, Religion, Peace, and that honorable title of Goodnesse' (Pendry, p. 183); rather than leaving himself open to the corrosive anarchy of 'all damnable sinnes' (Grosart, vol. III, p. 266). According to Richard Johnson, another peddler of metropolitan anxiety, 'the undoing of a number of good gentleman, citizens, trades-men and such like' was likely given the vast 'army' of 'shifters … within London'.[36] To protect himself, so Dekker claims, the male reader merely had to 'Read and Laugh; read and learn; read and loathe. Laugh at the knavery; learn out the mystery; loathe the base villainy' (Pendry, p. 183).

The squalor and hardship which characterized the suburbs became transcoded into phantasmic and fictive realms of the citizen-subject's imagination. Readers of *The Seven deadly Sinnes of London* were tendentiously asked, 'what hope hast thou to grow up still in the pride of thy strength, gallantness and health, having seven deadly and detestable sins lying night by night by thy lascivious sides' (Grosart, vol. II, p. 13). From such a perspective a man's integrity was figured as singular and separate, free from the morally degenerate grasp of the lascivious mire around him. Many writers concentrated on making such 'personal fears' a crutch for a new urban masculinity. Gender categories came to illustrate the imaginary topography of the city as the individual citizen looked for and after himself. As London grew into a metropolis (from the Greek: *metro* meaning mother or uterus; and *polis* meaning city state) its literature increasingly figured the city as a female persona. Following this trend, Dekker playfully alluded to London as his gargantuan mother: 'from thy womb receaved I my being, from thy brests my nourishment'; and later 'O London! (thou Mother of my Life) …' (Grosart, vol. II, p. 13, and vol. IV, p. 285). 'London', in Middleton's civic pageant *Triumph of Truth*, appears as 'a woman': she says, 'I am thy Mother' to the newly ensconced mayor, her 'honourable son' (Bullen, vol. VII, p. 236). Behind this grand maternal figure lay the complexities of representing and embodying the political father. Personifying 'the city as heroic matron', Manley argues, 'facilitated a symbolically submissive intermediary between nature and the higher claims of political culture.'[37] For the vigorously patriarchal James I, the picture of London as 'a gender-based model of obedient submission' both flattered and soothed his sense of royal authority.[38] London's oligarchic rulers, the City Fathers, though not always entirely happy to be 'under' the crown were, nevertheless, content with models of 'female' submission. They were particularly impressed with those images which 'suppressed the more dynamic aspects of urban life'.[39] These aspects included 'the potentially divergent powers and interests that were topographically epitomized by the city's subdivisions into a discontinuous terrain of holdings and jurisdictions, hidden tenements, alleys, byways, straight rooms, and cellars.'[40] All of these locations were associated with 'low life', prostitutes, and the suburbs.

Next door to the nurturing London-as-matron lurked London the threatening 'monster'.[41] Capitalizing on masculine unease, Dekker exploited the tension which these two images engendered. London could be represented as both chaste and wanton:

O London, thou art great in glory... Thou art the goodliest of neighbours, but the prowdest; the welthiest, but the most wanton. Thou hast in thee to make thee fairest, and all things in thee to make thee foulest: for thou art attir'd like a Bride, drawing all that look upon thee to be in love with thee, but there is much harlot in thine eyes. (Grosart, vol. II, pp. 10–11)

London could be a dream-come-true or a nightmare; a place where a man might lose or find himself. For many, the interconnection between these views was a profoundly discomforting thought. Like Lenton's view of the shopkeeper, the projection of masculine desire could easily become recycled as a 'harlot's' seduction. Dekker teased those men who want to purify their desire for wealth by imagining that they are marrying a fair 'bride', while all the time he's selling them a 'whore with a heart of gold'. Hippolito's schizophrenia is shot through with this dichotomy in *The Honest Whore, part I* as he tries psychically to separate his would-be 'fair' bride and his subliminal fear and desire for Bellafront. Meanwhile, in the Draper's shop, Candido is being continually aggravated by the unfulfilled desires of his far from obedient wife, as she tirelessly flouts his patient civic authority.[42] Candido's domestic conflict was a parodic jibe at the City's rulers who sought to interpenetrate the image of a governable London with that of a tractable woman.

Much of the language of urban identity tried to locate the citizen-subject as an 'impregnable' castle standing erect and above the miasma of corruption around him.[43] This resulted in an intense fear of engulfment. With suffocating unease Lupton reveals that 'London ... she is grown so great, I am almost afraid to meddle with her; She's certainly a great World, there are so many little worlds in her...she swarms four times in a year ....'[44] Yet such meddling was inevitable: to be a citizen meant to be part of the city, an integral part of London. With a grotesquely gastronomic metaphor Lupton exposes the apparent threat to the citizen's socio-sexual identity: 'Shee seems to be a Glutton, for she desires always to bee Full.'[45] Being inside, as part of the City's community, seems to agitate rather than alleviate social and gender relations. Although 'Her Citizens should love one another, for they are joyn'd together; onely this seemes to make them differ ...'.[46] The need for differentiation provoked such a crisis for London's citizen-subjects that many of their fears were quickly translated into a deep and ambivalent hatred for the prostitute.[47] The intensity of this anxiety produced extraordinary linguistic and social violence directed against prostitutes. Marston's Freevill – a name which invokes the Freedom of the City – graphically translates his fears of the 'whore', Franceschina: 'she's none of your ramping cannibals that devour man's flesh, nor any of your Curtian gulf that will never be satisfied until the best thing a man has be thrown into them' (*The Dutch Courtesan*, I.ii.90–3).[48] Utterly terrorized by his own feelings of inadequacy, Freevill thinks that her imagined sexual rapacity could both castrate and annihilate any man; he would be 'blown up', absorbed, erased without trace. Faced with such a terrifying psychological spectre, the citizen-subject required a secure vantage point, a place which could be his 'castle impregnable'. London's anxious citizen found himself peering nervously over the real and metaphorical walls of the City into the mass of seemingly unregulated space around him. Perspective became the key to legitimizing urban identity. Many beguiling offers were made in order to assuage the citizen-subject's fears as the malevolent and degenerate were fixed in their place outside the official sphere of the city. Complete clarity of sight was needed to locate the ostensible threat. A vast literature of classification and categorization proliferated during this period. Lanterns were shone into all the dark corners of the City to reveal what was there; it was mapped, unwholesome alleys were looked into, iniquities were laid bare, vices exposed, enormities made known, and immorality was scourged. London was, as Lupton wrote, literally 'carbonadoed' (cut open), so that its secrets could be discovered. All manner of writing was dedicated to 'Bringing to light the most notorious villanies that are now practiced in the Kingdome' (Grosart, vol. III, p. 63). It seemed as if there could never be enough description, comprehension, discovery, or revelation. Dekker vowed 'to repeate over againe the Names of all the Tribes' who lay 'within' London (Grosart, vol. III, p. 192). Stow completed the most comprehensive, encyclopaedic, and cartographic index of London which had ever been compiled. Like other, later, bourgeois writers of the city he had an 'obsession with completeness', as he sought, 'to capture his entire city, every bit of it, and so he wrote on and on ...'.[49] Stow's enterprise differed little in purpose from Richard Johnson's sycophantic muck-raking. Stow wrote to validate the bourgeoisie of the City, and its sense of security; Johnson, for the same reason, brought the attention of the City's magistrates to the 'sucking shifters' of the suburbs and London's underworld. While Stow catalogued the streets, Johnson sought to reveal the activities which went on there. He sought 'to lay before their eyes ... wicked meeting places ... abuses un-knowne unto them', about which he said, 'I thinke it a worke of much honesty to reveale them ... '.[50] No nook or cranny was spared, no stone unturned. Even the esoteric language of the 'underworld' had to be deciphered and known. Appearing long before regular dictionaries, canting dictionaries promised linguistic and social perspicacity for the anxious citizen reader. In *Lanthorne and Candle-light*, Dekker provided long sections decoding canting language, knowledge of which was deemed necessary otherwise 'strange people' 'might freely utter their mindes to one another' (Grosart, vol. III, p. 194). Even the untraceable mind was not to remain an undiscovered realm; it, too, needed to be mapped, investigated, and disseminated, in order to be fully comprehended. Although Dekker's canting index recycled material from Greene and Harman, its contemporaneity was not the issue. The purpose of the literature was not novelty but scrutiny and taxonomy, and for inducing a feeling that the reader knew everything about and within the city.

For the men of the City, clarity of sight was deemed an effective defensive posture; it demarcated psychic, social and topographical boundaries. Failure of perception severely disrupted the organizing principles of integrity and threatened disintegration. Dekker responded to the bunkered mentality with the appropriate metaphors: 'What armor a harlot weares comming out of the Suburbes to besiege the Citty within the wals' (Grosart, vol. III, p. 268). In an effort to heighten anxieties, Dekker constructed the invading prostitute as one able to borrow or steal the 'known reputation' of 'some cittizen ... as a cloake to cover her deformities', thereby contributing to the paranoid fear that 'all comers may enter, without the danger of any eyes to watch over them' (Grosart , vol. III, p. 268). Undetectable assimilation was the ultimate nightmare for the anxious citizen and drove him to new levels of surveillance. Imperfection and deformities may 'offend the eyes of goodnesse' but had better be seen in order to be eradicated.[51] Yet setting up mechanisms of scrutiny could not avoid fostering the internal doubts they were designed to alleviate. Mayoral pageants ritually staged perspicacity as the means by which imperfection could be eradicated: 'Vanish infectious fog', says 'Truth' in Middleton's pageant, 'that I may see/This city's grace' (Bullen, vol. VII, p. 252). Later in the same pageant 'a flame shoots from the head of Zeal', phallically burning all 'the beasts' (Bullen, vol. VII, p. 262) attached to 'Error'. In many ways, mayoral inaugurations were a celebration of an ultimate all-seeing and pure City Father.

III AN HONEST ENGLISHMAN LURKING IN THE SUBURBS?:
OR 'ONCE MORE UNTO THE BREACH'

> ... so upon the sea,
> What ribs of oak, when mountains melt on them,
> Can hold the mortise ...

> (*Othello*, II.i.6–8)

> Lastly the perturbations of the minde are oftentimes to blame
> both for this and many other diseases. For seeing we are not
> maisters of our owne affections, wee are like battered Citties
> without walles, or shippes tossed in the Sea, exposed to all maner
> of assaults and daungers, even to the overthrow of our owne
> bodies. (Edward Jorden, *A Brief Discourse of a Disease called the
> Suffocation of the Mother*, London, 1603)[52]

Images of men and their bodies destroyed or threatened by
engulfing forces are common in the literature of the period. This
threat to masculine security was often depicted as any type of overwhelming external pressure: a 'sea of troubles' against which
defence was futile. For many men in the City the body also encoded
anxieties about the insurgent dangers of an inner world. Passion,
'our owne affections', increasingly perturbed the mind. And those
perturbations were increasingly linked to a profound fear of what
was metonymically perceived as bodily appetites. The 'body', for
men like Thomas Hall, 'doth hinder men in their Callings.'[53]
Ironically it was their careers as men engaged in seeking and desir-
ing 'worldly profit' which structured that sense of hindrance:
'Neither the inticements of profit or pleasure should withdraw our
mindes' as one contemporary trader put it.[54] Consequently, it was
the 'distraction of minde by daungerous lustes' which threatened
masculine integrity and social identity.[55] According to one suspicious view of the commercial world, men should 'have to doe in
matters of profit no more then we must needes'.[56] But the more the
attempt to separate himself from 'licentiousnes', when involved
with 'dealinges in the world about commod[ities]', the more those
feelings became transcoded on to the body.[57]

Money, or gold, became an overdetermined vehicle for carrying
the fluidity of men's passions. Because both were connected to their
repressed emotions, gold, like passion, could never be fully under

control. Specie, gold, was the physical, material, strand which held the social fabric together: 'Gold is the strength, the sinnewes of the world' (*Old Fortunatus*, I.i.89). Yet its uncanny effects constantly rose to trouble the mind, as Dekker disconcertingly reveals in *A Knight's Conjuring*:

> (Golde,) the strange Magick of it drave me straight into a strange admiration. I perceiv'de it to be a witch-craft beyond mans power to contend with: a Torrent whose winding creekes were not with safety to be searcht out: a poyson that had a thousand contrarie workings on a thousand bodies ... (Robbins, p. 78)

Awesome and omnipotent, gold's most troubling effect is that 'mans power' is deemed useless in the face of his own ultimate desires. Gold had become a fetish: an incarnation and mystification of all the functions of social power. When exposed, the subconscious manifestations of greed and avarice reveal repressed connections between commerce and passion. Through the effects of acquisitive accumulation the city-dweller's body becomes a realm of fear. Gone is the concept of a collective social body. In its place are discrete and opposing bodies tensely linked via the function of money and an uncanny nexus of 'strange Magick'. The realm which is 'beyond mans power to contend with' is a demonized female world of 'witch-craft', of ever-flowing 'winding creekes', of bodily mistrust and hatred. Psychic and imaginative confusion ensues as the socially familiar function of trade is powerfully displaced into a terrifyingly nether world characterized by bodily dysfunction and anti-male and anti-individual error.

In such a mistrustful mind, the connection between profit and desire had to be reprocessed, and so the deleterious function of trade was projected on to the figure or body of the prostitute.

> Then she's a right strumpet; I ne'r knew any of their trade rich two yeeres together; Sives can hold no water, nor Harlots hoord up money; thay have many vents, too many sluces to let it out; Tavernes, Taylors, Bawds, Panders, Fidlers, Swaggerers, Fools and Knaves, doe all waite upon the common Harlots trencher: she is the Gally-pot to which these Drones flye: not for love to the pot, but for the sweet sucket within it, her money, her money. (*The Honest Whore*, part II, I.ii.134–40)

Representing Bellafront as the source of all kinds of nefarious social transactions incarnates a common unease about commercial activity. Through metaphors of liquidity, the prostitute's leaky body reifies the ostensibly promiscuous function of the trade nexus; thereby making a powerful metonymical connection between the money, desire, misogyny, consumption, and prostitution.[58] Not surprisingly, the effect of this produced an intense interest in the figure of the prostitute. Mutual and conflicting fascination and horror can be read in Nashe: 'the speech-shunning sores and sight-irking botches of their insatiate intemperance they will jestingly lay forth.'[59] Disgust at prostitution was similar to that for business; upon returning from London Richard Rogers noted that 'the chief anoiaunce was from that comon eye-sore, p[rofit]'.[60] But the City's scrutinizing energies were focused ever more on the body of the prostitute. Even the devil, when checking out 'all damnable sinnes', Dekker notes, 'lookes onely upon her body'(Grosart, vol. III, p. 267). Through the figures of citizen and prostitute, social geography and urban topography were inextricably linked. In condemning Bellafront, Hippolito indicts himself and all men who held his views: 'your body/Its like the common shoare, that still receives/All the towns filth/The sin of many men/Is within you ...' (*The Honest Whore, part I*, II.i.324–7).[61] Hippolito follows Augustine and Jerome ('a whore is one who is available for the lust of many men'[62]) in seeing the prostitute as a filth-filled annex ensuring men's purity.[63] The mind simply could not be trusted within the body. In *Match mee in London*, John talks about his desire in the following terms; 'my bodie (which was before a clean stream) growing foul/By my minds trouble ...' (*Match Mee in London*, III.ii. 135–7). Following suit, Marston's urbane Freevill refers to the prostitute, Franceschina; 'I lov'd her with my heart until my soul showed me the imperfection of my body ...' (*The Dutch Courtesan*, I.ii.93–4). Perhaps intentionally, Freevill discovers that it is his body, not hers, which really disturbs him.

As error incarnate, the prostitute was largely responsible for the assault on 'truth': Hippolito paradoxically admits; 'for a mingled harlot, Is true in nothing but being false' (*The Honest Whore, part I*, II.i. 314–15). My contention is that certain men in Dekker's London sought to conceive themselves and their City in terms of politico-intellectual abstractions and strategic disembodiment. Conceptualizing the body as the topos of epistemological error became a potent way of rationalizing urban identity. Although prostitution concerns a transaction between at least two people, its history, by and large, has been one of the indiscernible client.[64] It is the prostitute's body which principally represents the act. Karras indicates the common view, that a prostitute 'was defined as a woman who lived by her body'.[65] The prostitute's body not only bore the epistemological uncertainties ascribed to trade, but also the ontological stresses which accompanied the citizen-subject's fears. In the increasingly popular pamphlets of the time, page after page of underworld figures appeared before the eyes of the citizen-subject and the more they materialized, the less visible he became. Disembodiment, then, was part of the effect and function of reading.

Keeping the body and its passions out of site became translated into the City government's policies. In 1614 Middleton entitled the inaugural pageant for the incoming mayor, Thomas Myddleton (no relation it seems), a *Triumph of Truth*. During the procession 'Truth's champion', 'Zeal', appears to triumph over 'Error' and at this crucial moment says 'Bold furies back! or with scourge of fire,/Whence sparkles out religious chaste desire,/I'l whip you down to darkness …'(Bullen, vol. VII, p. 245). The thrill of purity is enacted as one of self-chastisement and banishment from within. Such a clampdown eradicated the 'elf of sin and darkness' which stirred up the realm where unchaste desire lurked; and which counselled his 'appetite to master' him (Bullen, vol. VII, p. 246). Earlier, another mayor had been counselled in the values of self-mastery; 'whereby he is to govern himself and the City'.[66] Vigilance against oneself was the only recourse, another writer revealed: 'there breaketh out of me much corruption … espec[ially] when I am not watchfull … I perceive … some riseing of hart against m[e] … .'[67] Patterns of concealment and alienation characterized his rebellious body. Strategies of surveillance were implemented, creating within his person the structures of a deep paranoia.

This scrutiny was at once excessive, visceral, and carried enormous social repercussions. In 1613 Richard Johnson wrote a pamphlet, *Look on Me, London*, and dedicated it to the aforementioned Mayor Myddleton. Its theme was simply embodied in the prologue written for the incoming mayor; 'I am an honest Englishman, ripping up the Bowels of Mischiefe lurking in thy sub-urbs and Precincts'.[68] Myddelton is likened to a moral butcher, metaphorically disembowelling all the internal corruption of the City as he inaugurates truth in nationhood, selfhood, and integrity. Graphic images of violent expulsion and bodily rupture mirrored officially designated policies. For example, London's indefatigable Recorder, William Fleetwood, 'went abrode' in an attempt to 'repress the evils' in the City, and thereby avoid 'great whoredoms'.[69] He launched countless searches. In one particular week of terror he reportedly captured over a hundred 'lewd people' whereupon the 'Master of Bridewell received them and immediately gave them punishment'.[70] His zeal for conducting surveillance of the City's 'other places' was unsurpassed: 'I am at the least the best part of a hundred nights a year abroad in searches'.[71] This fanatic examiner was actively encouraged and emulated by the City's rulers. In 1603, as Johnson recalls, Myddleton (then newly elected Sheriff) sought out 'the hidden evils harboured in the bowels of London [whereupon] ... your Lordship ... made visitations in the sub-urbs ... to enquire after evil livers, and by justice strove to root out iniquity'.[72] Later, in 1614, while acting as Lord Mayor, he wrote that:

> He had informed himself, by means of spies, of many lewd houses, and had gone himself disguised to divers of them, and, finding these nurseries of villany, had punished them according to their deserts, some by carting and whipping, and many by banishment.[73]

Surveillance and disruption were not merely tropes confined to London's literature. Day after day the 'search deeper into these wounds of a common-wealth' produced the systematic social violence directed towards prostitutes and the poor.[74] Neither was the scrutiny of London's netherworld confined to the zeal of individual mayors. From the latter half of the sixteenth century onwards there was an increase in institutional and governmental concern with who and what was deemed to be 'lurking' in the suburbs and precincts. Archer's recent book, *The Pursuit of Stability*, argues that there was a concerted attempt by the city's authorities to achieve 'a high level of knowledge about the contours of the underworld'.[75] But it was the pursuit of knowledge, rather than the knowledge itself, which functioned as the stabilizing force – at least as far as the authorities were concerned.

Discovering and disgorging the contents of the city's underbelly made the relationship between literary form and social practice dynamic. London was literally gutted to create new and popular forms of metropolitan satire. In *London and the Country Carbonadoed* (that is, cut or slashed open) Lupton promised a comprehensive exposition of the city and its characters. Political satire, too, freely borrowed from the language of dissection and extrusion. In his polemics, William Averill sought to 'drawe from the entrails and bowelles certaine filthie vapours'.[76] The pulpit was not exempt from such rhetoric. A late sixteenth-century sermon implored the listener to 'awake', and then 'thrust dilligently your sword of justice in to launce out all corruption and bagage which is gathered in the bowels ... .'[77] Finding those who were corrupt through 'good and perfect eye-sight', Dekker claimed to flay 'off their skins ... and show those abuses naked to the world' (Pendry, p. 290). Ruptured bodies purported to signify an unadulterated honesty; by stripping away the body's surface epistemological and representational error was discovered and averted.

This 'quest for an internal assurance of their election through the zeal for God's glory' according to Archer 'gave the Bridewell governors their impetus' for systematic punishment.[78] In 1599, Thomas Platter noted that:

> Good order ... kept in the city in the matter of prostitution, for which special commissions are set up, and when they meet with a case, they punish the man with imprisonment and a fine. The woman is taken to Bridewell ... where the executioner scourges her naked before the populace. And although close watch is kept on them, great swarms of these women haunt the town in the taverns and playhouses.[79]

If the goal of punishment was to stop prostitution, and whipping was considered remedial, why not scourge both client and prostitute 'before the populace'? No! The spectacle of the man's own bodily rupture (vagrants did not count as city-men) would have been too disconcerting. Scourging prostitutes and vagrants fractured those who were being punished, the men who organized and executed it remained symbolically and physically whole. The purpose of the disciplinary action was *not* to eliminate the 'problem of prostitution' as propagated through the official language of the city government (a view which many writers, both now and then, have too often accepted). More precisely such disciplinary action was conceived as corporal punishment for the prostitutes *per se*. Recidivism of prostitutes was expected, even considered 'natural' by many, and the deterrent value of whipping, if any, was rarely articulated publicly. Whipping was the actual goal of punishment rather than the means to eliminate the so-called crime itself. Whipping is always, in some sense, perpetrated as an act of purification. Carting and whipping prostitutes around the boundaries of the City was an act of social purgation which panoramically played out the individual psychic fears of the men who organized it. The ritual floggings in the streets and institutions of London enabled the spectators to fantasize about a sense of their own integrity. Having projected their feelings of disgust on to the person being flogged, they then felt purged by this spectacle of purification. Prominent City men like Thomas Myddleton became obsessed with these practices, and they structured their whole political life around them. Myddleton not only rounded up and punished vagrants and prostitutes in his younger days but later became governor of Bridewell after his stint as Mayor!

But it was not just a few members of City Hall who were locked into these brutal, anxiety-ridden, practices. For example, London's Nehemiah Wallington, an artisan turner, and Puritan, kept a detailed account of his own 'examined life'. His account became a vast and voluminous undertaking; 'less for the purpose of rereading and remembering than for taking stock, reviewing, maintaining awareness, achieving perspective'.[80] It was another document full of a compulsive taxonomic drive based on his need for vigilance and purity. An early relationship with a woman predictably ties him into the bizarre brotherhood of anxious city men. Upon nearing the object of what he calls his 'exceeding burning desire [he] did read much of the fearful sin of adultery, and would often be speaking to her of that grievous sin of whoredom'.[81] Typically he blamed a woman for seduction because he could not confront the depth of his own feelings. Out of fear, Wallington perceived his desire as 'a sty of filthiness within me which did boil and bubble up'.[82] Trying to contain these feelings, he threw himself into work, gave up the foods he liked, and collected writing which condemned 'adultery, fornication, uncleanness, wantonness'.[83] Deeply afraid of his own motives, he felt it both necessary and dangerous to scrutinize the very literature which troubled him. Wallington became so overwhelmed by his anxieties that he ominously contemplated doing 'something to [his] body'.[84] That he was prepared to castrate himself reveals the extent to which he perceived his own body as a danger to himself; and that such a drastic measure could purify the filthiness within him. When faced with his desires,

Wallington turned his faith into a vehicle by which he could douse his desire and 'allay and quench this fire'.[85] Wallington's dilemma could be construed as a classic case of the return of the repressed: 'his preoccupation with lust' gave him the feeling that he had 'a filthy, odious, and polluted heart'.[86] As Stallybrass and White acutely observe, 'disgust always bears the imprint of desire'.[87] What better example could be found than Nehemiah Wallington, who called on God to help him repress his feelings and found himself writing: 'I had rather that my nose were held over some filthy jakes than yield unto my delightfullest sin'?[88] Wallington's scatological prurience reveals his pleasure in being disgusted by the function of his body. Out on the street the same pattern could be found. Richard Johnson imagines visiting the parts of the city which offend him only so that he can shun them: 'and to keep myself more cleere from them, I will passe by those streetes, where these vile houses are planted, and blesse mee from the inticements of them ...'.[89]

But what if you could not tell where the 'enemy' lay? This proved to be a common feeling for many men of the period. Again, metaphors of liquidity excite fears of incursion: barriers were breached as the prostitute was imagined and re-imagined as a quintessentially protean form:

> When her villanies (like the mote about a castle) are rancke, thicke, and mudd, with standing long together, then (to purge herself) is she dreined out of the Suburbs (as though her corruption were left behind her) and as a cleere streame is let into the Citty. (Grosart, vol. III, p. 268)

Historically this represents the sixteenth-century ban on brothels in the suburbs which encouraged the subsequent mobility of prostitution throughout the capital. But its latent metaphors are tied to psychic terror. Images of disgust and contagion are mobilized to demonstrate that the once impervious castle/city/citizen has been penetrated. If the palace is only kept pure by the sewer, then there is always the risk that the invisible by-products of purity could seep back.[90] Rather disconcertingly Dekker switches around the language of purgation, suggesting that such contamination might flow both ways. Dekker presents this invisible threat as 'armor' which 'a harlot weares coming out of the Suburbes to beseige the Citty within the wals' (Grosart, vol. III, p. 268). Rather conveniently, only the author can make transparent that which is unseen. Almost through emotional blackmail, he speculates upon where and how 'she' might suddenly 'appear': 'And where must her lodging be taken up, but in the house of some cittizen, whose known reputation, she borrows (or rather steals) putting it on as a cloake to cover her deformities?' (Grosart, vol. III, p. 268). Who now would not read a pamphlet claiming to locate what he most feared? – even though integrity built upon this kind of expulsion can always be held hostage by the very fears which it continually has to express.

Its difficult to say to what extent writing about the city shaped or articulated perceptions and practices within London. Certainly writers like Dekker took advantage of these kinds of metropolitan anxieties. His picaresque underworld literature, so full of tricksters and huxters, was both a confidence trick and a trick in confidence. While promising to make his readers feel more secure, he often upset their looked-for sense of security. Dekker's 'greatest publishing success' was *Lanthorne and Candle-light*; first published in 1609, it enjoyed many reprints.[91] In its 'Epistle Dedicatorie' Dekker seduces the reader:

> Give me leave to lead you by the hand in a Wildernesse (where are none but Monsters, whose crueltie you need not feare, because I teach the way to tame them: ugly they are in shape and divelish in conditions: yet to behold them a far off, may delight you, and to know their quallities (if ever you should come neere them) may save you from much danger. (Grosart, vol. III, p. 180)

Supposedly offering a helping hand, the writer is actually making a deal with the reader in offering to become his metropolitan guide. His knowledge of the 'Wildernesse' renders all the fearful sights into a delight, but only after the reader has been transfixed, opened up to his horrors and their dangerous proximity. Only then can the writer assuage his fears. It was, undoubtedly, a strategy designed to catch the customers who browsed along London's bookstalls. The opening lines of such pamphlets called out to the reader. Once the reader was hooked, Dekker quickly delved into his anxieties:

> Who therefore would pity such imposters, whose faces are full of dissembling, hearts full of villainy, mouths full of curses, bodies of sores which they call the 'great cleymes', but laid upon their flesh by cunning ... Now whereas the Bellman in his privy search

found out the nests of these screech-owls, pulling off some feathers only to show their ugliness but, for want of good and perfect
eye-sight, not flaying off their skins as I here purpose to do, and
so draw blood, I will finish that which the Bellman by being
overwatched left lame, and show those abuses naked to the
world which he never discovered. (Pendry, p. 290)

The plague's graphic effects on the body become the root of a series
of metaphors about the punitive practices which the City engendered. Words are used to flay off the imperfections which impede
the view of the troubled spectator, thus purifying his perception
and shoring up his integrity. These scourging satires exploited the
same taxonomic urge, along with the need for complete surveillance, which encouraged the drama seen every day at the whipping
post and on every street corner, behind the whipping-cart, or in the
yard at Bridewell. In effect, Dekker wrote the expelled and chastised body – its 'faces', 'hearts', 'mouths', 'bodies', 'sores', 'flesh',
'skins', and 'blood' – back into view while claiming to contain it.
Only 'with the help of his lanthorne and candle' could he bring 'to
light, that broode of mischiefe which is ingendered in the wombe of
darknesse' (Grosart, vol. III, p. 66). And so the 'sight' of such a
'monstrous birth', of all that was 'fearfull' could 'utterly vanish'
through the illuminatory function of the text (Ibid.).
   Only the rational mind seeing from its phallic locations –
'Towers', 'Temples', and 'Pinnacles' – was deemed able to eradi-
cate all moral error. To do that required an absolute state of
consciousness:

> awaken out of thy dead and dangerous slumbers, and with a full
> and fearlesse eye behold those seven Monsters, that with ex-
> tended jawes gape to swallow up thy memory: for I will into so
> large a field single every one of them, that thou and all the world
> shall see their uglinesse, for by seeing them, thou mayst avoyd
> them, and by avoyding them, be the happiest and most
> renowned of Citties.   (Grosart, vol. II, pp. 14–15)

Sleep, and the death which it echoes, is a non-desiring, non-
sensory, and, of course, non-seeing state. Consciousness, sentience,
apprehension are overwhelmed by sleep, whereby the mind is subjected to the body. To be awake is to perceive and locate the world
rationally; to 'look after' the body's otherness. The instance of

awakening captures the terrible moment when the somatic self is realized as being part of the rational self. Dangerous slumbers could be understood to swallow up memory; and memory is the abstract essence, the true self, which structures the continuity of self and mind. A return to consciousness brings a fleeting remembrance of the body such that the perceiver is thrown into a continuous unblinking terror in order to maintain an exalted, rational, perspective. Nothing less than full consciousness will guard against utter extinction: to be awake is to be stark awake! However much sight operates to vanquish this monstrous realm, defeat could never be completely avoided. Like his own sleeping body, and his bowels, his eyes are something which the anxious man can never wholly see. As Achilles reveals in Shakespeare's *Troilus and Cressida*: 'nor doth the eye itself,/That most pure spirit of sense, behold itself ... ' (III.iii.105–6). The incorporeal mind could only contemplate its abstraction at the moment it was made crucially aware of its own bodiliness. Literature like Dekker's recycled and returned the transcoded body, even as the speculating, conceptualizing, imagining, mind of the reader attempted to efface it. Writing played a key role in negotiating certain anxieties about the body, not only in the literature which at once invoked and censored 'adultery, fornication, uncleanness, wantonness' (for men like Wallington), but also in the diaries and pamphlets written and read by men in the city.[92] The new metropolitan literature was well placed to provide both condemnation and titillation under the rubric of moral instruction. Ironically, Dekker often found himself alongside the very prostitutes his writing ostensibly condemned. Both were, after all, attempting to hustle a living by selling themselves through the images engendered in metropolitan male fantasies. For many men of the city, the stage was as a strumpet and the pen was an instrument of prostitution.[93]

## IV 'WA, HA, HO! AND WHO ARE HER CUSTOMERS?': MALE FANTASIES IN THE CITY

as that trade is most honourable that sells the best commodities; so the bawd above all. Her shop has the best ware, for where these sell but cloth, satins and jewels, she sells divine virtues, as virginity, modesty, and such rare gems, and those not like a pretty chapman, by retail, but like a great merchant by wholesale. Wa, ha, ho! And who are her customers? Not base corn cutters or sowgelders, but most rare wealthy knights, and most bountiful lords are her customers. (Cocledemoy in *The Dutch Courtesan*, I.ii.31–42)

Most studies of prostitution assume that it merely means sex for sale, but Lyndal Roper's question is important: 'what precisely were men buying?'

To say that, for example, men are seeking 'release from sexual tension', or that prostitution is a necessity in a society which delays marriage for its young men, confuses a theory about what male sexuality is like with a biological explanation, and masks the issues of power and aspects of fantasy involved.[94]

Obviously prostitution offered men the means to deal with their 'exceeding burning desire', which, in the case of men like Wallington, they often despised. For many men, scared by the potentially engulfing force of passion or the body, the attraction of prostitution was the controlled return of their own bodies. It was a re-engagement which appeared to be safely negotiated via the alienating function of the cash nexus. Paying for sex seems to offer the client the ability to remain discrete from all the messy business around his body, her body, and their emotional entanglements. Yet, as we have seen, the 'strange Magick' of 'Gold' invisibly connected all bodies through the seemingly uncanny function of the cash nexus. Ironically for some, it was the promiscuity of trade which produced the very anxieties which led them to disavow dispassionately their bodies. Prostitution, then, works across the tension of these two different perceptions.

Not surprisingly, the cultural history of prostitution has focused on the prostitute's moral turpitude and social contamination rather than the proclivities of the buyer. Clients are rarely seen or mentioned, nor are their motives or fancies interrogated. This tends to perpetuate myths about the innate sexuality of men; they are simply assumed to 'need' sexual intercourse. But what were men really seeking? Archer tells of the London financier, Horatio Palavacino, who sent his servant to pimp for him, to find 'some mayden to abuse who had not been dealte with before.'[95] That he was willing to part with the relatively large sum of 10 shillings testifies both to the extent of his fantasy and the incentives which 'the falling trade' had in meeting it. Virgin prostitutes were valuable precisely because they had not yet been traded ('dealte with'). A 'whore' selling herself as a virgin over and over again sponsored many an anxious laugh in the audiences of the new cynical city comedies. At the instant of being traded, even a virgin prostitute could not remain pure. Angelo, in *Measure for Measure*, precisely captures the dilemma as he imagines, and tries to enforce, a sexual transaction with the virgin Isabella: 'Dost thou desire her foully for those things/that make her good?' (II.ii.174–5). As Angelo, in his mind, rapes Isabella he also simultaneously tarnishes her forever. The play's revenge is that in that brutal transaction, made possible by the bed-trick, Angelo tacitly makes good his previous bargain with Mariana as he reneges on his promise to Isabella.

One of the newer and growing forms of metropolitan identity was the male consumer. Gentlemen, wealthy farmers, businessmen, merchants, ambassadors, courtiers, and so on, men who lived in or visited the capital, were all (like the hapless Froth in *Measure for Measure*) somehow aligned with the phenomenon of prostitution. Like the flâneurs whom they prefigured, these men-about-town employed their economic muscle to enable their 'visual and voyeuristic mastery over women'.[96] Many courtier-consumers assumed that any woman they saw could be subject to their purchasing power. Dekker tells the all-too-familiar story of a 'yong Farmer, who many times makes his wife (in the country) beleeve he hath suits inlaw, because he will come up to his letchery' (Grosart, vol. II, p. 255). London was the place *par excellence* where the consumer could flatter and privilege himself. However, the fantasy of London as a place for consumption was (and still is in modern scholarship) seen through the eyes of the men who made the purchase, or, as we say, 'choice'. Morse perhaps unwittingly testifies:

> Yet the attractions of London were considerable, and although being a stranger in the city could be a risky and expensive business they came all the same. Then, as now, London was an unparalleled entertainment capital, offering pleasure and diversion in abundance. Here, if you had the money, you could have exquisite and costly garments tailored in the latest imported fashion, you could sample the most exotic foods and spices, you could take your pick of ostentatiously dressed courtesans.[97]

Leaving aside the problem of how abundant the 'pleasure' might have been for the 'country wenches', the question remains; who could actually take their pick and why? In the minds of the consumer, shopkeeper's wives merged with their wares as objects for sale. Many contemporary writers registered the continuous fascination which courtiers had with the city's tradeswomen. Dekker's *Match mee in London* revolves around both courtly and royal fascination with a tradesmen's new bride who is, inevitably, still a virgin. Much of the action in *The Honest Whore, part II* concerns attempts by courtiers to prostitute the draper's young new bride; with as much gusto as they sought to enjoy 'whoe with the wenches' (that is, citizen's wives). Lodovico peremptorily comments upon the draper's wife as 'my fine yong smug Mistris' (III.iii.20). Meanwhile, his 'gallant' companion, Carolo, enlists the help of Bots and Horsleech, pimp and bawd; 'Ile give thee for thy fee twenty crownes, if thou canst but procure me the wearing of yon velvet cap', meaning the acquisition of Candido's wife for sex (III. iii. p. 22–3). Class antagonism mixed with sexual fantasies as the courtier-consumer sought to revenge himself upon the city's bourgeoisie by sexually dominating women of their class.[98] Shrewd, business-like, prostitutes such as Penelope Whore-hound catered for this as they 'attyred' themselves as 'Citty-dames' so that they could more easily 'besot Gallants' (*The Honest Whore, part II*, V.ii.351–7).

In *The Honest Whore, part I* the draper's journeyman, George, extols the values of his wares to his courtier-clients as if he were a bawd. His lawn is 'the purest shee that ever you fingered since you were a gentleman: looke how even she is, look how cleane she is, ha, even as the brow of Cinthia' (I.v.24–6). In return, the courtier downgrades the cloth by using misogynistic images of impurity and sexual disease. George responds with a phrase which is, in terms of the play, axiomatic; 'compare them I pray … compare virgins with harlots' (I.v.32–3). Through conjuring images of sexual prowess and spending power, George flatters his client's ability to choose. Within this economy, if lawn could be likened to (chaste) women then chased women could be likened to lawn. Another courtier in the play becomes a pimp as he tries to sell Hippolito the idea of taking a 'curtizan'. Echoing George earlier, he insists 'youle swear she is the prettiest, kindest, sweetest, most bewitching honest ape under the pole. A skin, your satten is not more soft, nor lawne whiter' (II.i.171–3).

Consumer knowledge within the city was sexualized. 'Knowing' multiplied its meaning from the sixteenth century onwards; it came to signify, not just the idea of being in the know, as in 'inside knowledge', or carnal knowledge, but also the fetishization of knowledge as mastery which accompanied metropolitan acculturation. To know the dark and dangerous parts of the city not only underpinned much of the pamphlet industry, but characterized a new urbane (masculine) hipness. Consumer knowledge consisted of not just knowing a good piece of cloth when you saw it, but also knowing which were the best brothels , of knowing 'the fashions ... [of the] house', and where they could be found (*The Honest Whore, part I*, II.i.153). Knowledge about commodities and their purchase was, and still is, the key to the City. Archer cites the case of a pimp, Melcher Pelse, who in contemporary accounts was 'a broker whoe is every day upon thexchange ... a notable bawde and doeth bringe strangers iiij at ones to lewde wemen.'[99] That the city was full of naive men beguiled by lewd prostitutes was a common metropolitan fiction; and one which still persists in modern scholarship.[100] Such a view merely reproduces the perspective of those men at the time who had such a vested interest in that viewpoint.[101]

As a historical postscript to this section, it is worth tracing some of the consequences of the prostitute's relationship with the solid citizen. Through Foucault and others, it is possible to see that as bourgeois repression became more culturally secured, the apparatus of discipline became more successfully internalized. Later, attitudes towards prostitution changed when the concept of the client's body was transformed. As disciplinary processes began to close off the bourgeois-masculine body, to construct its clean and impenetrable surface, the focus of containment shifted ever more to his own boundaries and their policing. This reconception created different 'bodily' needs and fears, and significantly changed his interaction with prostitutes. Once designed to control the mass of feelings he had displaced on to the body of the prostitute, whipping now became an instrument by which he chastised, contained, and policed, the limits of his own body.[102]

## V  MOLL: OPPOSER OF ALL MEN AND A ROARER IN THE CRYING GAME

SIR ALEXANDER    Who has bewitched thee, son? ...
SEBASTIAN        Sh'has a bold spirit that mingles with mankind,
                 But nothing else comes near it ...

(*The Roaring Girl*, II. ii.116 and 172–3)

In many ways Middleton and Dekker's *The Roaring Girl* offers a striking example of how the issues of sexual fantasy, prostitution, urban identities, city topography, and writing all intersect. Moll comes with all the baggage to make the citizen and man-about-town at once anxious and fascinated. As fluid as currency, 'She slips from one company to another like a fat eel between a Dutchman's fingers' (II.i.118); and she is just as slippery both sexually and semantically. In another sense, this 'civil city-roaring girl' is a motley crew rolled into one (*The Roaring Girl*, Prologue, 22). Moll is variously deemed a cutpurse, drab, whore, thief, bawd, drunkard, and moral reprobate. She appears as a paradigm of the city's low-life. For those pursuing social stability through a gender hierarchy, she appears as a troublesome cross-dresser, a transvestite. As a woman wearing man's clothes, she visibly upsets the so-called 'natural' order of things.[103] While Moll's cross-dressing has informed much debate about sexuality in the early modern period, her dressing as a man firmly signalled her as an immigrant, if not a vagrant. Her social status was crucial. The authors of a recent survey of cross-dressing note that in this period 'practically all our disguised women came from the lower classes', and many women 'dressed as men for traveling.'[104] No doubt there were good safety reasons for this, but what makes Moll unusual is that she makes no secret of the fact that she is wearing men's clothes. She flouts both class and gender categories, and wields a sword (both an aristocratic and male weapon) with more skill than most. Although many critics see her as an exemplary figure of both subversion and containment, I would like to explore her role as a dramatic figure of urban fantasy.[105]

Moll's nefarious background encouraged a correlation between her and the personification of London as a monstrous female. Similar to Jonson's Ursula, she represented the vigour of the unofficial side of the city; that which was opposed to pretension and civility. Moll seems to have been based on the 'real' Mary Frith, a notably boisterous character of London. In recreating her the writers drew on both the fictional and folk characters of Long Meg and Mother Bunch traditions. Long Meg of Westminster was a semi-mythical champion of the poor and oppressed who arrived in London via one of the infamous carriers, similar to those met by Horsleech and Bots, in *The Honest Whore, part II*.[106] The legendary Meg successfully challenged the carrier who tried to abuse her, whereupon, with considerable martial ability, she proceeded to right all manner of wrongs on behalf of the downtrodden. The charismatic Long Meg functioned as a quasi-romantic figure in the fantasies of the poor. She became their champion: one who took the chivalric emblems of their oppressors and turned them upon the class which traditionally employed them.

Both Meg and Moll were connected to much older dramatic figures like 'Mother Bombie' and 'Gammer Gurton' of early Tudor theatre.[107] All these characters were rooted in the folk heroine Mother Bunch;

> Now for *Mother Bunch*, the onely dainty, welfavoured, well pro-portioned, sweet complexioned, and most delightfull Hostesse of *England*, she was squared into inches, being in height twelve thousand and a halfe, wanting a fingers bredth jump, in bredth eleven thousand, and two inches, and a nayles bredth just; she spent most of her time in telling of tales, and when she laughed, she was heard from Algate, to the Monuments at Westminster, and all Southwarke stood in amazement, the Lyons in the Tower, and the Bulls, and Beares of Parrish-garden roard (with terror of her laughter) lowder than the great roaring-Megge, she was once wrung with the winde in her belly, and with one blast of her tayle, she blew downe Charing crosse, with Pauls aspiring steeple. She danced a Galliard on Tower-hill, and all the great or-dinance leapt for joy, and London shooke as it had been an earth-quake ... Shee was an excellent companion, an sociable, shee was very pleasant and witty, and would tell a tale, let a fart, drinke her draught, scratch her arse, pay her groat, as well as any Chymist of ale whatsoever. For this nobel *Mother Bunch* pro-ceeded all our great Tapsters, and fat swelling Ale-wives ... .[108]

Mother Bunch had the Gargantuan appetite of the people. Like the collective body she incarnates, her history is social rather than indi-vidual; she has lived for a long time (though not quite long enough to 'knit Powles a night-cappe' or to buy 'London-bridge a payre of pantofles' to keep his feet warm).[109] Her Rabelaisian body mocks the topographical pride of London even as she is integrated with it. Every laugh and pleasure in the city enjoins hers. In Moll the writers try to incorporate the whole diffuse essence of the unofficial city, and the unwritten morality embodied in London's folk. Although Moll's transvestitism enables us to interrogate specific and local attitudes to gender, it also fundamentally connects her to the whole community.

Having created such a big and complex character as Moll, the play demonstrates how this exuberant figure could become the vehicle for misogynistic, and therefore reductive, male fantasies. If we compare Laxton's perception with the representation of Mother Bunch we can see how her image is transformed:

> Heart, I would give but too much money to be nibbling with that wench: life sh'as the spirit of four great parishes, and a voice that will drown all the city: methinks a brave captain might get all his soldiers upon her, and ne'er be beholding to a company of Mile End milksops, if he could come on, and come off quick enough: such a Moll were a marrow-bone before an Italian, he would cry bona roba till his ribs were nothing but bone. I'll lay hard siege to her, money is that aqua fortis that eats into many a maidenhead: where the walls are flesh and blood, I'll ever pierce through with a golden auger. (*The Roaring Girl*, II.i.169–179)

In Laxton's account the celebratory images which Moll incorporates become negatively reduced. Her lively productivity is registered as an insatiable engulfing threat. Her plenitude becomes narrowed and sexualized into an insatiable lust. The universal spirit of the social body shrinks to mere flesh and blood. Finally, the symbolic magnificence of the city becomes savagely diminished through the pejorative account of the sexual act. In so doing 'the spirit of four great parishes' contracts into a sterile and partial focus upon the genitalia. The individual body is fragmented and fetishized through Laxton's deployment of his spending power. Laxton creates a monstrous image of what he sees as Moll's lust, one in which the wielding of his weapon, 'money', accompanies his fantasy of brutal territorialization.[110] In his imagination, Laxton's 'golden auger' will simultaneously penetrate and destroy Moll. His violation appears all the more reductive because Moll simultaneously encodes so many facets of metropolitan society. Through his savage impalement, he desires to silence the great voice and spirit of the city (and, significantly, the suburbs) while with violence he attempts to control both her female autonomy and her sexual ambiguity. Laxton (his name carries a sense of double impotence: Lackstone meaning no land, and no testicles) wants to control the city while he tries to eliminate his sense of class and masculine effacement. His rape-fantasy allows him to oppose and therefore end his troubles. Yet it is a fantasy in which he disavows the existence of

his own body; only Moll's body is 'flesh and blood'. Laxton operates through objects which symbolize him: money, power, violence.
Laxton's 'aside' to the audience appears as a most damning and
vicious indictment of the role of gallant-consumers in the city.
Laxton articulates a powerful male fantasy, or fantasy of male
power; one in which the penetration of the city, of knowing completely its topography, is wholly sexualized and structures his view
of women like Moll.

Laxton is, of course, the conspicuous villain, yet the drama of
Moll's representation as object of topographical and sexual prurience consistently pervades the play. She endlessly excites the peculiar fascination of the other male characters. Moll's appeerence is, at
first, just a rumour: 'There's a wench Called Moll, mad Moll, or
Merry Moll, a creature So strange in quality, a whole city takes Note
of her name and person … ' (I.i.94–7). Here Sebastian echoes the
overwhelming sense of her city-wide ambivalence and the way in
which she evinces inquiry. For all the scrutiny she appears uncannily elusive and her ineffability invites all manner of descriptions
and fantasies. Goshawk trips over his language in describing her as
'the maddest fantasticall'st girl: – I never knew so much flesh and
nimbleness put together' (II.i.186–7). Moll becomes both vector and
screen for the sexual anxieties and fantasies of the men in the play.
According to Jean Howard it is Moll's theatricality, the drama of
her cross-dressing, which agitates all manner of social categories
when connected to anxieties about social order. Even Moll's insis-
tent chastity ironically serves to excite attitudes about sexual
promiscuity because of its multi-faceted obfuscation. 'In the play
Moll is constantly read by the men around her as a potential
bedmate, a sexual prize', Howard argues, 'Even Trapdoor, the
servant hired to spy on Moll, assumes he can master her sexually.'[111]
Reading the mystery of Moll is precisely what the Fortune stages.
City-man Sir Alexander Wengrave offers the huxter Trapdoor his
own version of a golden auger; 'I'll tell out gold for thee: hunt her
forth' (I.ii.15). Trapdoor promises that he'll 'find her out' (I.ii.204).
Like Middleton's 'Country Wench', Moll is not an individual, she is
generic, a symbol of prostitution, unchastity, vagrancy, disorder,
and of the dread dissimulation.[112] As Wengrave says; 'For seek all
London from one end t'other' and you will find 'More whores of
that name than any ten other' (II.ii.150–1). For all the critical potential which the writers build into *The Roaring Girl*, it is the play itself
which ultimately offers up Moll for scrutiny. The Prologue invites

'the audience' to 'look/For wonders ... of a roaring girl' (Prologue, 1–2, 5). They hope 'a roaring girl ... Shall fill with laughter our vast theatre' (Prologue, 9–10). Moll is a screen for the imagination and perspective of the individual members of the audience: 'each one comes/And brings a play in's head with him' (Prologue, 4–5). They are asked, 'would you know who 'tis?'; as they come for the titillation of 'knowing' Mad Moll (Prologue, 29). Speculating on behalf of the audience, the prologue anticipates the play's disclosures; 'I see attention sets wide ope her gates/Of hearing, and with covetous listening waits,/To know what girl this roaring girl should be'(Prologue, 13–15). In the strange contract drawn up by the prologue, the audience's desire for entertainment is made to parallel the same social scrutiny and sexual inquisition which Laxton, and the other men, exhibit in the play.

Moll is both an embodiment of London's underworld and our guide. At ease in the city's primary world she moves effortlessly through the netherworld of pranksters, schemers, pickpockets and cutpurses. In the first scene of Act V Moll gives a group of gallants an underworld tour which includes a lesson in canting. Canting was a mish-mash of dialects and slang ostensibly spoken by London's rogues; its crucial attribute, as far as the authorities were concerned, was its opacity. For the modern editor of *The Roaring Girl*, 'the canting scene is an almost complete irrelevance'.[113] But its structural relation to the meaning of the play is crucial. Like the bewildered, mildly disgusted, and lightly titillated gallants who accompany her, the audience have indubitably come to see Moll in her element; canting with the low-life, knowing a con-man when she sees one, or besting a cutpurse. Mingling sexual excitement with linguistic flirting Moll teases both gallants and the audience:

| MOLL | And there you shall wap with me, and I'll niggle with you, and that's all. |
|---|---|
| SIR BEAUTEOUS | Nay, nay, Moll, what's that wap? |
| JACK DAPPER | Nay teach what niggling is, I'd fain be niggling. |
| MOLL | Wapping and niggling is all one, the rogue my man can tell you. |
| TRAPDOOR | 'Tis fadoodling, if it please you. |
| SIR BEAUTEOUS | This is excellent, one fit more, good Moll. |

(*The Roaring Girl*, V. i. 186–94)

All this nudging and winking implies that there is more to niggling than meets the eye. The tease excites as it releases tension about linguistic promiscuity, semiotic slippage, and the attendant dangers (albeit subtextual) of a threatening sexuality.[114] The elicited laughter brings both relief and a kind of perspicacity because the audience knows that it has been teased. Meanwhile the mystifying realm of the underworld is brought before the audience's eyes, precisely because it is mystifying, and only for the spectator to enjoy the pleasure of its demystification. What titillates is the process of revelation, not what is revealed. After all 'fadoodling' is just as euphemistic in this linguistic striptease as 'wapping' or 'niggling'. The thrill, or pleasure, comes from knowing the allusion, from finding out the 'truth' of the meaning behind the word; and all without risk. Voyeurism is, in essence, about looking – not seeing. Much of *The Roaring Girl* depends upon the exploitation of sexual innuendo. The basic plot revolves around an intimated, though non-consummated, sexual liaison between Moll and Sebastian. The secondary dramatic action involves the illusion of a sexual merry-go-round between the citizen's wives (Mistresses Gallipot, Openwork, and Tiltyard: all names with genital or sexual puns), their husbands, and the gallants. In the shop scene especially (I. i) the writers create a dense and amusing barrage of wordplay around sex and selling. But nothing actually happens! Everything disappears in the gap between niggling and fadoodling. The sceptical distance between word and action which constitutes innuendo is enhanced by the drama concerning Laxton's impotence and Moll's chastity. Their ironic liaison proves to be as full of sexual allusion and as empty of substantive sexual action as the rest of the play.

Having revealed her ability to decipher canting language, Moll elaborates further for the audience upon her 'knowledge of ... nasty villains' (V.i.285). Ostensibly in defense of her good name, she reveals how she came to know them; 'they to me show it' she says simply, and 'I show it you' (V.i.308):

> In younger days, when I was apt to stray,
> I have sat amongst such adders; seen their stings,
> As any here might, and in full playhouses
> Watched their quick diving hands, to bring shame
> Such rogues, and in that stream met an ill name:
> When next, my Lord, you spy any one of those,
> So he be in his art a scholar question him,

Tempt him with gold to open the large book
Of his close villainies: and you yourself shall cant
Better than poor Moll can, and know more laws
Of cheaters, lifters, nips, foists, puggards, curbers,
With all the devil's black guard, than it is fit
Should be discovered to a noble wit.
I know they have their orders, offices,
Circuits and circles, unto which they are bound,
To raise their own damnation in.

(*The Roaring Girl*, V.i.291–306)

'Watched', 'seen', 'spy', 'know', 'open', 'discovered': Moll's verbs
testify to the purpose of her speech; to bring to light 'knowledge in
those villanies' (V.i.314) in exactly the same manner as Dekker's
pamphlets. It seems highly likely that much of the contents of the
first scene of Act V would have found its way into pamphlet form if
the plague had closed the theatres again. Moll invites the audience
to take a safe but vicarious glance into all the corruption of the city.
The world they see is neither terrifyingly chaotic, nor threateningly
organized. Rather comfortingly it echoes the order, the imagined
order, of their own society. As such the underworld becomes a read-
able, knowable, 'Other'; a realm different enough to structure social
boundaries but not impinge on them. Just as Moll works to harmo-
nize the schismatic factions in the primary social world of the city in
the play (by bringing Sebastian and her namesake Mary together in
spite of their fathers), so she brings order to the dark side of city life.
In effect she neutralizes the fear of the suburbs. Appropriating the
role of Long Meg, she retrieves purses, restores property, rights
wrongs, in the same manner with which she facilitates marital
harmony for the disunited lovers. While Moll offers us an insider's
view of London's netherworld, we still get the apparent omniscient
security of the outsider's perspective. For example, it is always the
authorities' view (and sometimes the scholar's) that canting and
other slang languages (including its derivative, cockney rhyming-
slang) are designed for nefarious purposes, designed merely to
thwart, avoid, or challenge the authority from which it remains
obscure. Dekker's *Lanthorne and Candle-light* reveals how canting
derived as a 'gabling with strange tongues' in order to 'conspire together' and was 'bred in the Chaos' and 'mainteind … in disorder'
(Grosart, vol. III. pp. 187 and 189). But such languages develop as a

result of defensive and protective strategies of inclusion to counter the ostracism, disenfranchisement, and exclusion from the central cultural arena. With its inflection and corruption of linguistic norms, slang mocks dominant social discourse and is necessarily disrespectful of the establishment. From the authorities' view slang symbolizes a threat which is why they, rather than its users or practitioners, imagine that it indicates criminal intent.

In Moll the writers create a highly sexualized, hybrid, transvestite figure who effectively disarms the often subliminal sexual anxieties about the underworld, just as she ultimately placates those anxieties about herself. In part this is because she neutralizes her potentially disturbing sexuality: 'being awake, I keep my legs together' (IV.i.128). She is more sexually allusive than sexually active; linguistically more euphemistic than straightforward. Yet just as the oxymoronic and eponymous honest whore, Bellafront, emblematized a City ethos in earlier Dekker–Middleton plays, so Moll's characterization works along faultlines between the city–suburb axis and its parallel honest–dishonest locations. Although she appears in men's clothing and bears the sobriquet 'Moll', significantly she is no more prostitute than man. Yet Moll appears as no stooge on behalf of those who malign her and her kind. She constantly instructs and challenges those who seek to oppress her. The city man Laxton gets told in no uncertain terms; 'In thee I defy all men, their worst hates,/And their best flatteries, all their golden witchcrafts,/With which they entangle the poor spirits of fools' (III.i.90–2). As she beats Laxton she also rejects the ethos of the City and its values of money and exchange. In so doing she indicates the way in which male fantasies have become entangled with the function of (the) capital. In Moll's panoramic speech she defies Laxton's 'base thoughts' which figure 'each woman' as a 'fond flexible whore' (III.i.70–1). But Moll's vanquishment of Laxton is a pyrrhic victory, which she comes to realize with some frustration:

> If I could meet my enemies one by one thus,
> I might make pretty shift with 'em in time,
> And make 'em know, that she that has wit and spirit
> May scorn
> To live beholding to her body for meat,
> Or for apparel, like your common dame

That makes shame get her clothes to cover shame.
Base is the mind that kneels unto her body ...

(III.i.30–7)

However laudable her defeat of Laxton, the problem is larger than
two people and therefore requires a systemic solution. She can
never meet all her enemies, because their attitudes are part of the
very discourse of the city from which she is cast. More important,
perhaps, is the recognition that public opinion needs to change.
Wengrave, who once thought of Moll as 'a devouring flood', later
comes to realize his misperception;

> Forgive me, now I cast the world's eyes from me,
> And look upon thee freely with mine own ...
> I'll never more
> Condemn by common voice, for that's the whore
> That deceives man's opinion ...
> ... makes his heart unjust.

(V.ii.171 and 244–50)

He admits his perspective has been erroneously governed by a
widespread prejudice held in the city. Clarity of sight, once a
function which emplaced the 'whore', now appears free from such
deception. In what must be a critique of Puritan dogma (the
common voice) such linguistic hypocrisy is exposed. Now the
concept of dissimulation reflects upon those who ascribe others as
whores.

# 3
# London's Languages of Fashion

## I  FASHIONING THE FANTASTIC; FORMS OF ADDRESS

we followed him, like so may russet serving-men, to see the
event of all ... he was encountered by a most glorious-spangled
gallant, which we took at first to have been some upstart tailor,
because he measured all his body with a salutation, from the
flow of the doublet to the fall of the breeches; but at last we
found him to be a very fantastical sponge, that licked up all
humours, the very ape of fashions, gesture, and complement ...
that fed upon young landlords, riotous sons and heirs, till either
he or the Counter in Wood-street had swallowed them up ... Our
prodigal child, accompanied with this soaking swaggerer and ad-
mirable cheater, who had supt up most of our heirs about
London like poached eggs ...    (Bullen, vol. VIII, pp. 78–9)

First (to be an accomplisht gentleman, that is, a gentleman of the
time) you must give o'er house-keeping in the countrey, and live
altogether in the citie among gallants: where, at your first appearence, 'twere good you turnd foure or five hundred acres of
your best land into two or three trunkes of apparell. (Buffone in
*Every Man Out of His Humour*, I.ii.37–42)

Of the large numbers of people who migrated from the country to
the city none were more noticeable than London's gallants; or
'Guls', 'Conies', 'Phantastickes', as they were also known. Although
dispossessed workers, forced to migrate, bore the brunt of the city's
judicial and punitive practices, the 'country gentlemen' who came
to make their way in the city were also made to bear the responsibility for social upheaval and the stressful consequences of economic change. Buffone's account is common, decline of the rural
way of life is literally thrust on to the shoulders of the gallant and

his search for metropolitan accomplishment (something, ironically, Jonson also sought). As stereotypes, gallants were charged with liquefying the hitherto permanent assets of the country and translating them into so much sartorial ephemera. The past, too, seemed apparently lost in the moment when the 'accomplisht gentleman' completely turned his back on country life. Widespread moral condemnation ensued, and satirical writers like Middleton seized on the figure of the gallant to castigate his deportment and manners; a way of life which was increasingly seen by London's citizens as aristocratic profligacy. In his *Father Hubbard's Tales* a dispossessed ploughman spells out the dire social consequences of his master's actions; 'thereby that world was turned upside down since the decease of my old landlord, all hospitality and good housekeeping kicked out of doors, all thriftiness and good husbandry tossed into the air, ploughs turned into trunks [breeches], and corn into apparel' (Bullen, vol. VIII, p. 75). As capital drained from the country, through the departure of the old landlord's heir, all sense of social cohesion seemed to dissipate. Middleton's ploughman (a long-standing symbol of feudal humility) describes the breakup of feudal social structures by condemning excessive expenditure.

In keeping with this general critical tone, Dekker offered his own opprobrium:

> for that true humerous Gallant that desires to powre himselfe into all fashions (if his ambition be such to excell even Complement itselfe) must as well practice to diminish his walkes, as to bee various in his sallets, curious in his Tobacco, or ingenious in the trussing up of a new Scotch-hose:/All of which vertues are excellent and able to maintaine him, especially if the old worme-eaten Farmer, (his father) be dead, and left him five hundred a yeare, onely to keepe an Irish hobby, an Irish horse-boy, and himselfe (like a gentleman).[1] (Grosart, vol. II, pp. 229–39)

Dekker's critique posits the gallant as a new being, one who feeds off the carrion-like body of the rural patriarchy. But his moralism is somewhat tongue-in-cheek because this is caricature rather than outright condemnation. To be a gallant one had to be a connoisseur, a cognoscente, of metropolitan goods and services. Clearly, the figure of the gallant functioned as a vector for the massive changes taking place in the city's self-fashioning, and dress codes quickly characterized the enormous stress of transition. Images of

finely dressed city gallants helped them to occupy a space which
was overlaid with meanings of cultural transposition. What was at
stake in the new relationship between literature and the social
space which the gallant and his fashions inhabited?

In response to that question, let us look at some fashions in
language and its forms of address. Here, Jonson, Middleton, and
Dekker offer different viewpoints on contemporary fashion:

> So that we may conclude wheresoever manners and fashions are
> corrupted, language is. It imitates the public riot. The excess of
> feasts and apparel are the notes of a sick state, and the wantonesse
> of language, of a sick mind. (Ben Jonson, *Discoveries*, 964–8)

> At last, to close up the lamentable tragedy of us ploughmen,
> enters our young landlord, so metamorphosed into the shape of a
> French puppet, that at first we started, and thought one of the
> baboons had marched in man's apparel. His head was dressed
> up in white feathers like a shuttlecock, which agreed so well with
> his brain, being nothing but cork ... His doublet was of a strange
> cut; and to show the fury of his humour, the collar of it rose up so
> high and sharp as if it would have cut his throat by daylight ...
> His breeches, a wonder to see, were full as deep as the middle of
> winter, or the roadway between London and Winchester, and so
> large and wide withal, that I think within a twelvemonth he
> might very well put all his lands in them; and then you may
> imagine they were big enough, when they would outreach a
> thousand acres ... Thus was our young landlord accoutred in
> such strange and prodigal shape, that it amounted to above two
> years' rent in apparel. At last approach the mercer and the mer-
> chant, two notable arch-tradesmen, who had fitted my young
> master in clothes, whilst they had clothed themselves in acres,
> and measured him out velvet by the thumb, whilst they received
> his revenues by handfuls; for he had not so many yards in his
> suit as they had yards and houses bound for payment, which
> now he was forced to pass over to them ... (Thomas Middleton,
> *Father Hubbard's Tales*, Bullen, vol. VII, pp. 68–72)

> Good cloathes are the embrodred trappings of pride, and good
> cheere the very *eringo-roote* of gluttony: so that fine backs, and fat
> bellyes are Coach-horses to two of the seven deadly sins: In the
> bootes of which Coach, *Lechery* and *Sloth* sit like the waiting-

maide. In a most desperate state therefore doe Taylors, and Cookes stand, by meanes of their offices: for both those trades are Apple-squires to that couple of sinnes. The one invents more phantasticke fashions, then Fraunce hath worne since her first stone was laid; the other more lickerish *epycurean* dishes, then were ever servd up to *Gallonius* table. Did man, (think you) come wrangling in to the world, about no better matters, then all his lifetime to make privy searches in Burchin lane for Whalebone doublets, or for pies of *Nightingale* tongues in *Heliogabulus* his kitchin? No, no, the first suit of apparell, that ever mortall man put on, came neither from the Mercers shop, nor the Merchants warehouse: *Adams* bill would have been taken then, sooner then a Knights bond now; yet was he great in no bodies bookes for satten, and velvets: the silk-wormes had something else to do in those dayes, then to set up loomes, and be free of the weavers ... (Thomas Dekker, *The Guls Horne-booke*, Grosart, vol. II, pp. 209–19)

Any similarity of opinion on manners and dress among these three passages is mediated by the form of their expression, by the way they are fashioned. Each has a very distinct emphasis. Dekker's writing style is just as 'lickerish' and embroidered as the fashions it describes. For example, his prose playfully harnesses a rag-bag of metaphors, archaisms, similes, anecdotes, and allegory, into a dense colloquial narrative which ironically flows with the same excess it is attempting to admonish. In addition, the trades which are made complicit with the extravagance of dress and food are corrupted by the very superfluity upon which they depend. In contrast, Jonson's criticism is made with detached authoritative sobriety. His writing claims an authenticity for fashion yet dare not risk the vulgar assault on language which would accompany its enunciation. He will not jeopardize the word for fear of its being compromised or adulterated. Jonson's rhetorical strategy is monological, brooking neither contrariety nor other voices through a style which tries to be always and apparently unambiguous. Its aims are probity and perspicacity. Addressing his reader in this tight, highbrow form, he attempts to remove himself, his audience, and his word, from the infection of the 'public riot'. Jonson avoids the problems of excessive representational turpitude by simply not being drawn into it. Shunning ridicule, satire and the vices of description, he relies instead on a rhetoric of moral-literary disdain. Deviation from the authorial line means nothing less than irrationality, mental instability, and treason; or worse, immersion in the linguistic mêlée which is everyday speech.

*Pace* Jonson, Dekker's style is tailored in and for that public riot. It is implicated, complicit, and inside the audience and objective of its prose. It drips with the corruption and excess so studiously purged from Jonson's.[2] Middleton, on the other hand, while aware of the potential 'wantonesse of language', stands at a certain ironic distance from the object of his invective. Happier with a plainer prose style, his writing appears less stained by the tools of its critique. Unlike Dekker's language, where social antagonism becomes manifest in argumentative linguistic juxtapositions, Middleton's prose inscribes a morality through perspective, enabling us to see through the borrowed eyes of 'us ploughmen'. Mediation of the ploughman's viewpoint comes through the controlled form of its exposition rather than from refashioning peasant colloquy. A sense of moral dignity is given to the ploughmen who haplessly become witnesses to the mechanisms which dictate their fate. Middleton's style is tied to his moral passion which, in turn, inflects our view of the ploughmens' disenfranchisement. By making aristocratic prodigality a vector of disreputable socio-economic activity, Middleton articulates their perception by writing about clothing through acute and vicious similes, metaphors, and analogies. In seeking to translate himself through dress, the prodigal, as the 'cut' throat of the doublet collar suggests, gives himself a self-inflicted wound. *Father Hubbard's Tales* evokes an extraordinary image of barren landscapes and rural desolation encoded in the description of 'breeches' being 'full as deep as the middle of winter'. In his intimately panoramic prose, the decay, however, signals a dynamic transfer of social energy as the young landlord and his one-time vassals come to remake themselves in the city. Fancy breeches stand for the cultural distance between the City and Winchester, as fashion aesthetics are realized through social perspective. Driven from their livelihoods by their young master's prodigality, the ploughmen perceive clothes in the currency of rents and the lost acres of their traditional way of being; 'his glorious rapier ... drunk up the price of ploughland in very pearl' (Bullen, vol. VIII, p. 70). Heralding a profound shift in social resources, this sartorial refit functioned as a rueful allegory of social change. More comically perhaps, Dekker makes the merchant and mercer part of a post Lapsarian mockery, animating gallant profligacy as an apparent catalyst of social corruption. Excessive consumption on dress seems like an old-fashioned form of gluttony. Through an almost affectionate use of the old-style morality tradition, Dekker depicts the excesses of upper-class consumption as that which corrupts the service industries. His half-serious moral joke about an 'Apple-squire', a cant term for pimp, points to the sinful origins of clothing and also reveals how the cash nexus had contaminated class relationships. Even so, terms like Apple-squire have a humorous tone which Middleton's title, 'arch-tradesman', does not.[3] Instead, Middleton reveals the merchant and mercer as calculated and culpable agents of social transformation as he dissects their avaricious behaviour. For Middleton, 'the lamentable tragedy' of the ploughmen is deepened by the intersecting aspirations of two groups: prodigal gallants and greedy merchants. Both Dekker and Middleton saw greed as a corrupting force which perpetuated class antagonism and underpinned social conflict. Middleton's critique is sharper, more precise, because he wants to expose and rid corruption from the group to whom he was aligned, and in which he had a stake. More than Dekker, Middleton was materially connected to London's guildsmen, traders, craftsmen and citizenry; its middle class. Similar to Jonson's savage views of the Court (a Court he never quite thought worthy enough), Middleton presented an equally ferocious critique of London's bourgeoisie – though he still kept plenty of spleen for chastising the role of gallants and rakes. As such he makes the gallant a victim of his own ineptitude and air-headedness, while still implicating the tradesmen as an integral part of that exploitation. In this process fashion and social criticism are one and the same.

Both Jonson and Middleton display a firm grasp on their material because they write, at least rhetorically, from a more identifiable place. Although an avid writer of the city, Dekker's work is more ambiguously placed, more pressured by the complex insecurities of his own position as a professional writer. Sometimes he adopts the distancing stance of moral finger-pointing, at other times he seems to be intimately proximate to those socially accused. This sense of ambivalence and frustration about the social place of his writing has made Dekker's writing difficult to locate with any precision.[4]

## II GROTESQUE, CARICATURE, SATIRE

For the writers above, mobilizing the language of fashion was not simply about fads in style but a participation in the trends of a widespread social argument. Jonson's disgusted and elevated with-drawal, Middleton's meticulously controlled caricature, and Dekker's narrative hyperbole, all target the excesses of fashion in an attempt to challenge or redefine social attitudes. Modes of liter-ary expression were often borrowed from the terms of fashion: 'Bombastic', for example, became an abusive term by which one class attacked the pretentious style of another.[5] On a wider stage, fashion could be seen as a resource which was both indicative and instrumental in structuring social change in the city. Fashion tips rapidly increased during this period as metropolitan London wit-nessed an explosion of behavioural manuals and gentlemanly advice. My starting point for exploring the meanings implicit in the languages of fashion, manners and style, is Dekker's unique pam-phlet, *The Guls Horne-booke* (1609). Born out of his fraught authorial position, this off-the-rack piece of writing entered the market as a parody, a critique, and an intervention, of advice and behaviour in the city. An immediate best-seller, it appealed to the vanity of those whom it purported to ridicule, the city's gallants, while presenting itself as an indispensable read for those in social competition with them. A fashionable book which ridiculed fashion was precisely the kind of ironic and irresistible item which many Londoners would have found appealing. No one could afford to ignore the codes and importance of fashion in the city. Even Dekker, who lampooned the excess of manners and fashion in *The Guls Horne-booke*, spent seven years in King's Bench prison for debts to his tailor![6]

Much of the underlying satirical force which underwrites *The Guls Horne-booke* develops from its apparent and critical exposition of extravagance and or lack of constraint. A wide range of gallant styles, manners, and behaviour are discovered one after another in various places in the city. As Christopher Breward observes, 'late sixteenth-century aristocratic dress was nothing if not fantastical'.[7] Manners and behaviour followed suit: whether the 'Gul' is being advised to 'discourse as Lowd' as he can in an ordinary, 'to laugh alowd in the middest of the most serious and saddest scene of the terriblest Tragedy' at the theatre, to protest himself 'to be ex-treamely in love', or, at 'Paul's Walk', to publish himself in 'phanta-sticke fashions', *The Guls Horne-booke* operates by presenting unacceptable social behaviour as spurious gentlemanly advice to the 'Guls' and gallants who began to hang around the city in in-creasing numbers (Grosart, vol. II, pp. 238 and 251). A restraining critique seeking to bridle excessive behaviour appears implicit in the *Horne-booke*'s presentation. In addition to ridiculing the behaviour and fashions of London's upper crust, the *Horne-booke* provides a sustained mockery of all types of flamboyant self-representation. Yet for all this, the writing is complicit with the extravagance it is exposing. As a vector for moral restraint, then, *The Guls Horne-booke* is formally at odds with its own 'phantasticke fashions'. Holding restraint and riot in tension created the special comedic and satirical texture of *The Guls Horne-booke*. Such writing, like gallant fashion, drew its energies from deep-rooted cultural conflict embedded in verbal and sartorial expression. It seems appropriate to ask: what was at stake in this conflict?

Aristocratic fashions in early modern London, and the gallant fashions which followed them, were a curious amalgam of styles. Upper-class dress formally incorporated and displayed vestiges of armour through gauntlets, plumes, sword-bearing, and, in particular, the sculpted effect of the doublet (usually made of leather or shiny material such as silk or satin). These chivalric echoes nestled alongside a meticulous superfluity of styles which Dekker exposed to comic description in the *Horne-booke*. Ornamentation and embellishment of a variety of materials were combined with extravagant gusseting and generously cut sleeves and breeches, all of which produced an extraordinary effect of extravagant and conspicuous consumption. Symbolically displaying the residue of armigeral forms through an affectation of luxurious flamboyance was an attempt to create a sense of self-confidence in the wearer. 'The period', as de Marly says of seventeenth-century aristocratic dress, 'saw a lot of swagger'.[8] Yet writers like Dekker saw that swagger as flatulence, and such self-confidence as arrogance. *The Guls Horne-booke* was offered as an instrument to deflate and expose the arrogant affectations of upper-class and gallant behaviour. Aside from the evocation of armour, the overall effect of the ornate, even baroque, style was to deny any firm shape or outline. Smooth-surfaced items of dress were pleated, bombasted, underfolded, or designed to shimmer. Decorative detail was extensive and included a variety of cloth textures, deep gussets and folds, material pulled through slits to make ornate puffs, conglomeration of national styles, pinking, spiking, extensive use of protruding and ornamental lace, printed garters, ties, ribbons, feathers, and bows. All combined to produce deliberate overstatement and sartorial effusion. According to Breward; 'the disintegration of the body's natural contours and any sense of coherent harmony within the design of the components of fashionable dress and its colour and pattern as a whole continued into the final decade of the sixteenth century ... .'[9] Such a stylized disjuncture pointed to a fundamental conflict within elite modes of representation, as these contradictory fashion tropes were created to mediate and articulate two different but related aesthetic forms: grotesque and baroque. This resulted in, what Breward calls, 'a complicated profusion of styles'; and out of this medium was woven *The Guls Horne-booke*.[10]

Of particular significance in Dekker's satire is the way in which grotesque relates to a certain transgressive epistemology of the body. His parodic description harnesses, for example, the grotesque energy associated with disease in order to condemn gallant behaviour. Especially targeted are those, as he says, 'whose bodyes, either overflowing with the corrupt humours of this ages phantasticknesse, or else being burnt up with the inflamation of upstart fashions' (Grosart, vol. II, p. 214). Underwriting these images of bodily effusion is, of course, Bakhtin's formulation which argues that 'the grotesque body is not separated from the rest of the world ... it is not a closed, completed unit; it is unfinished, outgrows itself, transgresses its own limits.'[11] Throughout *The Guls Horne-booke*, aristocratic fashions are deemed to express pejoratively these characteristics as bodily definitions continually reveal their unfinished qualities. Gallant fashions presented bodily transgression through an exaggerated distortion of the body's shape which was both desired and admired. It was an aesthetic which linked them to 'the collective ancestral body of the people'.[12] Although Bakhtin's explanation of grotesque forms was derived from the bodily energy of popular culture, aristocratic sensibilities also partook of that same sense of a collective social body. Somewhat paradoxically, baroque fashions were an elite version of those grotesque aesthetics.[13] Gallant fashions modelled baroque into a form of class-specific nostalgia. The culture in which grotesque idioms acquired their meaning was also the one in which the ruling landed aristocracy were deemed to be more socio-economically secure, precisely because its relationship with the lower class was more integrated, though no less fraught. One of the ways in which the bourgeoisie challenged the aristocracy was by exploiting, widening, and inhabiting the gap between the upper and lower classes. As the strong social and personal bonds which interconnected all members of a feudal society dissolved, so did the aesthetics which accompanied them. Gradually the artistic link between grotesque and baroque was put under more and more strain by the reconfiguration of class identities. As the lower class moved from service work for the gentry (on the land or in the house) and became a work force of labourers, the grotesque became increasingly degraded and demonized. Social and economic forces within the metropolis hastened the demise of the ties between upper and lower classes as well as the identities which went with them. In addition, the metropolitan arena, along with its expanded resources, enabled and required a specifically urban affect for those with aristocratic roots, wealth, and sensibilities. As Breward notes: 'transformation, elaboration, and the cultivation of artifice begin to describe the nature of elite modes of dress at the end of the sixteenth century.'[14] For the elite, dressing the conflict between city and heritage meant the creation of some extraordinary styles.

We could argue, then, that the upper class had three main problems in creating a socially viable fashion mode which incorporated, expressed, and enabled the reconstruction of their identity. Most importantly, they had to display their wealth as a significant and hierarchical form which differentiated them from other classes; this includes what Breward has called 'the rhetoric of power'.[15] More tricky for elite dress codes was the need to allude to grotesque forms whilst avoiding the overwhelming effect of its all-embracing cultural energy. At the same time, although in competition with the bourgeoisie, they required a style which denoted their right to lead, or 'head', society and the body politic. One specific item of dress was designed to negotiate all these socio-sartorial pressures. Not surprisingly, then, it became one of the fashion modes which characterized the period. I am referring to the ruff. Ruffs developed from what had previously been the more simple 'standing collar'. By the late sixteenth century 'the head was completely encircled by starch and goffered linen or the increasingly popular cutwork standing ruffs'.[16] Designed to feature and privilege the head, the ruff held its wearer erect and encouraged elevated noble deportment. Once on, the ruff enforced considerable upper-body restraint, as it limited back and neck movement. Lack of bodily freedom emphasized and displayed the fact that the wearer was a person of leisure. Carrying on a mundane trade or business while wearing a ruff was either difficult or impossible. Apart from concealing the disfiguring effects of disease, the ruff had absolutely no utilitarian function. At a stroke it removed the wearer from any taint of practical labour. Rather, it displayed the wearer's power to purchase the labour of others. Ruffs required considerable sartorial engineering. Dekker's personal jibe at Gallants, calling them 'stiffenecked reba- toes', refers to the bracing collars under the ruff which were them- selves often held in place by supporting wires called pickadillys.[17] Like much of the aristocratic fashion at the time, ruffs relied on labour-intensive processes such as lace-making, embroidery, pinking, and poking (giving it its folded shape with special hot pokers), as well as all the other factors of their tailoring. Noticeably beyond the means of most people, the ornate ruff developed not just to enhance the wearer's deportment but to exemplify and demonstrate a specific set of social relations. Its importance in the new metropolitan arena, where the aristocracy were forging a new identity, was crucial. Servants in the country house, or workers on the demesne, were obviously not as highly visible as lace on the streets of London. Wearing an extravagant ruff was a clearly visible sign that you required servants to help you dress properly. In a lo- gistical sense, if you were of the upper class, you could not dress yourself even if you wanted to.

Perhaps the most important aspect of the ruff was the extraordi- nary effect it produced, demarcating the head from the body. Especially with the large ruffs, the great 'millstone ruffs' in Dekker's account, the head appeared to be completely separated from the body. With their heads literally above the crowd, members of the ruff-wearing class paraded themselves around the fashionable walks of London. A disembodied head appeared to solve the problem of the potentially overthrowing energies of the grotesque. Separating the head from the realm of the body enabled it to be elevated from the effusive vigour associated with the body and all that went on there. In mockery, Dekker indicates that 'the Head is a house built for Reson to dwell in' (Grosart, vol. II, p. 224). This comment underlines what an important device the ruff was, because reason, as we know, appears antithetical to the grotesque body. Reason, and what Bakhtin called 'the material bodily lower stratum', could – albeit in a state of tension – coexist in a single fashion statement, providing there was a stratified form of discretion.[18] It appears that a hierarchy of fashion- able forms was designed to protect the head from the body.

In such an economy, women's bodies were increasingly made to bear those energies associated with the reproductive, regenerative, and unfinished body. Increasingly women were deemed more 'nat- urally' grotesque, at a time when such forms were becoming more negatively represented. Social threats 'from below' were often read through the topography of the lower body. From the view of those ruling society this made a woman's body doubly dangerous, thus the effect of bodily separation and demarcation in women was heightened. Upper-class women found themselves having to ward off the aesthetics which tied the grotesque to reproduction and sexuality, often by addressing the rhetoric which required them to be both 'fruitful' and 'chaste'.[19] A number of fashion modes for upper-class women developed to accommodate and negotiate this conflicting cultural rhetoric. Through the use of light colours like silver and white, and by extensive use of gauze and lace, a shimmering aureola effect was created which gave the upper body especially an ethereal, almost angelic, quality, a peculiar weightlessness. But women were not completely allowed to float off into the hyper-platonic realm of the court poet's imagination, heirs were needed. And so the body was anchored by the farthingale, which was a huge wooden or metal frame holding the dress out in a wide, flat circle. Beginning just above the hips, the farthingale alluded to, as it simultaneously obscured, the fecundity and substance of the lower bodily stratum. At the same time it created the effect of an upper body barely connected to the lower body; one seemingly able to detach itself at any moment and leave the threatening lower part standing. The farthingale had developed earlier from the highly artificial and angular 'X' look for women.[20] As Breward says 'a severe, triangular aspect to the female outline was established in court circles by the middle years of the sixteenth century.'[21] This severity destroyed any curves about the woman's outline and erased her waist, while the intersection of the X marked the very spot which was the focus of so much attention. The sharply tapered stomacher which provided the upper part of the frame for the 'X' look reduced the impression of a reproductive, and therefore, grotesque, belly: such an outline, of course, emphasized both virginity and chastity.

Under Elizabeth the emphasis shifted again as the stomacher was extended so that the point went past the navel to indicate the pudendal region. Stomachers were worn to great iconographic effect by Elizabeth; a virgin queen who required a shift in emphasis from her never-to-be productive womb to the, almost unimaginable, 'fair thought' that lay between her legs. The longer stomacher helped Elizabeth present herself as the primary symbolic focus of sexual-political desire while remaining continuously unattainable. To make sure her courtiers got the point, Elizabeth would often tie

jewels on to her clothes to indicate that most symbolically inaccess-
ible place: in the 1588 George Gower portrait, Breward observes
'the pendant pearl at Elizabeth's crotch calling attention to the
famed virginity of Gloriana'.[22] Elizabeth also redeployed the expansive impression which the farthingale created; in 'The Ditchley
Portrait' by Marcus Gheeraerts the Younger (1592) she appears to
cover the world with her kirtle.[23]

Apart from Elizabeth's special relationship to the ideology of
dress, in many ways aristocratic fashion developed to restructure
their changing relationship with others in society. Ultimately, they
still wished to model and incorporate a harmonious, non-
bourgeois, vision of society through dress codes. But the expression
of baroque, grotesque, and extravagant styles took different forms
and meanings as they came into contact with city culture. The logistics of a social life in London were far removed from the ideological
seat of aristocratic identity, the country estate. Consequently the
aesthetics of the grotesque and baroque narrowed into caricature
and satire as they impacted upon the more anonymously competitive world of the city. Sumptuary laws were written in extensive
detail to enforce elaborate hierarchies. As laws they were largely
ineffective and were very rarely prosecuted, but they did reflect
aristocratic anxieties about hierarchy in a rapidly changing world.
Fashion became the very medium of competition between and
within various groups in the metropolis. Dress codes charted all
manner of paths between individual aspiration and class approba-
tion, and were the perfect vehicle for both envy and ridicule. Yet
fashion, for the upper class in particular, became a sartorial game
fraught with many problems. The doublet, for example, while
standing as a vestigial emblem of the breastplate (and all the
martial chauvinism which that entailed) had to avoid being a mere
parody of the good old days. Such an ensemble could not draw too
much attention to the fact that the wearer probably spent more time
in litigation over rents, or in administration, than in legitimate
chivalrous pursuits. In spite of this, many portraits of the period
have the subject's armour not-so-discretely displayed in the background, demonstrating the continued importance of encoded references to chivalric activities, even or especially when not actually
pursued. A woman's midriff, then, was not the only abdominal site
which sought to renegotiate social tension and grotesque forms: the
upper-class man's belly also came in for some reshaping. What was
apparently required was the idiomatic display of grotesque without

its full-blown incorporation. The rambunctiousness of a Falstaff-like figure could be partly invoked because, like the mythical 'land of Cockagne', he encoded a lost realm of plenty and harmony. Such a nostalgia for 'merry old England' was compromised in an urban milieu with its endless moments of disjunction; and the invocation of grotesque in this atomized world undoubtedly tapped a desire for a time of more secure identities. What was needed by the upper class was a form of grotesque shorn of its full cultural potency. This aesthetic balancing act was performed by one of the most bizarre fashion items of the period: the peascod belly, a pouch filled with cotton which was strapped around the waist to look like a paunch. As a fashion statement the peascod belly mirrored and parodied one of the central grotesque idioms, the full and extended belly. Coincidentally, it also echoed the breastplate armour bulge of the more portly members of the aristocracy, especially those of the past. Here we can see how stoutness, an 'emphasis on bulk', once a representative idiom of the *common* wealth, became reduced to an image of the *singular* wealth of its bearer.[24] Peascod bellies are best described in the contradictory or paradoxical terms which brought them about: that is, as a pseudo-grotesque fashion. Sufficiently extravagant to be condemned by the bourgeois Puritan hack, Philip Stubbes, this false, padded, simulated belly 'was as much as 5lb in weight, and the extension was bombasted, quilted, and bedecked with slashes, prickings, and cuts.'[25] Peascod bellies reveal how grotesque forms become truncated when they encounter the dynamics of metropolitan society. Once idiomatic of the collective body, the ancestral body of the people, bellies in the city became axiomatic of individual self-expression which arrogantly mocked the forms from which they were derived. Tainted by personal infra-class rivalry, the false belly expressed the insecurity of individuality as it sought to render substance to its wearer. Strangely, then, the peascod belly at once symbolized the demise of grotesque and heralded the birth of new kinds of urban satire and caricature.

The relationship between gallants, 'Guls', and the court, produced an interactive and competitive cycle of dress styles; 'Put off to none', advises *The Guls Horne-booke*, 'unlesse his hatband be of a newer fashion then yours, and three degrees quainter' (Grosart, vol. II, p. 234). Aspiring to be 'three degrees quainter' produced caricature, camp, competition, and always the next fashion mode. Fashion metaphorized the interface between individual competition and social display:

If therefore you determine to enter into a new suit, warne your
Tailor to attend you in Powles, who, with his hat in his hand,
shall like a spy discover the stuffe, colour, and fashion of any
doublet, or hose that dare be seene there, and stepping behind a
piller to fill his table-bookes with those notes, will presently send
you into the world an accomplisht man: by which means you
shall weare your clothes in print with the first edition. (Grosart,
vol. II, pp. 234–5)

In the city where 'every mans eie heere is upon the other mans
trencher' those seeking social accomplishment entered into a tense
form of interaction with others (Grosart, vol. II, p. 245). 'Urban life',
according to Pelling, 'added new dimensions to attitudes to the
body as the city became the main arena for competition among
social aspirants.'[26] It was a competition which led to an increased
'stress on personal good looks and accomplishments'.[27] In turn, this
led to an extraordinary 'preoccupation with dress and artifice'
which underscored many of the exquisite fashions of the
Elizabethan and Jacobean Courts and their environs.[28] Much business – 'obtaining of suits', 'Interest with the King', the getting of
'offices', and 'mightie credit' – was done, it seems, largely, and
sometimes 'onely', 'upon the privilege of hansome clothes'
(Grosart, vol. II, p. 239). Adopting the right guise or identity, often
through high artifice, might considerably enhance or establish your
socio-political standing. In this world, everyone was in costume.
According to Breward, 'fashionable costume referred not so much
to the three dimensional body hidden underneath, responding
instead to the dictates of portraiture and constant display ...'.[29] *The
Guls Horne-booke* indicated the contradictory pressures which required 'the individual to summarize his estate in his own person',
and this often led to fashions which collapsed under the weight of
'a new flamboyance'.[30]
Dekker suggested that being on display could bring all kinds of
danger. His fashion-monger arrives at the theatre and finds the
clothes he has bought have turned him into a commodity:

for if you should bestow your person upon the vulgar, when the
belly of the house is but halfe full, your apparell is quite eaten
up, the fashion lost, and the proportion of your body in more
danger to be devoured then if it were served up in the Counter

amongst the Powltry: avoid that as you would the Bastome.
(Grosart, vol. II, pp. 250–1)

As place and fashion are juxtaposed we can see how the force of the
collective body threatens to overpower that of the individual body
in this confrontation.[31] Yet the victory of the 'Rabble with a full
throat' does not quite materialize in this account (Grosart, vol. II,
p. 250). Although challenged and made anxious, the gallant's character is allowed some definitive form. Eventually that self-
conscious 'awareness of the snares and limitations of the body'
helped to construct an ironical distance between those bodies.[32]
According to Pelling, satire can be seen 'as a particularly urban
product, requiring a "crowded society" for its generation'.[33]
Paradoxically, it was also that same sense of distance which structured many of the new satirical forms of the growing metropolis, so
that while exposure to the energy of the collective body might overwhelm the quality of the individual body, Dekker leaned on the tradition of grotesque to chastise the gallant's ambition rather than his
individuality. City satire tended to flatten out the grotesque when-
ever it was propelled by the exigencies of individual antagonism
and personal competition. The problem, according to Rhodes, was
that Dekker 'could not easily use grotesque imagery for the
purpose of social criticism, [his] ... concern with the real social
issues of the time reined in any desire to imitate the exuberant,
sprawling grotesque of Nashe's writing.'[34] Dekker's urbanity governed his adaptation of grotesque, especially as he tried to avoid
the poverty which overwhelmed Nashe for remaining true to the
spirit of those earlier forms.[35] Rhodes' analysis of the grotesque,
however, registers the debt which *The Guls Horne-booke* owes to
those forms and 'traces of earlier influences'.[36] *The Guls Horne-booke*,
for example, was a mediated version of its source; a scurrilous and
vigorously grotesque pamphlet called *Grobianus*.[37] *Grobianus* was a
stylistic *tour de force* of bodily idioms which violently satirized aristocratic behaviour. Its power derived solely from the expression of
bodily energy via its most basic functions (spitting, defecating,
sweating, drinking, farting, and so on). Though it purported to
censure upper-class behaviour, its ferocious celebration of the
body, the unfinished body, also qualified its own critique. Dekker's
most significant point of departure from *Grobianus* stemmed from
his need to capture the ethos and aesthetics of urban life and space.
With its cheek-by-jowl bodily agitation, the city inevitably agitates

many of the elements of grotesque, but it also contains its oppositional forces: urbanity, civility, politeness, and the regulation of
manners and behaviour. Whereas grotesque endlessly seeks to participate in a collective body as part of its utopian fantasy, satire
derives its social and artistic energy from factional and individual
attacks upon each other which, in turn, serve to delineate and demarcate character. For all that, Dekker's satire is deeper and richer
for its residual grotesque tendencies.

It was Dekker's subtle shift in use of the grotesque towards caricature which heralded a different approach to satire. Caricature indicates a point of departure from the aesthetics of collective forms;
it conceptualizes social distance, it is a discriminative force in a way
that grotesque cannot be. Caricature articulates a critique based on
specific mimicry and enhances rather than erases character. In early
modern London, social aspiration was measured by the reproduction of manners and behaviour, as Dekker reveals in *The Guls
Horne-booke*:

> [if] your Lords use it; your Knights are Apes to the Lords, and so
> too: your Inne-a-court-man is Zany to the Knights, and (mary
> very scurvily) comes likewise limping after it: be thou a beagle to
> them all, and never lin snuffing, till you have scented them ...
> (Grosart, vol. II, p. 251)

Aping Lords, being zany to knights, becoming three degrees
quainter, was symptomatic of the extravagance of gallant manners,
style and behaviour. The characters so brilliantly lampooned in *The
Guls Horne-booke* are themselves already caricatures. Without digni-
fying the identities which they desperately sought, *The Guls Horne-
booke* tacitly privileges the identifiable social roles which city
gallants craved. Ironically, then, it does this through its primary
function of mocking courtly fashions and ridiculing gallant behaviour. *The Guls Horne-booke* cannot help but authenticate, even if it
does not dignify, the Guls, the target of its rhetoric.

With little comfort for the budding gallant, it seems highly likely
that *The Guls Horne-booke* appealed to the very people it ostensibly
targeted. Caught between the competitive world of the city and the
potential indifference of the Court, what better role to adopt than
one of tailored distress and disillusionment? Social dishevelment
was matched with sartorial derangement as maudlin displays of
abandoned love became a widespread fashion.[38] In Shakespeare's

As *You Like It*, Rosalind offers up this darkly narcissistic state as spurious advice to a would-be lover:

> your hose should be ungartered, your bonnet unbanded, your sleeve unbuttoned, your shoe untied, and everything about you demonstrating a careless desolation. But you are no such man: you are rather point-device in your accoutrements, as loving yourself than seeming the lover of any other. (*As You Like It*, III.ii.368–74)

Appearing as a perennially jilted lover became paradigmatic of the courtier who suffered personal, emotional, and social trauma upon exclusion from the Court. Adopting a posture of self-devastation was symptomatic of aristocratic identity but it was fraught with many psychological and social problems. Investment in an identity of social and mental turmoil exacerbated the very problem of (in)security which had encouraged it. As a way of being, this imminent collapse into self-centredness was an extremely fragile prop for personal identity and quite unstable as a class emblem. In *The Guls Horne-booke* Dekker rather viciously poked fun at such cultic excesses. His eponymous Gull is advised to 'protest your selfe to be extreamely in love' in order to appear 'most Gentlemanlike', but in doing so he runs the risk of becoming a mere narcissistic cipher (Grosart, vol. II, p. 256). Dekker teases the 'Guls' about the conceit which accompanies such 'careless desolation' and loss:

> Put on therefore either no apparel at all, or put it on carelessly: for looke how much more delicate libertie is then bondage, so much is the loosenesse in wearing of our attire, above the imprisonment of being neatly and Tailor-like drest up in it. To be ready in our clothes is to be ready for nothing else. A man lookes as if he be hung in chaines ... (Grosart, vol. II, p. 220)

Melancholics were malcontents. Yet abandonment of being neatly 'drest up' is neither a social victory nor an act of dissidence. All the wearer does is flaunt his sense of disentitlement and the failure of his aspirations. Why do it then? What was at stake in this behaviour? For one reason, gallant fashions mingled both caricature and a sublimated form of protest. Malcontents became increasingly numerous from the latter sixteenth century onwards as they cathected deep-seated anxieties about all kinds of social inclusion and exclusion, along with a sense of helplessness in the face of someone or something more powerful. Many gallants trod a fine line between avid and often sycophantic emulation, sarcastic caricature, or malcontented rejection. Much of this was registered through the metalinguistic forms which fashion makes available. A characteristic malcontent was one who attacked the style and values of the class or social group to which he aspired, precisely because his ambition had been thwarted, or went unrecognized.[39] Both in spite and because of this a certain reputation could be found embodying, or wearing, these dissembled emblems of social stress: 'As for thy stockings and shoos,' advises the *Horne-booke*, 'so weare them that all men may point at thee, and make thee famous by that glorious name of a Male-content' (Grosart, vol. II, p. 223). Fame and reputation appear to accrue precisely because of the wearer's protest at being dispossessed. In a formal sense *The Guls Horne-booke* followed a similar pattern to the attitudes of the 'Guls' it mocked. The writer, too, desired to be part of a social world which so often rejected him. Although Dekker attacked London's gallants, he thoroughly understood their fragile social position. He clothed in words (caricature, satire, emulation, and rejection) the same forms which they expressed in fashion.

### III   ALL BUTTONED UP: CLAIMING THE CLASSICAL BODY

Metropolitan London, then, was a highly transformative medium for the acquisition of cultural identity. Though internecine courtier competition structured a variety of dress codes within the city, they were not the only arena of sartorial contention in London. Fashion also encoded rivalry between classes and concomitant claims for social identity and superiority. While poking fun at the cosmopolitan excesses of aristocratic fashion, along with some cheap nationalistic jibes, Dekker spuriously harks back to the good old days of England:

> There was then neither the *Spanish* slop, nor the Skippers galligaskin: the *Switzers* blistred Cod-piece, nor the *Danish* sleeve sagging/down like a Welch wallet, the *Italians* close strosser, nor the French standing coller: you trebble-quadruple *Daedalian* ruffes, nor your stiffenecked *rebatoes*, (that have more arches for pride to row under, than can stand under five London Bridges) durst not set themselves out in print ... (Grosart, vol. II, pp. 210–11)

Within the scope of its mockery, there lies behind this sentiment a City bourgeois perspective positing a morally legitimate, anti-decadent past. It is a view that denoted 'Simplicity' and 'Honesty'; values which were being overwhelmed by ludicrous anti-English foreign fashions of the kind now sported by London's gallants.[40] It appears that only modesty could uphold a proper, sober, national, and metropolitan identity for the city's 'meere' Englishmen. Caught between moderation and flamboyance, Dekker's pamphlet is underwritten by the same social conflict: 'I altred the Shape, and of a Dutchman fashioned a meere Englishman' (Grosart, vol. II, p. 199). Altering shapes, and especially bodily shapes, was precisely what was at stake in the political vernacular of London's fashion.

Conflict between the power blocs of Court and City provided the broad stage for the conflict about sartorial shapes, but the argument was by no means confined there. The images, claims, and critiques pertinent to this altercation were tied to the aesthetics of the so-called 'classical body'. According to Bakhtin the 'new bodily canon' of the Renaissance inaugurated the classical body; a body around which the legitimation of civic identity and class conflict circulated. This non-transgressive classical body was figured in contradistinction to the grotesque body:

> The new bodily canon, in all its historic variations and different genres, presents an entirely finished, completed, strictly limited body, which is shown from the outside as something individual. That which protrudes, bulges, sprouts, or branches off (when a body transgresses its limits a new one begins) is eliminated, hidden, moderated. All orifices of the body are closed. The basis of the image is the individual, strictly limited mass, the impenetrable facade. The opaque surface and the body's 'valleys' acquire an essential meaning as the border of a closed individuality that does not merge with other bodies and the world. All attributes of the unfinished world are carefully removed, as well as the signs of inner life.[41]

This formulation had an enormous impact on fashion in the early seventeenth century. Following Bakhtin, Stallybrass and White stress the relationship between politics and corporeal form. Accordingly:

> the classical body denotes the inherent form of the high and official culture and suggests that the shape and plasticity of the

human body is indissociable from the shape and plasticity of discursive material and social norm in a collectivity [and that] high
languages attempt to legitimate their authority by appealing to
values inherent in the classical body.[42]

All manner of social and cultural topographies can be charted
through a high–low dichotomy of bodily aesthetics. Although
Stallybrass and White convincingly demonstrate the strong interconnection between the emergent bourgeoisie and the 'high' classical body, they do not account for, nor fully address, the way in
which different forms of the 'elevated' body were in conflict with
one another. London fashions in the early seventeenth century captured that moment of contention as the period witnessed a lively
ideological quarrel over who had access to, and who could define,
the 'classical body'. Art, fashion, and behaviour became a particularly challenging arena in which social conflict was played out. At
Court, the masque reigned supreme as an exclusive art form which
elaborately deployed classical motifs.[43] Poise, balance, harmony,
high-fashion, Greek and Roman mythical forms, upright and geometric bodies, and the maintenance and reinforcement of hierarchies, operated as vectors for claiming the 'high'. This was
undergirded by upper-class fashions of elevated deportment: high
heels, stiff-necks, and an exaggeratedly erect stance and gait. Heads
were affectedly tilted back, enabling the poser to look down his or
her nose – thereby ensuring that, whatever their height, everyone
appeared to be beneath them.

But, in London particularly, other groups were laying claim to
the 'high', 'classical', body through devices of fashion and social
bearing. Eschewing aristocratic flamboyance, Puritans, City-
Fathers, and the upper bourgeoisie in general, were reworking their
social and political demands through a different bodily aesthetic.
Their 'classical body' was separated off from others, it was hermeti-
cally sealed. As Bakhtin has argued, such a body was closed-off,
shorn of embellishment and grotesque idioms. Being solid became
the quality most admired by the bourgeoisie. The term stood (and
still stands) for individual integrity; accompanied by the body's
opacity and inpenetrability. As we saw earlier, Candido's 'minde'
is like 'A wall of Brasse' exemplifying his emotional stability, his
social 'togetherness', and the removal of what Bakhtin called 'all
the signs of inner life' (*The Honest Whore, part II*, V.ii.493). In
*Measure for Measure*, Angelo, too, is likened to 'characters of brass'

(V.i.12). All this corporeal impenetrability is a characteristic of what Norbert Elias has termed *homo clausus*, or enclosed man, who operated as a prime vehicle for the 'civilizing process' of Western culture.[44] Bodily enclosure was achieved through the circumscription of any form of sartorial effusion or stylistic excess. At its extreme was the radically plain Puritan fashion of self-discipline and restraint.[45] Yet the use of simple materials was not confined to Puritan zealots. Smooth-buttoned unfussy doublets, unstarched and practically unadorned collars lying flat upon the shoulders (called the 'plain falling band'), unembellished shoes, plain stockings, all characterized solid burgher fashion of the period. At its fringe, these fashions were rigorously policed through anti-extravagant critiques put about by men like William Prynne and Thomas Hall, who, 'in defence of plaine apparell', saw gallant fashion being 'against the modest, civill, and commendable custome of our own Nation' (Hall, pp. 76 and 27). For men like Hall, plain fashion was an inscription of inner security; it endorsed a realm of impeccable virtue, and complemented 'the inward adorning of the mind, with humility, faith, obedience' (Hall, p. 56). Against the 'selfe-conceited, fantastic fooles of the World' are measured 'grave men, who expresse inward vertues of their minds by outward modesty, humility and gravity of their Haire, Habit, Gestures, Actions &c' (Hall, p. 75). Clothes and actions were fashioned as defence mechanisms to keep out the corrupting world.

In following the cult of Elizabethan puissance, 'male dress' as Breward notes, 'had forsaken a stylised masculinity in favour of an attenuated and skimpy effeminacy'.[46] Such fashion, which led to the disappearance of the cod-piece for the first time in several hundred years, combined loyalty and obedience to Elizabeth, the ostentatious display of the elite, and a remarkable effective way to differentiate social groups from one another. Much was at stake, especially for those attempting to challenge the aristocracy. Many in the City, not least those with Puritan sympathies, thought that a vigorous programme of discipline aimed at securing the 'masculine' body was the key to structuring a 'true' national identity. Defining masculinity was and is one of the prime indicators of cultural legitimacy.[47] Accordingly, Hall attempted to downgrade the flamboyant, and especially 'all gayish attire' as hallmarks of effeminacy (Hall, p. 102). Privileging solid bourgeois masculinity effectively devalued all other forms of identity. Although the 'Gay' aristocracy was the main target, the so-called 'Exorbitancies of many Women' were also thrown in the anti-bougeois masculine camp, along with the intractable poor and the riff-raff (Hall, p. 99). *Homo clausus* was founded on a rejection of the effeminate, downgrading the lower-classes, and the exclusion of women. Pamphlets like *Hic Mulier: Or, The Man-Woman: Being a Medicine to cure the Coltish Disease of the Staggers in the Masculine-Feminines of our Times* (London, 1620) and *Haec-Vir: Or, The Womanish-Man: Being an Answer to a late Booke intitled Hic-Mulier* (London, 1620) agitated the charges of gender indeterminacy leveled at the upper class and their followers. More serious than either of those pamphlets was William Prynne's *The Unlovelinesse of Lovelockes* which contained over 100 relentless pages indicting and convicting effeminate aristocratic hair-styles and behaviour.[48] Uptight critics like Hall and Prynne, Puritan hacks like Stephen Gosson, John Stubbes, or Philip Stubbes with his appropriately titled *Anatomie of Abuses* (1583), and a host of sulphuric preachers about the city, all employed a spectacular extravagance in their own styles of writing and speaking which they so assiduously condemned in others. Monitoring bodily and linguistic effusion was, ironically, accomplished with much exuberance. Hall attempted to strike the double blow of disgracing aristocratic dress while forever tarnishing the utopic elements of the 'vulgar' culture of common folk, that which Bakhtin described as 'the collective gaiety of the people'.[49] Having chastised the aristocracy, manners of sobriety were also deployed to demarcate the bourgeoisie from all things plebeian. This was achieved, according to Foucault, through the strict policing of the subject's body via surveillance, discipline, and punishment; which sought to clean up the boundaries of the body through changes in social conduct and manners.

In developing my argument I have, perhaps, dwelt on the extremities or fringes of early modern fashioning. Certainly not all the aristocracy dressed as lavishly as they could, no more than all members of the bourgeoisie were Puritans who followed Prynne and Hall. Many people in the metropolis did not easily fit into a specific pattern. Fashion is a language which can be used for negotiation as well as altercation. Social and political interaction between and within Court and City compromised any wholly inclusive or exclusive fashion statements. Fashion argued, intermingled and cross-fertilized different forms which inflected the contention and cooperation of various groups within London. Through a complex assembly of different fashion codes, the smart

Londoner had the opportunity to mix and match, to mediate the various factions, social and political, in a form of address which would be difficult to express in other ways. By assembling opposing styles, fashion could be made to cut across firm sectarian boundaries thereby compromising or evading simple class affiliations. For example, Edward Alleyn – actor, impresario, property speculator, entrepreneur, a man with connections at court and interests in the city – was someone who could not be defined or confined by a particular social group or ethos. As such he appeared to be dressed accordingly, blending an extravagant ruff with a dark and sombre cloak of civic sobriety.[50] Furthermore, rich and ambitious merchants, while favouring plain materials, still chased courtly extravagance by choosing sumptuous fabrics like silk and velvet and decked themselves out in gold chains and rings. Attempts were also made within the courtier class to induce restraint in habit and manners, as in Castiglione's *The Booke of the Courtyer* (1528). Whether such elite books, or even the more everyday manuals, had any effect is difficult to say. In principle, then, there were two central motifs of the classical body: the upper class elevated 'high' and the mental and physical enclosure of the 'sealed'. Although these distinctions became increasingly conjoined or homogenized by the post-Restoration period, in the early part of the century they were still relatively polarized.[51]

## IV   HAIR: SHAVED HEADS AND LOVELOCKS

Headwear (including hairstyles and hats) was also an index of the social and political skirmishes which were conducted on the streets of London. In *The Honest Whore, part II* Candido arrives 'wearing a long hat' known as a copotain (I.iii.intro). Along with full-bodied plumed hats, these tall hats were very fashionable at the turn of the century being worn by courtiers and certain figures among the urban elite such as the wealthy leaders of the premier companies. Not surprisingly the play's gallants are upset about Candido's assumption of such headgear along with the aspirations it indicates. And this is why they so assiduously seek to take him down a peg or two. When worn by London's citizenry the copotain captured some of the increasing self-confidence which the City was developing. In the ensuing altercation with the indignant courtiers about hats, Candido eventually defends another hat, one which was a more ubiquitous symbol of the City's freemen, the 'flat cap' (*The Honest Whore, part II*, I.iii.19–22). In doing so, Candido inadvertently undermines his own millinerial pretension as he states the case for the citizen's flat cap. The cap's flatness invokes forthrightness, plainness, unadornment, refusal of ostentation, as Candido says, it 'swels not hye,/For Caps are Emblems of humility' (I.iii.40–1). Upon this hat, Candido builds a political claim for the city;

> Of geometricke figures the most rare,
> And perfect'st are the Circle and the square,
> The Citty and the Schoole much build upon
> These figures, for both love proportion.
> The City cap is round, the Schollers square,
> To shew that Government and learning are
> The perfect'st limbes of a State:
> For without them all's disproportionate.
> If the Cap had no honor, this might reare it,
> The Reverend Fathers of the Law doe weare it.
> It's light for Summer, and in cold it sits
> Close to the scull, a warme house for the wits;
> It shews the face boldy, 'tis not made
> As if a man to looke out were afraide...

(*The Honest Whore, part II*, I.iii.50–63)

Somewhat pretentiously, Candido draws the relationship between citizenship and statecraft by making rational fashion homologous with sound government. Discipline, through schooling and learning, is quite simply configured as the mathematically enclosed body of the state. Education and utility are valued more than birth and degree. A state of perfection is achieved by subjecting the body ('perfect'st limbes') to the impenetrable discipline of the circle and square, both geometrically flawless. Anything less, he fears, renders the world disproportionate. It is a discourse of purity, 'most rare', in which Candido endorses City society through the aesthetics of the City cap. It is a way of seeing which depended upon the principles of the classical body as a symbol of government; a body which 'was far more than an aesthetic standard or model' according to Stallybrass and White, for it 'structured from the inside as it were, the characteristically 'high' discourses of philosophy, statecraft, theology and law...'[52] That structuring principle is graphically depicted by Candido's near terrifying image of enclosure; a circle within a square.

If millinery was the premier side-show of early modern head-wear in London, hair was the main event. Less easily changed than a hat, hairstyles were a prime index of class alignment or factional affiliation. Candido flatly states:

> He to the Cap was call'd; that is, was made
> Of Rome a Freeman, but was first close shorne,
> And so a Citizens hair is still short worne.

*(Candido in The Honest Whore, part II,* I.iii.45–7)

Those who cropped their hair in this manner were being deliberately confrontational. At a stroke, or snip, shorn hair created unambiguously sharp distinctions between certain social and political groups. With a degree of understatement de Marly notes that hair 'became an area of dispute' in this period.[53] Nor should we forget that the coiffurial styles of 'roundhead' and 'cavalier' were to symbolize the forthcoming Civil War. But hair was more than an emblem of sectarianism, it became tangled up in deep-rooted epistemological conflict. In Candido's presentation of 'close shaving' we sense a philosophy, a social model, a way of seeing and organizing the world (I.iii.48). Shaving the head was radically dynamic: it signified a symbolic entry into an exclusive social order. Furthermore, cropped hair erased effusion and eliminated any sense of a disorderly state. It was (and still is) the most visible token of the closed body, and, at times, of misanthropy. Only the most rigid disciplinary strictures could adequately purge and then fence-off the deleterious effects of extravagance. Short hair was worn to face down the styles and values of those which it opposed. 'For long hair, it is an ensign of pride, a banner,' says Jonson's Zeal-of-the-Land-Busy, 'and the world is full of those banners, very full of banners' (*Bartholomew Fair*, III.vi.27–8). And they should all be banned, we can hear him say! The bearer of a shaved head attempted to keep the world out and himself in. For many early modern London citizens, hair was reined in along with any outward display of emotion or exaggeration. More than a mere social gesture, close shaving incorporated its political philosophy within the very forms of its expression.[54] If courtiers fashioned themselves 'like unto the world' they then became illegitimately blurred, or disproportionate 'ragged Rascals'; in Hall's terms, personal security could only be achieved by uptight self-fashioning (Hall, A1 and p. 69).

Dekker found considerable literary mileage in this coiffurial conflict. In *The Guls Horne-booke* he teases the gallants for their long hair, not by offering to give them a hair-cut but by encouraging them to grow it faster, to flaunt it: 'it is now high time for me to have a blow at thy head, which I will not cut off with sharp documents, but rather set it on faster' (Grosart, vol. II, p. 223). Aside from the implicit image of decapitation, Dekker takes a swing at the head as an upper-class political icon. In keeping with the *Hornebooke*'s style, he ironically adopts the position of defending the gallant's hair through rational argument. The Citizen may have his cap as 'a warme house for wits', but the gallant, rather ridiculously it seems, had his hair:

> To maintain therefore that sconce of thine, strongly guarded, and in good reparation, never suffer combe to fasten his teeth there: let thy hair grow thick and bushy like a forest, or some wilderness; lest those six-footed creatures that breede in it, and are Tenants to that crowne-land of thine, bee hunted to death by every base barborous *Barber*; and so that delicate, and tickling pleasure of scratching, be utterly taken from thee ... (Grosart, vol. II, p. 224)

Unkempt hair stood for an iniquitous way of life. Lazy, lice-ridden, landlords languished in the fear of being cleaned up at the city's barbers. Even the gallant's scratching his flea-bites appears to be a spuriously sybaritic pleasure which would be denied once his hair was cut. Behind this mock defence of long hair lay a subtext of rigid control and personal constraint. By implication shaggy hair signified a fuzzy metaphysic, and so attacking long hair plucked out epistemlogical uncertainty. Much of *The Guls Horne-booke* appears to be a metaphorical shaving, a cutting off with 'sharp documents', a trimming of social pretension, of those 'Guls' it targets. But, by redoubling the irony, Dekker satirizes the position of the mocker, denying him the certainties he seeks. In parodic mimicry of the language of condemnation, *The Guls Horne-booke* bristles with the frizziness it claims to crop. Dekker's satire depends upon undermining the position from which he appears to speak.

> When your noblest Gallants consecrate their houres to their Mistresses and to Revelling, they weare fethers then chiefly in their hattes, being one of the fairest ensignes of their bravery: But

thou, a Reveller and Mistress-server all the yeare, by wearing fethers in thy haire, whose length before the rigorous edge of any puritanicall paire of scizzers should shorten the breadth of a finger ... (Grosart, vol. II, p. 226)

Juxtaposing moral laxity with reprimanding rectitude, the dignity of noble aspirations is reduced to a pejoratively hedonistic lifestyle, while vestigial emblems of class become mere gestures of idleness and dronery. Gallant fuzziness is made to face-off the spectre of 'the base barborous Barber' ferociously bent on hacking at long hair. City writers like Gosson and Stubbes *were* those base barbers. Dekker spoofs the whole altercation by playing the role of trimmer himself. As a lateral jest, he ponders the wisdom of cutting off all that hair; what could you do with it? It would be, for example, an un-Christian act, a 'Mahumetan cruelty ... to stuff breeches and tennis-balls' (both articles of aristocratic fashion) with the shorn hair (Grosart, vol. II, p. 227).

One of the contemporary contradictions of coiffurial contention was that those metaphorical wielders of 'puritanicall scizzers', rather surprisingly, wore their beards long. The rationale behind this is best explained by Thomas Hall: 'Long haire is *contra decus virile* ... not so a long Beard ... A decent growth of the Beard is a signe of Manhood, and given by God to distinguish the Male from the Female sex, this is a badge of Virility, the other of Vanity' (Hall, p. 48). So the beard's principal virtue was that women could not grow them, thank God! Hall's version of masculinity acquires immeasurable comfort and assurance from this: 'onely for beards' can sex be 'distinguished' (Hall, p. 49). For City-men like Hall, symbolizing masculinity was politically crucial: cod-pieces, for example, were much too plebeian and vulgar (too lower body), and the aristocracy had already claimed fighting and loving (war and chivalry) as a major field in which to play out masculine virtue. For the City Fathers only beards and sobriety were left, which is why they donned with pride their anti-feminine hirsuteness. Shaving, or shaping, your beard left you open to the charge of un-Englishness, or worse, being a non-Christian: as one contemporary political stylist put it; 'Neither will I meddle with our varietie of beards, of which some are shaven from the chin like those of Turks, not a few cut short like to the beard of marques Otto.'[55] In spite of the beard's anti-feminine qualities, Hall was well aware of the 'danger' of hirsute displays: that long dangly beards might also become part of the same economy of representation as long hair. It is precisely this anxiety which Dekker plays upon in *The Guls Horne-booke* as he brings the various protagonists together with some mischievous puns and allusions:

> You then, to whom chastity has given an heire apparant, take order that it may be apparant, and to that purpose, let it play openly with the lascivious wind, even on the top of your shoulders. Experience cries out in every Citty, that those self-same Criticall *Saturnists*, whose hair is shorter then their eye-brows, take a pride to have their hoary beards hang slavering like a dozen of Foxetailes downe so low as their middle. (Grosart, vol. II, p. 228)

Equating beards with long hair compromised the very purpose for wearing them. If the beard connoted order, propriety, and firm gender distinctions, then Dekker's ferocious mockery upset that. More troubling for these men was the use of excremental, bodily and animalistic metaphors, which invoked the horribly transgressive grotesque idioms which connected the head to the lower body and other bodies, and which compromised and embarrassed personal security. Dekker calls upon this promiscuous image to raise the ire of the so-called 'Criticall Saturnists' because they were, of course, the same critics who deplored the theatre. Their beards, distinctive symbols of their cunning and authority, are part of the same lasciviousness which they detest. He asks, 'why should the chinnes and lippes of old men lick up the excrement, which they vyolently clip away from the heads of yong men?' (Grosart, vol. II, p. 228). He reveals how the politics of aggressive discipline pursued by the City Fathers fed upon what it putatively detested.

Dekker continued to satirize London's oligarchic rulers by tarnishing the symbols of their authority with disturbing images of their own behaviour. Of the City Fathers, he asks:

> Is it because those long beesomes (their beards) with sweeping the soft bosomes of their beautiful yong wives, may tickle their tender breasts, and make some amends for their maisters' unrecoverable dulnesse? No, no, there hangs more at the ends of those long gray haires then all the world can come to knowledge of. (Grosart, vol. II, p. 228)

Dekker joined the tradition of criticizing the social practice of merchants and the city's upper class who sought to measure their social virility through the procurement and marriage of much younger women. In *The Seven deadly Sinnes of London* he condemns the acquisition of these trophy wives as a 'cruelty' by asking, 'what glorye atchive you in these conquests ... enforcing May to embrace December?' (Grosart, vol. II, p. 71). Rather than operating as the chief emblem of their probity, their beards are made to appear as instruments of lust and sexual immorality. Even this, Dekker smugly admits, cannot make them interesting: they are lascivious because they are dull, and dull because they are lascivious. As the primary tool which arrested 'the confounding of Sexes', the long beard indicated profound sexual anxiety (Hall, p. 25). For the men of the City, all kinds of masculine anxieties became entangled in long hair: 'O, no, long hair is the onely nette that women spread abroad to entrappe men in; and why should not men be as far above women in that commodity, as they go beyond men in others?' (Grosart, vol. II, p. 227). Engulfment, once again, seems to be the main fear. Nothing, it seemed, could be worse than having hair like a woman, as Harrison admits whilst admonishing 'English' aristocratic styles: 'our heads, which sometimes are polled, sometimes curled, or suffered to grow at length like a womans lockes ...'.[56] In *The Guls Horne-booke* Dekker agitated the City men's fear of women's desire as well as their (barely disguised) homophobia, along with the anxiety of 'overflowing' and corrupt 'bodyes' which lay outside men and manners. The convergence of these ideas gathered momentum in the ensuing decades. Hall saw 'disease in the haire' whereby it 'seizeth specially upon women' (Hall, A5). Securing masculinity meant surviving this diseased ensnarement, expelling both the grotesque and the so called effeminate. Through the charge of effeminacy, a deep bourgeois antipathy developed around their views of long hair. Writers like Rowlands expressed the view that 'Your gallant is no man unless his hair be of the woman's fashion, dangling and waving over his shoulders'.[57] Conflict between an effusive 'high' and a closed-off integrity produced a number of stylistic extremes. For the aristocracy and those who aped them it meant a charge into ever more extravagance. Some of the 'The Mode' fashions of the 'Cavalerian garbe' sported by the aristocracy in the middle years of the seventeenth century achieved a degree of magniloquence rarely seen either before or since (Hall, B2). They were suitably opposed by the parsimonious fashions echoed in the 'just reproach of those that are called Puritans and Round-heads' (Hall, E2). Extravagance appealed to the upper class because it gave them a much-needed sense of identity, something which Hall and Prynne's diatribes ironically shored up rather than undercut.

Achieving and maintaining this flamboyant identity for the gallantry required increasingly inventive forms of embellishment. A particularly distinct mode, and therefore one of the most contested, was the lovelock. Corson writes: 'One of the most curious and inexplicable fashions of the seventeenth century was the lovelock, a single lock of hair, much longer than the others, hanging down over one shoulder'.[58] It was worn by aristocrats and gallants alike. Shakespeare's patron, the Earl of Southampton, sported a particularly fine example. According to *The Guls Horne-booke*, for those gallants seeking a 'conspicuous Eminence' it was an essential accoutrement: 'by which meanes, the best and most essenciall parts of a Gallant (good cloathes, a proportionable legge, a white hand, the Persian (Parisian) lock, and a tollerable beard) are perfectly revealed' (Grosart, vol. II, p. 248).[59] With its asymmetry, its 'gayness', the lovelock emphasized rejection of the contemporary norms of masculinity. Worn almost exclusively on the left side, this queer style invoked a darker, exotic, or rebellious, bias. It also disrupted and annoyed the geometric equilibrium, or balance, so avidly sought by Puritans. For them it was both unnatural and abominable. The lovelock conveyed a certain sensibility: an artistic or poetic bent, as well as a sense of bravado. Sporting a lovelock brashly stated to the world that the wearer embraced the very effeminacy abhorred by his class rivals and was exclusively a court fashion. Diatribes against lovelocks, such as Prynne's massive tract, *The Unlovelinesse of Love-lockes*, sought to downgrade aristocratic masculinity.[60] Many of these attacks, including Prynne's, simultaneously denigrated women. Appearing at the moment when ruff wearing started to decline among the aristocracy, the lovelock proved to be just as durable because it represented a distinctive voice in a deep-rooted cultural argument. Although it apparently condemns this fashion item, *The Guls Horne-booke* acknowledges perhaps the most important role of the lovelock, and for that matter other aristo-gallant fashions, the overwhelming need for display. Lovelocks were crimped, scented, tied with bows or clipped with rosettes, platted, and so were nothing if not exquisitely flamboyant. Dekker distinguished the 'Guls' through the very flamboyant forms they cultivated, while parodying the discourse of rationality at which they were at odds. Small wonder the *Horne-booke* remained on the bookstalls well into the Restoration period.

## V THEATRUM MUNDI: GULS IN ST PAUL'S WALK

*What whispering is there in Terme* times, how by some slight to cheat the poore country Clients of his full purse that is stuck under his girdle? What plots are layd to furnish young gallants with readie money (which is shared afterwards at a Tavern) therby to disfurnish him of his patrimony? what buying up of oaths, out of the hands Knightes of the post, who for a few shillings doe daily sell their soules? What laying of heads is there together and ... What damnable bargaines of unmercifull Brokery, & of unmeasurable Usury are clapt up? What swearing is there, yea, what swaggering, what facing and out-facing? What shuffling, what shouldering, what Justling, what jeering, what byting of Thumbs to beget quarrels, what holding uppe of fingers to remember drunken meetings, what braving with Feathers, what bearding with Mustachoes, what casting open of cloakes to publish new clothes, what muffling in cloaks to hyde broken Elbows, so that when I heare such trampling up and downe, such spetting, such halking, and such humming (every mans lippes making a noise yet not a word to be understood) I verily beleeve that I am the Tower of *Babell* newly builded up, but presently despaire of ever being finished, because there is in me such a confusion of languages. (Grosart, vol. IV, p. 51)

St Paul's Walk was the unofficial cultural centre of early modern London and, without doubt, it was England's most popular tourist site. Both denizens and visitors went there to engage in the social and cultural practices which the new metropolis made available. Dekker's description of 'Paul's Walk' makes place and human interaction mutually dependent. In this context people function as a social space and the place designs and structures their behaviour. In this way of seeing interpretation amounts to social experience. We see the flip side of commodity exchange, a world of unconfined bargaining, money-getting, matched by unfettered social intercourse. He looks askance at the City's underlying forces and values, away from official forms of exchange. Yet in that glimpse we see that Paul's Walk functioned through the same ethos as the city. It was, after all, 'like a common Mart where all Commodities (both the good and bad) are to be bought and solde' (Grosart, vol. IV, p. 52). In this medium, language, too, was up for grabs. Dekker's relentless string of questions draws the reader into this commingling, dialogical, metropolitan space. There was no secure vantage point, no privileged individual perspective, no unadulterated voice, by which the viewer-reader could remain separate. To be in the 'Walke' was to be immersed in the heteroglot, to enjoy, despite the author's caveat, the 'confusion of languages'. This was where you could really mix it:

> For at one time, in one and the same ranke, yea, foote by foote, and elbow by elbow, shall you see walking, the Knight, the Gull, the Gallant, the upstart, the Gentleman, the Clowne, the Captaine, the Appel-squire, the Lawyer, the Usurer, the Cittizen, the Bankerout, the Scholler, the Begger, the Doctor, the Ideot, the Ruffian, the Cheater, the Puritan, the Cut-throat, the Hye-men, the Low-men, the True-man, and the Thiefe: of all trades and professions some,/of all Countreyes some ... (Grosart, vol. IV, p. 51)

Immersion in the heterogeneous crowd was a universal, rather than a utopic or even democratic thrill. Although you could take pleasure in being at once the same and different, it was a materially competitive world. To occupy this unique arena, where social resources could be transmogrified, was to inhabit the very essence of the city. The vigour, the contention, the comparisons, the dynamic juxtapositions, the rubbing together of cheek and jowl, this was where the city took place, in its potential for an infinite number of interactions denied by other types of social space. Under the intentionally thin guise of revealing iniquity, Dekker celebrates this fluid realm where everyone was challenged, by the sheer impact of interaction, into becoming someone different. 'In the city', Raban notes, 'we are barraged with images of the people we might become', and so in this environment, 'identity is presented as plastic, a matter of possessions and appearances...'.[61] You could borrow the experience of someone else as you proffered your own; you could perform as you enjoyed the show. It was the overwhelming need to be someone different which made St Paul's Walk the gallant's unofficial headquarters. Behind Dekker's facetious moralism in *The Guls Hornebooke* was a fast understanding of the fluidity and performance of

urban identity. For him, London's thoroughfares were analogous to
its theatres and in many ways to be a 'true' 'Gallant' in the city was
to be an 'artificial person'.[62] In his apparently censorious descriptions of the Guls, Dekker, who always championed the theatre,
cannot but acknowledge the gallants' theatricality. Identity formation in the metropolis made necessary the relinquishment of older
forms while adopting new roles, and for many this became a way of
being. What was required, then, was 'a case of Faces ... supplyed by
Arte' (*If This be Not a Good Play*, IV.i.11–15). Display was so much a
key to gallant identity that the practice of 'sitting on the Stage' was
extensively lampooned by Dekker in chapter IV of the *Horne-booke*
(Grosart, vol. II, p. 248). London theatres, particularly the private
ones, actually catered for this craving for gentlemanly display by
making available (at a suitable price) seating upon the stage. Back
out on the 'Walk', Dekker figured the continual need for such
display as an ongoing social drama. 'Paul's Walk becomes a theatre;
'Guls' are advised to 'observe your doores of entrance, and your
Exit, not much unlike the pliers at Theatres, keeping your
Decorums, even in phantasticality' (Grosart, vol. II, p. 230). In positing himself as writer-director, Dekker offered the gallants a medium
in which they could recast their identity. Spoofing alternative in-
structional literature – like the many advice manuals for gentleman
– *The Guls Horne-booke* aimed for urban relevance; 'Powles is your
Walke; but this is your Guid' he claimed (Grosart, vol. II, p. 198).
For all the 'Guls', gallants, dilettantes, peacocks, and paparazzi, the
*Horne-booke* ostensibly offered them information, their most valuable
asset. Failure to know how he 'should behave himself in Powles
walkes' meant that he would misread the city (Grosart, vol. II, p.
229). Inexperience at interpreting social codes exposed the gallant to
immediate danger; 'because your London experience wil cost you
deere before you shall have ye wit to *know what you are*' [my empha-
sis] (Grosart, vol. II, p. 235). Knowledge was identity in the new city.
*The Guls Horne-booke* advertised itself by selling knowledge as the
city's chief commodity. For the outsider unversed in city-lore – like
the 'meere country gentleman' – it was essential to know how to act,
to know where and what to buy, and, most importantly, to know
what to wear. Within an arena of increasingly complex patterns of
social interaction, reading the growing maze of signs, codes and
hidden messages which marked identity became ever more difficult.
Failure to appreciate the right codes could, potentially, have embar-
rassing or disastrous consequences.[63] Knowing the fashions was the
prime evidence of acculturation for London's newly arrived country

gentleman. Primarily rooted in the stress of rural–urban transitions, much of the popularity of the period's 'coney-catching' literature was underwritten by anxiety about city knowledge. A stereotypical metropolitan huxter, the coney-catcher always deployed his, or sometimes her, superior nous to prey on 'rabbits', conies, the gentlemen who came from the country. Ironically, many of those cast off the land became recast in the fiction of the period as those who preyed on the class who threw them off.[64] Conflict over an erstwhile existence on the land was immediately translated into ferocious urban competition. Metropolitan cunning and wit became an indispensable form in the new literature which grew out of this conflict. While tragedy tested virtue, comedy tried wit. Interpreting intelligence was a matter of social class: if the hallmark of the gallant was his wit and fashion sense (and this was to reach its apotheosis in Restoration theatre), then that of the coney-catcher was cunning and conning. Scholars rivalled sharpers, as educated men of letters pitched themselves into the fray against an underclass of hucksters – or so it seemed. According to his 'coney-catcher', Robert Greene's literature of exposés pretended to operate on behalf of the gallant against the trickster's skills: 'Tis by wit that I live and will live, in dispight of that peevish scholler, that thought with his conny-catching bookes to have crosbyt our trade ...'.[65] Greene's writing openly parades its apparent contradiction – that the literature was trying to ensnare the same conies as the tricksters it was advising against. In the stakes for metropolitan identity, the writer became another coney-catcher; offering those who valued their wit the chance to outwit their protagonists.

This contradictory space occupied by the likes of Greene, and later by Dekker, became writ large in St Paul's Walk and its environs. For it was here that writers like Dekker were negotiating a different relationship with their readers. While Jonson was 'trying to dignify an emergent place for authorship at a distance both from the aristocracy and the plebeians', Dekker remained within the medium of the city, its streets, taverns, and walks; in short, he kept at least one foot in the public riot and a partial voice in the heterogeneous crowd.[66] Though Jonson wrote that same metropolitan space with as much vigour and insight as anyone, it was precisely the removal of writing from that arena which made it 'Literature' (within a classical canon) and which contributed to the advance in the status of the author. With more engaged complicity, Dekker continued to write the interstitial and changing places of the metropolis. St Paul's

Walk, for example, 'was not only a centre of informal business, but of communication of all kinds, and for the transmission of political and social information, ... eventually, the face-to-face contact which had taken place in the nave, or in front of the cross in the precinct, gave way to broadsheets, books, and the theatre, as a means of collecting and disseminating information.'[67] As well as occupying that transitional place, by the manner and type of information it circulated, Dekker's writing helped to create it.

Somewhat spuriously, then, *The Guls Horne-booke* offered the city's newly arrived 'gentleman' the opportunity to reinvent himself by 'casting open of cloakes to publish new clothes' (Grosart, vol. IV, pp. 50–1). For all Dekker's facetious exposition of the 'Guls' position, he knows that he and they have much in common. Just as 'Gallants' become 'cheape and ordinary' if 'seene above foure turnes' (Grosart, vol. II, p. 231), so, too, in St. Paul's do the writers who 'trouble the *stationers* shops in *Paules Churchyard* ... out of a *Meere* and *Idle vaine-glory* will ever be *Pamphleting* ... [or others] that being free of Wits Merchant-venturers, do ... (for gaine onely) make 5. or 6. voiages to the *Presse* ...' (Grosart, vol. III, p. 178). Both 'Guls' and authors are commodities which, it seems, lose their value from too much exposure. In pandering to their whims Dekker reluctantly recognizes that the writer is as much compromised by such exposure as the reader. The city appears as a medium which insistently requires the production of novel forms. Demand for new fashions in writing or dress was presented as a self-priming pump producing an endless flow of new styles. Away from Westminster and the court, or from their rural roots, London's 'Guls' achieved a kind of immanence within the city at St Paul's Walk. Following their marginalization from other centres of metropolitan power, they sought to occupy other, less official, places and operated through the media of style and gossip, alternative forms of social intercourse at St Paul's. Although ambivalently located within the City, they deliberately took up urban space, semantically, topographically and culturally. Of course, it was this outlandish display of presence, of ambiguously located marginality, which made them truly metropolitan. Through encoding the multivalent and multifaceted aspects of city life, and precisely because their display could not exist anywhere else but in a metropolis, they became a peculiar kind of 'accomplisht gentlemen'; the kind which inhabited City comedy and other drama from the turn of the century onwards. Like the dandies and flâneurs who came after them, they were quintessentially urban. Their identity, as *The Guls Horne-booke* makes clear, was a matter of style and behaviour; yet so much also depended upon having a translatable resource or income. Many 'Guls' occupied a highly ambivalent space between the landlord, or rent-taking class, and the variety of occupations which could be found in both court and city. For all its mockery of these 'Guls', *The Guls Horne-booke* cannot conceal the fact that it occupied the same ambivalent space as those it subjects to ridicule. Both gallants and writing represent the translation of social stock: either land into clothes or education into gossip and popular literature. Both functioned through the idea that hipness could become a source of metropolitan capital. 'Guls' and pamphlet writers like Dekker were part of the backwash of a metropolitan culture which increasingly privileged information. Precisely because he did not have a large stock of social resources, a gallant had to be in the know, he could not be ignorant, he had to hold, encompass and display the currency of style. Failure to do this meant that he was out of stock, out of print, culturally and socially bankrupt. In the information economy you could either gull or be gulled. One question remains; had Dekker, the 'poore scholler,' been caught at his own expense, commodifying himself so that his writing could bolster the identity of others, or had he successfully gulled them into buying his pamphlets?

# 4

# Breaking Loose from Hell: Devils, Despair, and Dystopia

Hell hath no limits, nor is circumscribed
In one place; for where we are is Hell,
And where Hell is, there must we ever be.

(Mephistopheles in *The Tragical History
of Dr Faustus*, Scene 5, 121–3)


## I  WORDS GONE TO HELL

Perhaps more than any other form, Thomas Nashe's rhetorical style influenced the shape of Dekker's prose and pamphlet writing. Yet unlike Dekker, Nashe never managed to locate himself as a writer in the new metropolis. Often his work was inflected by that sense of dislocation: 'This is the lamentable condition of our times, that men of art must seek alms of cormorants, and those that deserve best be kept under by dunces ...'.[1] Much can be understood about the place of metropolitan literature and culture by exploring the subtle differences between these two writers, in particular their nuanced expeditions into the meaning of Hell. This chapter examines the deployment of Hell as a cultural narrative; not simply as a theological concept but as a complex social structure which refracts ideology through urban space and city topography. In tracing the cultural contours of Hell, writers like Dekker and Nashe drew together the seemingly disparate strands of the city – theatre, plague, poverty, and prison – which tied life and literature so closely together.[2] Telling the story of Hell enabled the writer to find a language through which to indict and criticize the social system within which he had to work. The writer was able to reveal the dark side and effects of metropolitan life, to make them topical, with the kind of verve and wit often denied him elsewhere.

In writing which often flashed dystopic images before the reader, both Dekker and Nashe self-consciously located themselves upon the axes of social change. *Pierce Pennilesse, His Supplication to the Divell* can be seen as a climacterical moment which captures and condemns the shifting relationship between writer and society. Nashe opens his *Supplication* with a profound mixture of frustration, despair, and thwarted ambition:

> Having spent many years in studying how to live, and lived a long time without money; having tired my youth with folly, and surfeited my mind with vanity, I began at length to look back to repentance and address my endeavours to prosperity. But all in vain. I sat up late and rose early, contended with the cold, conversed with scarcity; for all my labours turned to loss, my vulgar muse was despised and neglected, my pains not regarded or slightly rewarded, and I myself, in prime of my best wit, laid open to poverty. Whereupon, in a mal-content humour, I accused my fortune, railed on my patrons, bit my pen, rent my papers, and raged in all points like a madman. In which agony tormenting myself a long time, I grew by degrees to a milder discontent and, pausing a while over my standish, I resolved in verse to paint forth my passion; which best agreeing with the vein of my unrest, I began to complain ... [3]

Material poverty overshadowed then cut short both his spirit and his life. Without recognizing these circumstances it would be difficult to understand the driving force of Nashe's work. Overwhelmed by what he sees as the destruction of 'men of art', his writing becomes a bitter form of self and literary expression. With regret, he declares that 'those that most stand on their honour have shut up their purses'.[4] Heretofore, he reckoned, 'Men of great calling take it of merit to have their names eternized by poets'.[5] But, resentfully, he acknowledges that the covenant between poet and society which, he felt, might have been enjoyed by 'Gentle Sir Philip Sidney', has been sundered.[6] Facing the social deterioration of poetics, Nashe resorted to no obsequious muse; rather, a virulent linguistic irony became the vector of his self-abasement and subsequent rage, one which simultaneously targeted his ambition and impotence. Nashe turned the emblem of his disenfranchisement, his poverty, into a symbolic and mock-heroic virtue which stood for the values lost by his patrons. In bitter conceit, poverty represented an extended principle of value: he is poor because he is a writer, and virtuous because he is poor.

Yet it was a principle which subsequently became embarrassed by the success of his *Supplication*. Nashe later disavowed the project in his epistle to the publisher because the literary success of the *Supplication* was meant to be its failure.[7] The social entitlement of the poet became nullified precisely because he had been forced to make his *Supplication*. If you had to ask your patron for patronage it would not be worth having. Such a move would invalidate the bond before it could be confirmed because patronage was an ideal, it could only be bestowed, never requested. Frustration at this intangible rejection becomes transformed by Nashe into a spurious request as he proceeds to make a supplication to a mock patron, the Devil. Such a request parodies its own hubris. It blatantly chastises those who have neglected him, and derides the system upon which they have reneged. The ensuing ascerbic exuberance of his poetics is therefore a showcase for what he calls the 'prime' of his 'best wit'.[8] In this way Nashe negotiated the tricky problem of presenting a literature which bit the hand which he felt should have been feeding him.

After opening the *Supplication* with a profound image of dejection and disconsolation, he resolves to 'complain' in verse, a high art form. But 'Since none takes pity of a scholar's need', and because, he says, 'I am quite undone through promise-breach', he abandons poetry for reasons similar to those which caused his poverty.[9] Having then 'tossed' his 'imaginations a thousand ways', he ostensibly tries to find 'any means to relieve ... [his] estate'.[10] Upon this moment of poetic failure he concludes 'that the world was uncharitable, and I ordained to be miserable'.[11] In the four stanzas of his truncated poem Nashe realizes that the author's position in relation to the patron is akin to that of the subject before God. At once 'Promise-breach' represents the rift between patron and poet, and for the irrevocable schism, after the Fall, between Man and God. So 'damnation and despair' prevail as the condition of the writer who is ordained to the same misery as the divine subject. No more could he ask God for salvation than he could a patron for patronage. With a bathetic pun Nashe states, 'Adieu, unkind, where skill is nothing worth'; his allusion to an unkind God also stands as a valediction of his devalued place in society.[12]

By staging the failure of verse, Nashe precipitates not only his bizarre *Supplication* but an almost despairingly hubristic turn to the apocrypha of Hell. In that ridiculous journey, in which he sought out the Devil, he censured all the forces which made 'Men Labour Without Hope'.[13] Nashe did not have to travel far to cast his diabolic vitriol: his mistrust of London, not least because of its ethos of commercial activity, led him to collate Hell and the city.

Given that Nashe himself contributed to London's growth when he moved there from East Anglia, there is a certain irony in his observation that 'hell, which at the beginning was but an obscure village, is now become a huge city.'[14] Caught in the very social milieu to which he had turned, he viciously burlesques the idea of self-exploitation that characterizes the city:

> These manifest conjectures of plenty, assembled in one common-place of ability, I determined to claw Avarice at the elbow, till his full belly gave me a full hand, and let him blood my pen (if it might be) in the vein of liberality; and so, in short time, was this paper-monster, Pierce Penniless, begotten.[15]

Nashe's *Supplication* appears as a monstrous literary birth; its muse-mocking production gives further evidence of his special ability to deploy acute grotesquerie to rail at those who have it in their power to enfranchise him but refuse to do so. His anti-patronistic taunts are relentless because he needs, and believes in, patronage so strongly. In his railing, Nashe reveals a deep radical conservatism which, when coupled with the virtue of an empty belly, denied him the easy comfort or popularity that could be had peddling a literature of nostalgia. Not for him the delights of pastoral literature, or the rewards it might bring. For Nashe, mistrust of the city could not be translated into halcyon-calms or the metaphorical herding of sheep. Instead he concentrated on the vivid, micrographic, evidence of social decay. Working through the meticulous dissection of that decay, the *Supplication* unflaggingly etches the deterioration of the writer's place in and upon society. In choosing such a journey, the *Supplication* draws upon the primordial symbol of exclusion – that of being sent to Hell – and turned it into a magnificent inscription of writerly bravado. With symbolic irony, he chose the discourse and rhetoric of Hell, itself in flux and decay, in which to inscribe the dilemmas of his socio-literary status. Because he steadfastly refused to claw at the available rewards of commercial success open to him, he was trapped in a tragic double bind: the more he was unable to appeal to potential patrons the more he railed at them, consequently the less appealing he became. Ironically, for Nashe, it was to be the commercial publishers of the future which awarded him an albeit muted literary reputation.

Inspired by Nashe's *Supplication*, Dekker's *A Knight's Conjuring* imagines Nashe arriving in Elysium – now a 'Colledge' for poets – where he is 'still haunted with the sharpe and Satyricall spirit that followed him heere upon earth: for Nashe inveyed bitterly (as he was wont to do) against dry-fisted Patrons, accusing them of his untimely death' (Robbins, p. 156). Dekker depicted this as a moment of 'Barbarisme' in which 'the sacred Art of Poesie [had] falne', and so he perceived that the 'old Religion', patronage, had irretrievably broken down (Robbins, pp. 156–7).[16] Following Nashe's tragic death, Dekker realized he needed a different strategy, and so in *Newes from Graves-ende* he launched an all out and systemic assault on 'dry-fisted Patrons':

> *To Him, that (in the despite and never-dying-dishonour of all empty-fisted Mecæn-Asses) is the Gratious, munificent, and golden Rewarder of Rimes: singular paymaister of Songes and Sonnets: Unsquint-eyde Surveyor of Heroicall Poems: Chiefe Rent-gatherer of Poets and Musitians: And the most valiant Confounder of their deperate debts. (to the comfort of all honest Christians) The now- onely-onely-Supper-maker to Enghles & Plaiers-Boyes, Syr* Nicholas Nemo, *alias* Nobody. (Wilson, p. 65)

Although Dekker's railing was 'like Nashe', and employed similar vituperative anti-patronistic language, there are some crucial differences.[17] While Nashe's invective charts the disintegration of entitlement, Dekker rarely positioned himself in that way. When satirizing the patron–author nexus, Dekker's rhetoric is more liberal and does not spend itself seeking forms of idealism. His writing is thus more loosely charivaric, more freely ironic, more of a caricature, than Nashe's vicious grotesque. Dekker's description of the patronizing class depicts them as the walking wounded, as socially crippled as they are crippling. He employs a rag-bag disposition of the rent-gathering caste for whom Nashe had laid aside the profits of the pamphlet trade. In contrast, Dekker invested in the same pamphlet trade in order to make a living by lampooning them. Their different use of satire was more than simply a matter of aesthetics. Nashe was a pessimistic idealist who violently turned on the social principles he valued if and when they faltered in any way. Dekker, on the other hand, was a pragmatic optimist, one who satirized class-bound idealism especially if or when it congealed into pretension or became ossified as dogma. Nashe intended satire to function as a literary form which at least recognized the bonds between people; whereas for Dekker satire operated as a way of loosening the constraints – as he saw them – favoured by the aristocracy.

In Chapter 3 we saw how Dekker and the gallants were tied together, a correlation which was forged at the point where social identity and urban space intersected. And just as St Paul's Walk was the supreme place in which to publish yourself and your clothes, it was, as Feather says, 'the very heart of the book trade'.[18] Yet as it developed, the trade continued to marginalize the already disenfranchised writer. Feather notes that 'By the end of the sixteenth century literature, in the broadest sense, had become a commercial commodity', he continues, 'the rewards of that commerce, however, were for the printer, publisher and bookseller rather than for the author.'[19] Dekker, therefore, became a writer during the period when the industry was undergoing important changes: the bookseller-publishers were wresting control of the business from the printers.[20] Scanning through the title pages of Dekker's early publications reveals the prominence of the printer's name. These names disappeared later, so that by the Jacobean period they were replaced by those of the seller. Dekker's books move from 'printed by' to 'printed for' at some point around the publication of *The Wonderfull yeare* (1603). This shift in power within the business occurred at a time when professional authors, like Dekker, were becoming an increasingly important component of the publishing industry. 'New' books were increasingly required as the market for literature rapidly developed. But the power of the business still lay with those who held and controlled the copyrights and the patents, the 'copy-owning booksellers'. In spite of the punters' keen appetite for new matter, the publishers' grip on the industry ensured that writers like Dekker did not benefit from its expansion. Controlling patents facilitated the concentration of the publisher's power, particularly in the production of the regular religious and law books, but also the ABC's, and, significantly, the contents of the more conventional Horn Books. Dekker's *The Guls Horne-booke*, then, was a parody of the customary material from which the publishing industry derived the source of its economic power while being part of the new wave of (increasingly secular) leisure books necessary for its development. Though there was a change in the product, the rewards still favoured the copy-owners and not the authors. 'The trade itself became involved in the process of causing books to be written', Feather argues, 'beginning the shift away from patronage to payment'; and, of course, into a business.[21] Dekker's writing, which never received any consistent patronage, was precisely situated within that shift. And it was a shift that Nashe could never quite manage.

Dekker's failure to acquire any substantial patronage was dramatically spelt out when he created his figurative mock-patron, '*Syr Nicholas Nemo*, *alias* Nobody'. Deeply stressed by various factors within the book trade, Dekker often made impassioned pleas lamenting the lowly status of writers and their disenfranchisement. Without security he was forced to look hard at the bottom line:

> *Knowledge* and *Reward* dwell far a-sunder. *Greatnes* lay once betweene them. But (in his stead) *Covetousnes* now … no paymaister to *Poets* … *Merit goes a Begging*, and *Learning* starves. *Bookes*, had wont to have *Patrons*, and (now,) *Patrons* have *Bookes*. The *Snuff* that is *Lighted*, consumes *That* which *Feeds* it. A *Signe*, the *World* hath an ill *Eare*, when no *Musick* is good, unless it *Strikes-up* for *Nothing*. I, have *Sung* so, but wil no more. A *Hue*-and-*Cry* follow, his *Wit*, that sleeps, when sweete *Tunes* are sounding. But tis now the *Fashion*. *Lords*, look wel: *Knights*, *Thank* well; *Gentlemen*, promise well; *Citizens*, *Take* well; *Gulles*, *Sweare* well: but *None*, *Give* well. (Dedication in *If This be not a good Play, then the Devil is In It*)

This was written about the time when Dekker was on his way to prison for debt. Full of frustration, his belligerent invective charts the fraught relationship between writer and society, author and reader. Gone is Dekker's much-noted ebullience along with his long, eclectically fluid, panoramic sentences. We can see that the style and rhythm are fractured with italics, punctuation, and parentheses, as his prose signifies a disjointed and disconsolate writer. Dekker's gritty elaboration of this particular 'dissociation of sensibility' exhibits a certain tongue-in-cheek resignation about a past in which he never quite believed. In the period in which it was virtually impossible to make a living solely from writing, Dekker was working largely without the support of a patron. Yet his writing was locked into an industry which increasingly needed, and later valued, the author for its own business and profit. Dekker was therefore forced to develop a new readership for his work, to find '*Patrons*' for his '*Bookes*'. Many of his plague pamphlets were underwritten by the impetus to capture different kinds of metropolitan consumers. Dekker's response to his own role in these changes was often bitter. He reluctantly admits to having 'Sung' for his 'Supper' from would be patrons, often emptily concluding that he 'wil no more'. But without a proper social or literary place for the professional writer this snub proved to be difficult to sustain.

In spite of his rhetorical departure from Nashe, Dekker lamented the lack of patronage; it was still something he 'resented, yet hankered after'.[22] Having to rely solely upon the vicissitudes of consumer interest, while working within the iron-grip control of the industry by the copy-owners, produced considerable anxiety. Some of the resulting tension became translated into the hostile discourse of hellish torments. 'You (that are Readers) are the most desperate and fowlest players in the world, you will strike when a mans backe is towards you'; he continues, 'Readers, you turne your selves into Lictores, Executioners & tormentors' (Grosart, vol. II, p. 6). Like the gallants he wrote about, Dekker developed a love–hate relationship to the marketplace of bookstall and theatre. Literary authenticity depended less on authorial skill than upon the ability to defend oneself in the dog-eat-dog world of point-of-sale popularity: 'Reade over but one leafe (deare Nobody) & thou putst upon me an armor of proofe against the rankling teeth of those mad dogs (cald Booke-biters) that run barking up and down Powles Church-yard, and bite the Muses by the shinnes' (Wilson, p. 73). Changing from one patron to many proved to be a tense and ironic relationship for both writer and reader. They came to consume, and the writer wrote to be consumed: 'The Snuff that is Lighted, consumes That which Feeds it'. For Dekker, the class which failed to invest in him was not worth saving, unless it was as a ludicrous object of satire. Accordingly, the whole relationship between poet and patron had become not only risible but decidedly squalid. Dekker's dedications strip away the patina of reputability with which the poet traditionally glossed his relationship with his patron, leaving only the ghastly mechanics of socio-economic stress. It was an irrevocable step, one that broke the writer's fascination with an organically whole vision of society. Dekker's

'Epistle Dedicatory' is as long as *Newes from Graves-ende* itself, and is one of the longest of its kind; certainly within Dekker's *oeuvre*. It adumbrates and pre-empts the ensuing poem, rather than conventionally introducing it, as the plight of the professional poet in London is perceived through the poetic horrors of the plague. Following Nashe's esoteric obsession with pickled herrings (the staple, Lenten food of the dispossessed), Dekker sets up a rhetorical attack upon 'the whole barrel of pickled patrons' (Wilson, p. 65).[23] In an attempt to make a virtue of necessity, Dekker's 'Epistle' avidly admits that the love between poet and patron has not only been lost but has dilapidated into the type of moral corruption which had plagued Man since the Fall; 'Liberality has bin a Gentleman of a good house, and an ancient house', states Dekker, which had since 'falne to decay, and to repaire it requires too much cost' (Wilson, p. 67).[24] Liberality once meant hospitality, but now it had become a 'worme-eaten name' (Wilson, p. 65). Dekker finally sinks the idea of the good old feudal days: 'Its a name of the old fashion: It came up with the old Religion, and went down with the new' (Wilson, p. 67).[25] Without the ethos of the 'good house', the liberal house, there could be no patronage, nor any real gentlemen.

In an unveiled threat to the great, Dekker explains that the plauditor could be as capricious as those who would be, and had been, served by the immortalizing function of verse. He mischievously states that 'verses should have more feete' so that they can run away (Wilson, p. 70). Hitherto, that which had been elevated by 'glorious praises' was not guaranteed forever to be ensconced in a house of fame, it could be razed or demolished. Dekker supposes 'that Dukes, Earles, Lordes and Ladies, should have their Il-liberal names torn out of those bookes whose Authors they sent away with a Flea in their eare' (Wilson, p. 71). With relish the writer continues: 'And the stile of *Nobody* in Capitall Romane Letters' [should be] 'bravely Printed in their places' (Wilson, p. 71). Breaking this bond between writer and patron was something Dekker contemplated with more palpable enjoyment than Nashe. Though he may not have assiduously clawed at the elbow of avarice, he might have been content to nudge it occasionally. With an affectionate tribute, Dekker acknowledges Nashe as he parodies him:

Being in this melancholy contemplation, and having wept a whole ynck-horne full of Verses in bewailing the miseries of the time, on a suddaine I started up: with my teeth bit my writings,

because I coulde eate my words: condemnd my pen-knife to the
cutting of powder-beefe and brewes .... (Wilson, p. 69)

Following Nashe's literary gnashing, this melancholic spoof of
amusing contemplation nevertheless displays a certain grotesque
energy. In mock recantation, the joke turns on the moment when the
writer literally has to eat his words because his writing has brought
him nothing but pickled herrings, poverty and disapproval.

The Epistle Dedicatory of *Newes from Graves-ende* was an extended demystification of the role of the writer in society. Typical
of Dekker's Jacobean prose style, he imagines a writer (himself) at a
pseudo-court of poets competing for the attention of the archetypal
non-patron, 'Nobody':

> Thus had every one a flirt at thy praises: if thou hadst bene begde
> to have plaid an Anatomy in Barber-surgions Hall, thy good
> parts could not have bene more curiously ript up: they div'de
> into the very bowels of thy hartie commendations. So that I, that
> (like a Match) scarce gave fire before, to the dankish powder of
> their apprehensions, was now burnt up my self, in the flames of a
> more ardent affection towards thee, kindled by them. For
> presently the court brake up, and (without a quarter-dinner) all
> parted: their heads being great with childe, and aking very pitti-
> fully, till they were delivered of *Hymnes, Hexasticons, Pæans*, and
> such other *Panegyricall* stuffe, which every one thought 7. yeare
> till he had brought forth, to testifie the love that he bore to
> *Nobody*: In advancement of whose honour (and this was sworne
> upon a pen & ynck-horne in stead of a sword, yet they al write
> *Tam marti quàm mercurio*, but how lawfully let the Herads have an
> eye toot) they vowd & swore very terribly, to sacrifice the very
> lives of their invention; And when they wanted ynck (as many of
> them do wanting mony) or had no more (like a Chancery-man)
> but one pen in all the world, parcell of their oath was, to write
> with their blood and a broome-stick before they would sit idle.
> (Wilson, pp. 72–3)

Like much of the Hell literature inherited from Nashe, he allows
the symbols of writing and social violence to complement each
other. With ferocious intimacy, Dekker's poetic post-mortem draws
an image of the atrophied corpse of patronage and presents it
through a formal act of self-destruction. If he goes, they go!

Authors appear as rivalrous vultures or dissecting doctors when competing for the favours of Nobody. Writing appears trapped in the entropic corpse of courtly society, as the enshrined and romantic notion of the poets muse is barged out of the way. Even the grotesque has become somewhat self-serving as the disembowelling rituals of punishment embellish the competition between the writers who seek to present their various flatteries. For all its edgy humour, Dekker's words reveal the intense energy of literary and social frustration. The poet's rapacious curiosity rips up the cadaver of patronage as he searches for the very 'panegyricall stuffe' needed to appease and please him. Such images contain the deepest hostility towards those who have to be flattered. In addition the writer is consumed in the process of inventing such flatteries, burnt up producing the artefacts of social flirtation as he quite literally spends himself in a meaningless act of self-consumption. Competition drives the quill to the viciousness of 'ardent affections' rather than to the realm of literary and social integrity. Necessity here becomes reductively, though metaphorically, the mother of linguistic invention as we imagine the pregnant head of the writer delivering its gestations. That writing appears to be so combative serves to rupture the status of the 'old Religion', including those chivalric codes which had hitherto nourished it. Instead of easing the transition from chevalier to courtier, the pen mocks the mighty symbolic sword of aristocratic sensibilities. Writing with blood and broomstick appears both risible and quixotically bathetic: poetics become as prosaic as manual labour, and poets have become lowly housekeepers. Once the supreme metaphor of social bonds, and the poets' spirit, blood now signifies something merely utilitarian and therefore squandered. Social and symbolic violence appear endemic to a system in which 'poets' virtually have to spend their blood in order to be writers.

For all the energy of his complaint, it should be stressed that Dekker's Epistle was still meant as a *tour de force* of ribald humour. A position of disinvestment and disengagement was crafted through satirical form as his writing sought a constituency outside the conventions of patronage, and attempted to define a different relationship with its readers. This produced an understandable hypersensitivity to the vagaries and ravages of 'Booke-biters' who 'bite the Muses by the shinnes' (Wilson, p. 73). If the pure art of Poesie had to be abandoned to the appeal of popularity then the writer, particularly the playwright, had to be mindful of the

'Audience with hard hands' (Robbins, p. 157). Writing for a living produced a special kind of Hell: 'To come to the presse is more dangerous, then to bee prest to death ... for the payne of Tortures, last but a few minutes, but he that lyes upon the rack in print, hath his flesh torne off by the teeth of Envy, and Calumny' (Grosart, vol. II, p. 89). Through the diabolical strains of economic coercion Dekker realized he could not afford Nashe's disdain of these book-biters; a poverty-stricken death was too high a price. Away from the nexus of patronage, Dekker envisaged writing as a product of the tools of his trade. His mock dedication to 'Syr Nicholas Nemo, *alias* Nobody' is a stylized display of the patron's erasure. Dekker's 'Answere to Pierce Pennylesse' is that, like patrons, 'the Divell ... cares for nobody' (Grosart, vol. II, p. 91). This 'Nobody' became a recurring curse which forced Dekker to reconceive the social value of his writing. 'Nobody' is figured as nobody in particular, a nominal relegation of the patron's role. 'Some-body', then, meant not just anybody but a concerted pitch to a general clientele; and Dekker proceeded to develop a rich and panoramic narrative style specifically to accommodate this general audience. If he failed to make a living it was not because he missed his target, but because of the concentration of power and control of the book trade. Dekker inscribed a new social contract for writing, one in which the writer was more artisan than retainer. Poetic production within the mechanics of exchange began to seem more like labour than the ardour of one's muse. Rather than trying to reinstate the policy of unspoken munificence or recondition 'Liberality', Dekker sought instead to liberate gold from the purse of his readership. Perhaps his *'mercurius'* was now ironically invoked as a figure of both eloquence and commerce.

## II BREAKING LOOSE FROM HELL?

The social reproduction of seriousness is a fundamental – perhaps the fundamental – hegemonic manœuvre. Once the high language has attained the commanding position of being able to specify what is and is not to be taken seriously, its control over the language of its society is virtually assured.[26]

In his effort to relocate the socio-economic position of the writer, Dekker took on deep-seated social and theological anxieties. Often turning to images of London's plague-hit streets as a way of interpreting such cultural and moral landscapes, he mapped the interlocking realms of Hell and the city not only to produce popular literature but also to structure space for his subtle and complex dissident voice. It was a voice which, among other things, often found itself caught up in the conflict and contradictions of the Reformation. A keen defender of Reformation politics at a grassroots, though not presbyterian level, Dekker was a much less comfortable advocate of the forces of 'hierarchy and court' which bolstered mainstream ecclesiastical polity. Like many Londoners he remained uneasy at the concept of the Church being deployed as a vehicle for consolidating monarchical power. For the most part Dekker's city-based discontent with theological matters allowed him to flirt with Puritanism but never to go steady. As an ideological force, purification of the Church – which was after all the main plank of the Puritan programme – provided an antidote to Popery, was a thorn in the side the Court, and reinforced some strands of popular nationalism. In spite of Dekker's avid opposition to Catholicism, for a writer (particularly a play-writer) purity as a cultural force was too stifling as a social programme and inappropriate for the theatre. In general Dekker's writing tends to be suspicious of extremist or doctrinaire positions, whether rigidly hierarchical or inflexibly puritanical. What follows is an examination of the discrete narrative strategies and the ironies of literary form which underpinned his challenge to a variety of extremist attitudes which developed out of the Reformation.

It was through the imaginative topography of Hell that much of the period's conceptual and theological energy was directed. It was often there, in Hell, that Dekker located his populist literature. Among other things, Dekker's writing contained an ambivalent relationship to Calvinism. Calvinistic principles provided the crux of Puritan belief, and informed their understanding of the Reformation's political and theological matter. Although debate about the importance of Calvinism to Church orthodoxy and the ecclesiastical establishment, not to mention the position of the monarch, is still ongoing, it seems appropriate to qualify the post-Tyackean stress on Calvinism as an 'established orthodoxy' by evaluating its importance within the political establishment as G. W. Bernard has done:

> Before any theology can be claimed as a norm, as dominant, as established orthodoxy, it has to be set in the context of this

monarchical church, that is in the context of a church controlled to the limits of their power by rulers with an obvious and consistent interest in promoting comprehensive, eirenic, politique policies in order to hold together a religiously divided society and church.[27]

Anglican sympathies enable Bernard to conceive the history of ruling-class theology as one built on a tradition of pragmatic proto-Arminianism: 'surely the monarchical religion that very largely characterized government policy from Henry VIII, throughout Elizabeth's reign and now under Charles I and Laud was in this sense deeply and ineradicably "Arminian"'.[28] In effect he minimizes the history of social and theological conflict – a conflict in which the Reformation played a large part. Somewhat tendentiously Bernard dampens the significance of radical positions which later helped to form that centralized tradition. Leaving aside the theological niceties of the Cambridge debate, or the governmental consequences of James meeting the Puritans at Hampton Court, the political and ideological impetus necessary to remove the residual force of Catholicism from English culture cannot be accounted for via the trickle-down eirenic fancies of smooth religious transitions. This is especially relevant when reading history, ideology, or theology from the perspective of the ruling class. There is more than a touch of Whiggism about this so-called 'tradition' of Arminianism, despite the fact that Christopher Hill and others continue to stress the dissidence of early modern Protestantism. It seems likely that the monarchy sought the establishment of a reformed Church without its irksome radical elements. It is also likely that Dekker and others wanted a popular Protestantism without unpalatable sectarianism. One way or another, all positions had to negotiate the force of Puritanism.

One of Dekker's literary tactics was to use the landscape of Hell to explore the indigestibility of Calvinistic tenets, in particular that of double predestination (that God had predestined a few members of humanity to salvation, the elect, and condemned the remaining majority to damnation). It was upon this altar that Calvinist doctrine laid its concept of Hell. Disciplines of terror are especially important in theological systems which, like early modern predestination, offered so little to so many. The less heavenly carrot Calvinism offered, the more Hellish stick was required. As a way of policing conceptual boundaries, the inclusivity of Hell (that there was no alternative) was absolutely crucial. Its discipline had to reach everyone. Because it could be no other than a total system, humour always had the potential to cut deep into its structures.

Within the frame of double-predestination, most people were consigned to the wastes of everlasting torment. The drama of a despairing reprobate was both socially cathartic (for those wracked with anxiety) and a form of subconscious security (for those who avidly believed in the elect). In short, the reprobative figure anchored the ideology of predestination. Dekker savagely undermined any sense of security which the privileged elite might have entertained by agitating the anxieties which sprang from doubt. Dekker's Charon (in *Newes from Hell*), for example, wields a ferociously democratic oar as he ferries the once rich and powerful over the Styx. Imagining one's betters on their way to Hell's torments could be a poignant moment of class vengeance. Those whose social position might have encouraged them to foster feelings of being favoured in the afterlife are reminded that their temporal superiority might be just that, temporal. Doubt was held up and played out in the images of retribution. Time and again those who had most to gain were shown losing the most. This potential destruction of the fortunes of the well-heeled and upper class probably contributed as much as anything to the later downgrading of these tenets of Calvinistic doctrine, at least in its unadulterated form within the post-Reformation church. Uncertainty about the cosmic afterlife's ability to maintain the privileges of terrestrial life, a factor enhanced by Dekker's descriptions of the journey to Hell, paved the way for a more compassionate belief-system such as Arminianism.

Constructing and interpreting Hell was a most serious business. For some, any enjoyment or pleasure was a matter of religious disbelief. Even a smile might be considered smirking in the face of God. That laughter signifies levity, while profundity accompanies seriousness, appears to be one of the more durable aspects of Western civilization.[29] Yet Dekker consistently exploited the weighty aspects of levity and at times tried to explain, even theorize, this position. In *A Knight's Conjuring* he says: 'If you please to read me over, you shall finde much morall matter in words merily set down: and a serious subject inclosde in applications that (to some, whose salt of judgement is taken off) may appeare but triviall and ridiculous' (Robbins, p. 69). For Dekker, the 'serious subject inclosde' was, of course, Hell, which was itself an enclosingly serious subject. Behind Dekker's promotion of merry words lay a deep and abiding resistance to despair. This was not so much a counter-weight to the Calvinistic notion that despair was itself a sin, but a form of objection to the iron grip which that state generated. It was an impossible hubris to imagine oneself as one of the elect; thus despair was damnation and damnation was despair. Humour, then, can be seen as much a political strategy as it was a psychic necessity. For this reason we can see why the forces of seriousness were marshalled against it. Through the ethos of City government, sobriety was an insistently political force invoked in the name of God. I am not suggesting, of course, that the gridiron of Calvinistic thought could be simply overthrown by a few laughs, but the consequences of slipping the shackles occasionally, even as a fantasy, was a possibility which Dekker's literature sought to offer.

In keeping with Tyacke's basic drift (that Calvinism represented an orthodoxy), John Stachniewski seeks to rectify our understanding of early modern literature by tying it to religious despair; arguing that 'the brighter side of Protestantism had attracted disproportionate attention'.[30] For Stachniewski the uncompromisingly exclusive nature of Calvinism, doubts about election, and rigid authoritarianism, produced an overwhelming impact upon the writing of this period. So powerful and encompassing was this disconsolate grip that 'the dynamics of major literary texts can be effects of the pressures exerted by a collective imagination, to which the organizing intelligence of individual artists is largely subordinate.'[31] The imprisonment of language, therefore, governed by Calvinism's seizure of the political unconscious, produced an inescapable sub-text of despair. Furthermore, it appeared to do so in a manner which has now become familiar to students of early modern literature:

In fact both the narrating subject and the subject of narration are moving targets of analysis; the language of the text implicates the author in conflicts in the description of the self so that there can be no aloof controlling consciousness. While the quest for stability (itself culturally imposed) is clearly one dynamic in the text it is pitted against other forces which are far from submissive to authorial intention. These forces nucleated in the collective projection of the Calvinistic God. It is this communal construct, whose presence was not solicited by any individual but nevertheless

had potent effects inside the psyche, that my book's title, the persecutory imagination, identifies.[32]

Literature, then, operates through the closed-circuited function of
theological and ideological power. Any effort or intercession by the
author-subject is rendered useless, delusive, or subsumed, when
channelled through writing. Stachniewski's readings of texts from
Bunyan, Donne, Burton, and Milton locate despair, in either its self-
vauntingly (but finally doomed) optimistic form, or in its depress-
ingly melancholic (even suicidal) pessimistic form. It is an iron-clad
despair which offers any and all potential ideological escapees only
conformation of the inescapability of the cosmos organized by
a Calvinistic God. In Stachniewski's account, the author becomes a
mere vector for the transference of the psychic energy of despair
through what he dubs 'the persecutory imagination'. Self-
consciousness, textual reflexivity, literary licence, or authorial intention, are all grist to the mill of despair and delusion. The
subjected writer is limited to articulating, often blindly, his own
subordination and that of everyone else.

No reader of early modern literature would doubt that there was
a powerful self-enclosing discourse operating in the culture of that
period; or that it provided aesthetic, political, and rhetorical, effects
to which many critics have responded. While Stachniewski offers a
highly comprehensive analysis of the complex patterns of religious
despair, together with their material and social manifestations in
madness, (attempted) suicide, and profound anxiety, it seems
doubtful whether the Calvinistic strait-jacket was as securely fas-
tened as he supposes. Although Stachniewski provides the necessary corrective to the 'brighter side' of Protestantism – a rosy gloss
coloured by the views of Anglican sympathizers after the Civil War
– like the New Historicists before him, he tends to remain somewhat enthralled by the structures and systems of his own analysis.
Writer and reader are held in a grim awe by the thought of an omniscient glance from a Calvinistic God. Yet it seems that Dekker and
other writers were aware of the hegemonizing strategy of
Calvinism and wrote about its darkly contradictory aspects.

Any belief system which utilizes death as a major resource – and
Christianity was and is undoubtedly one – will be stressed when
large numbers of its community die. The plagues which hit London
in the early 1590s and again just after the turn of the century, including the deaths of 1603, were the worst since the Black Death of

the fourteenth century. Not only were customary rituals attached to death severely ruptured during such a time, but the metaphysics upon which they are based inevitably became distorted. Death provided a moment when Christians could cohere as a community and focus on the grand organizing principles ordered for life and afterlife. The miracle of a diseased body renewed was a key component in 'The Ordre For The Buriall Of The Dead' in *The Book of Common Prayer* (1549), one of the chief components of the Reformation practice.[33] Large numbers dying in the streets in the most horrible manner had a propensity to strain or heighten theological and epistemological principles.

Protestant theology had, from its reformatory inception, worked hard to reshape the notion of Hell, to replace the realm it perceived as the gothically physical with the apparatus of psychical terror. The manifest form of the reprobate was a crucial part of the machinery of this conceptual shift. In many ways the terror which Protestants internalized became projected, or inflicted, upon others, usually the less powerful. Reprobates were made to function as dramatic paradigms of the morally corrupt and sure-to-be-damned un-elect. In *The Decline of Hell*, D. P. Walker argues that this was made possible by reconfiguring of the idea of 'eternal torment'; one in which Hell and the reprobate were contingent.[34] Stachniewski broadly concurs:

> That Calvin conceived of the experience of the reprobate as a forestaste of hell indicates the intensity of the despair for which his theology provided. Indeed he impatiently dismissed those who, like preachers of the late medieval church, concentrated their terrorizing eloquence on the physical torments of hell as having 'crassae imaginationes'. Hell, as for Luther, was essentially psychological. It was the pain of eternal rejection by God. And since rejection could be communicated to the reprobate in this world, hell was the literal experience of the despairing reprobate.[35]

London's plague-ridden streets tended to over-mire terror in its disturbingly physical form. Such a physicality, however dire, could not be controlled, or used simply as an instrument of control, because the ludicrous and farcical which also attend it could never be sufficiently contained. During times of stress, repressed unseriousness often reappeared, usually as a moment of farce. The physical manifestations of such a moment consistently troubled theologians because of their impact upon strategies of terror. This is why 'physical torments' were continuously and necessarily remodelled in order to remove all elements of absurdity. Writers like Nashe who insisted upon conjuring up the physical, the 'grossly palpable', were held accountable for this laughing matter and charged with disbelief, heresy, and the catchall category, atheism.

A large measure of the terror which can be elicited through the apparatus of a collective persecutory imagination comes from an anticipatory unknowing, itself a product of paranoia derived from such an imagination. Stachniewski observes that the proportional increase in suicidal tendencies related to religious anxiety of the period stem from this suspense: 'I thought hell to come, could not be worse than what I felt' said one typically bereft Calvinist of the period.[36] In part, descriptions of Hell sought to give the beleaguered psyche some form of imaginative purchase. Dekker's 'Hell' literature constructed objects and places through which anxieties could be played out, and seemingly unspeakable fears could be articulated. For many, it seems that the 'worm of conscience', while furnishing the interior life of the self and providing evidence for that life, too often fed solely upon itself, leaving that valued interiority utterly disabled. Easing the potential consequences of self-annihilation which this 'worm' carried, Dekker projected a Hell they could see rather than one which solely inhabited them:

> I will ingenuously and boldely give you the Map of a country, that lyes lower then the 17. valleyes of *Belgia*, yea lower then the Cole-pits of *Newcastle*, is farre more darke, farre more dreadfull, and fuller of knaverie, then the Colliers of those fire-workes are. The name of this straunge Countrie is *Hell*; In discovery of which, the Qualitie of the King-dome, the condition of the Prince, the estate of the people, the Traffique thither (marie no transportation of / goods from thence) shalbe painted to the life. It is an *Empire*, that lyes under the *Torrid Zone*, and by that meanes is hotter at Christmas, then tis in *Spaine* or *Fraunce* (which are counted plaguy hotte Countries) at Midsummer, or in *England* when the dogge daies bite sorest: for to say truth (because ti's sinne to belie the Divell) the *Universall Region* is built altogether upon Stoves and *Hotte-houses*, you cannot set foote into it, but you have a *Fieri facias* serv'de upon you: for like the Gals-house *Furnace* in Blacke-friers, the bonefiers that are kept there, never goe out; insomuch that all the Inhabitants are almost broylde like

*Carbonadoes* with the sweating sicknes, but the best is (or rather the worst) none of them die on't. (Grosart, vol. II, pp. 97–8)

His intent in *Newes from Hell* was to fabricate a cognitive Hell from a symbolic one through a deepening familiarization. While familiarity did not necessarily breed contempt, it certainly drew some of the teeth of terror. Dekker's Hell was not one of everlasting torment but a trumped-up version of the world which everyone already inhabited. It was a vision which alleviated stress by offering an entertaining caricature of what was most feared, as its affective irony loosened Hell's grip upon the imagination. A prosaically located horror, 'painted to the life', however uncomfortable, could not at the same time be an unimaginable terror. But it was more than just Dekker's conceptual definition which had the effect of delimiting Hell, it was the inescapable worldliness, or physicality, of his organizing metaphors and similes which worked to offset the metaphysics of fear which they are ostensibly there to invoke. His topographical references indicating a wider/deeper/darker/hotter realm bend the narrative of Hell into a humour of camp excess.

As Dekker translated the everlasting torments of Hell into a variety of mock-scary forms, the imagination was restructured as a resource which could loosen the shackles of fear. Crass imagination also became a way through which he forged a contract with the audience: 'In what colours shall I laie down the true shape of it?', he implores, 'Assist [my] Invention' (Grosart, vol. II, p. 128). Through rhetorical questions, Dekker's appeal to the collaborative function of writing and thinking thwarts the enclosing effects of a private, discrete consciousness. Imagination and anxiety need not be an individual burden, they could be made social. Whether they liked it or not, Calvinist divines depended upon the organizing power of the imagination, and precisely because of this Dekker was able to hijack some of that imaginative energy.

Feelings of social exclusion and isolation were the building blocks of Hell. Hell was the 'lamentable condition' of 'the unhappie prisoner ... his Indictment is Impleadable, his evidence irrefutable, the fact impardonable, the Judge impenitrable, the Judgement formidable: the tortures insufferable, the manner of them inutterable' (Grosart, vol. II, p. 128). In Hell, the prisoner symbolically represents the psychological experience of being excluded from God and the community of the elect. Thus, the prisoner's condition metonymically instates the authority of that God and thereby privileges the elect. Though tracing the party line here, Dekker was also playing a game with the audience's imagination. In order to explain this he asks his readers to contemplate 'the very height of all worldly pompe that thought can aspire' only to tumble from this elevated state 'into the bottome of a lake, whose depth is immeasurable, and circuit incomprehensible' (Grosart, vol. II, p. 128). This fall is made 'clammy and palpable' by a plethora of horrible Dante-esque images:

> Into what gulf of desperate calamitie, wold not the poorest begger now throw himself headlong, rather than to tast the least dram of this bitterness, if imagination can give being to a more miserable place than this described? Such a one, or worse than such a one, is that, into which the guiltie soules are led captive, after they have their condemnation. And what tongue is able to relate the grones and ululations of a wretch so distressed? a hundred pennes of steele wold be worne blunt in the description, and yet leave it unfinished. (Grosart, vol. II, pp. 129–30)

In the face of this narrative failure it seems almost churlish to remind ourselves that Dekker had promised earlier that Hell 'shalbe painted to the life', yet it was part of Dekker's writing strategy to indicate such a shortfall. He appears genuinely ambivalent about the power of the imagination to represent the state of Hell by indicating the impossibility of such a project, yet the ostensible direction of his narrative is to encourage the mind to grapple with the inconceivable. Most importantly, he does not attempt to elicit despair through this type of description because, for him, the imagination was not meant to be overawed and subjected by the image of infinite horrors. His muse appears compassionately recalcitrant rather than hopelessly abject. Dekker licenses the reader to think about the unthinkable, to flirt with danger in order to side-step a seizure of the imagination. Even the most zealous Calvinist would find little to disagree with in Dekker's writing. Yet he deliberately avoids terrorizing his reader into helpless submission by continually pointing up his own rhetorical failure to do so. Despair was induced by enforcing the futility of man's intellect in the face of God's universe and the magnitude of the cosmos. Despair could only become a certainty when the imagination is relinquished to a system which wholly circumscribes it. The 'landmarks of Hell' were translated by Dekker into 'the landmarks of London'.[37] By

building the 'Universall Region', Hell, 'upon Stoves and Hotte-
houses' and other mundane artefacts of the city everyone knew,
Dekker upset the grandeur of Hell, and teased its ability to reify
despair. A number of critics have cast Dekker's writing as orthodox
or conservative, yet underneath that patina of conservatism is a
deep mistrust of the apparatus of dominance and discipline. While
the instruments of these forces are paraded before our eyes, the
manner of its presentation undermines their effect. Often his descriptions of the demonic were borrowed from the very sermoniz-
ing language, the proselytizing terror, which he was imaginatively
renegotiating. There was more than a whiff of brimstone in
Dekker's narration of Hell, but his rhetoric always gave off a
parodic odour.

Yet Dekker's engagement with systems of control was not simply
confined to comic strategies. For Stachniewski the subordination of
individual artists to the combined pressures of a collective imagination reflected wider social patterns. Patriarchal authority was, it
seems, inevitably intertwined with the ideology of Hell, and was a
beneficiary of its social effect. Religious doctrine and absolutism
(the divine right of kings) mutually reinforced one another.
Theology and patriarchy operated together like a vice holding the
mind in subjection and despair:

> Walzer is surely correct, then, to say that 'the defence of secular
> repression and the assertion of 'the claims of God' are so closely
> woven together that it is extremely difficult to disentangle them.
> The two sources of power and oppression were associated ... in
> the imagination of the victims of despair. No theological outlet
> existed for feelings of protest or resentment against the power of
> the father, father-surrogates, or God. And this could nurture an
> intolerable tension in individuals between their expanding self-
> awareness and the submissiveness demanded of them.[38]

It was through the language of Hell that Dekker located some of
those 'feelings of protest', while simultaneously exploiting and ex-
pressing that 'intolerable tension'. More than inverting the figures
of power, Dekker spread 'a confusion of languages', a dispersal and
dissipation of images, in his presentation:

> These *Territories*, notwithstanding of *Tartarie*, will I undermine
> and blow up to the view of all eies, the black & dismal shores of

this *Phlegetonticke Ocean*, shal be in ken, as plainely as the white (now unmaydend brests) of our owne Iland: *China*, *Peru* and *Cartagena* were never so rifled: the winning of *Cales*, was nothing to the ransacking of this *Troy* that's all on fire: the very bowels of these Infernall Antipodes, shall be ript up, and pulld out, before that great Dego of Devels his owne face: Nay since my flag of defiance is hung forth, I will yeelde to no truce,/but with such *Tamburlaine-like* furie match against this great Turke, and his legions, that *Don Belzebub* shall be ready to damne himselfe, and be horne-mad: for with the conjuring of my pen, al Hell shall breake loose. (Grosart, vol. II, pp. 100–1)

All manner of topical, topographical, political, and historical subjects are spliced into this diatribe.[39] His description compresses the infinite, the multifarious histories and narratives of Hell, into literary inspiration and psychological release in a moment of sheer exhilaration. By taking on the Devil, and his spirit, the writer invokes the charismatic and legendary Tamburlaine, a character of unbounded ambition, pretension and ruthlessness. In many ways the dramatic Tamberlaine embodied the contradictory self-vaunting and submissive attitude to religion induced by Calvinism. In Marlowe's well-known play, in which he is the eponymous hero, he challenges the might of religious authority, 'Come, let us march against the powers of heaven', only later to realize that he has to back down; 'Ah, friends, what shall I do? I cannot stand'.[40] According to Sinfield, 'the basic challenge of Tamberlaine and other tragic heroes is their determination to identify and pursue their own goals without deference to God or humanity.'[41] Sometimes Dekker played with this position: 'I will ingenuously', 'I will yeelde to no truce', 'will I undermine' he resolves, as if the act of description itself was volitional, one that flouts the underlying logic of cosmic predetermination. But it is an act that realizes and recognizes the force with which it is engaged and from which it was produced: 'For with the conjuring of my pen', he admits with ironic trepidation, 'al hell shall break loose'. His writing taps into the apocalyptic moment of despair grounded in the theology of the Reformed Church. 'Militant Protestants were deeply influenced by apocalyptic theology', argues Julia Gasper, and 'this led them to envisage the world as a dualistic struggle, whose ultimate outcome must be the triumph of the True Church.'[42] Yet why, Dekker implies, should that victory be accomplished through the creation

of a Heaven of misery? In the inverse image of a diabolically apocalyptic moment the writer entertains a fantasy of liberation. The
imaginative instant when Hell breaks loose ties it to the same
moment when the narrator breaks loose from Hell.

But what kind of escape could it be? Stachniewski's argument anticipates these evasions, deeming them inevitably futile or ineffective. Optimism is therefore merely an 'illusion', perhaps even 'the
essential attribute of despair'; any successful resistance would reinforce the bars of the 'psycho-theological prison'.[43] It may be, as he
says, that 'confronting the persecutory imagination meant facing
up to the impossibility of facing it down'.[44] Yet Dekker's writing
appears more than aware of this dilemma and does not really fit
that frame. The place where psycho-theological strategies of power
were being most heavily enforced would also have been the point
where they were most brittle. A doctrinarian Hell depended upon
its inflexibility for its ideological strength. Any movement or
rupture in its narrative strategy would have rendered it vulnerable. Of course, Dekker's dissentient commentaries on the manacles
of the mind were necessarily oblique. His flag of defiance, the truce
against which he will not yield, the object of his *'Tamburlaine-like*
furie', was, overtly, *'Don Belzebub,'* the Devil. As a good, 'militant
Protestant', it would have been unthinkable to defy God openly,
not to mention being politically and personally dangerous.
Nevertheless, we have to see the 'great Turke', *Don Belzebub,* as one
of a number of the father-surrogates against which, Stachniewski
believes, there existed no ideological outlet for feelings of protest or
resentment. Throughout the Hell pamphlets Dekker levels an
attack on *'Don Pluto'*, the 'lying *Cretan'*, *'his Infernallship'*, *'Don
Lucifer'*, 'Captaine of the damned *Crew'*, *'Grand Sophy of the Whore of
Babylon'*, *'Cavaliero Cornuto'*, *'Colonel of Conjurers'*, *'Cacodæmon'*,
*'Monsieur Malediction'*, or 'Lieutenant of Limbo'. Many of these
names satirize military leaders, as if the Devil is one who unjustly
conscripts the army of the damned. A deep antipathy developed
between those who could be conscripted and those in authority
who organized their conscription. In 'Elizabeth's army ... the re-
cruitment system was riddled with corruption and graft and operated so that vagabonds, misfits, and prisoners, who traded their
sentence for service in the army, filled the regiments.'[45] Choosing
between hunger and death in prison or death and hunger in the
army must have been a close call, though there was a chance of de-
serting from the latter. That Dekker figures so many upper-class

army officers as parodically in charge of Hell enables him to satirize both forms of authority. Above all, such mock titles of authority express displaced feelings of resentment against fathers in general. They all, of course, take reference from the ultimate father, God. Although secular patriarchal power and the overwhelming claims of God are so 'closely woven together' that it would be difficult to tease them apart, problems would necessarily arise when either cultural force had differing or competing claims. This was an endemic problem, especially because the ethos of Protestantism depended upon religious insubordination. For all its vigorous drive for mastery it began by defying a central and incumbent authority. This kind of dissentient voice both shadows and, paradoxically, highlights Dekker's 'militant Protestantism'. Just how consciously displaced were Dekker's jibes at the trappings of patriarchal authority is difficult to say, but it is likely that sublimated aggression towards a Calvinistic God was often redirected towards literal and symbolic fathers; including, of course, patrons and the government.

In his ostensible revelation of diabolical machinations – 'I came as a spy to betray him ... to discover his stratagems' – Dekker, surprisingly, draws a parallel between the function of his writing and the gunpowder plot; 'will I undermine and blow up to the view of all eyes ... *These Territories*', that being, the Devil and Hell (Grosart, vol. II, p. 95).[46] With a reference to England, 'our owne Island', and a clear indication of James' accession through the image of 'now unmaydend brests', this political map would have been instantly recognizable to the Jacobean reader. We are invited to 'ken' (to see and know) the 'Infernall Antipodes' and 'that great Dego of Divels' as plainly as we see England and its rulers. The narrator's self-appointed brief is similar to that of an Elizabethan spy, to 'discover', to disclose, 'the *Qualitie* of the King-dome, the condition of the Prince, the estate of the people'. While such a correspondence appears sufficiently oblique that it could not with certainty be a direct attack upon the king, it seems sufficiently suggestive to ensure that it was. Once again, Dekker's often muted or cryptic anti-authoritarianism is cryptically located through the proximity of topical allusions. Gasper argues for a direct correlation, claiming that 'King James was the "Dego of Divels"'.[47] Broadly her analysis focuses on Dekker's concern for the abuse, or potential abuse, of tyrannical or absolutist monarchical power. His exposition of the Devil's 'stratagems' were a neat way for him to condemn the activities of those in power. In Hell 'the seven deadly sinnes are there in as great authority' as they are outside (Grosart, vol. II, p. 116). Their examination draws attention to the inherent dangers in the structure of hierarchical power. Through this kind of subterranean antipathy towards the monarch we can see how images of the Devil accommodated deeply disguised anti-authoritarian feelings while appearing to remain within an orthodox frame.

Hell narratives were a form of indictment as they enabled Dekker to depict a distorted, dystopic vision of society. Against this, he enjoyed presenting learning as a form of moral illumination and writing as intrinsically anti-diabolic. Exclusion from Hell of the writer-educator is depicted with delicious irony, because 'the Divell can neyther write nor reade', and because 'all the Scriveners ith' towne he had at his becke' drawing up contracts for souls (Grosart, vol. II, p. 93). Dekker's narrator claims to write for the Devil only in order to discover him from the inside, 'to betray him, then as a spirit to runne of his errands' (Grosart, vol. II, p. 95). Nothing less than the writer's soul and survival are at stake as he openly sets his 'wits ... against this Captaine of the damned Crew' (Grosart, vol. II, p. 95). That the Devil cared neither for learning nor 'Poets' was turned around in the epistle and 'Prologue' of *If This be not a Good Play* (1612) to indicate that not caring for 'New-playes' (the poet's 'Works') could itself become a diabolical charge. Even though it was finally staged at the Red Bull, it was the rejection of this play by the Fortune Theatre which pointed to both his literary disenfranchisement and his slide towards debt; a condition which eventually resulted in his imprisonment.[48] With a sense of portentous irony Dekker prefigures both his literary and social Hell in *Newes from Hell*. Dekker's relationship with the theatrical administration was just as fragile as that with his (usually non-existent) patrons. 'And it best becomes me' he wrote to Edward Alleyn from the King's Bench prison in 1616, 'to Sing anything in praise of Charity, because albeit, I have felt few hands warme, thorough that complexion, yett imprisonment may make me long for them.'[49]

With ironic acrimony, Dekker notes of Hell/London that 'it is an *Iland*' which now nurtures '*Usurers*' and their ilk (Grosart, vol. II, p. 98):

very fewe Poets can be suffred to live there, the *Colonel* of *Conjurers* drives them out of his Circle, because hee feares they'le write libells against him: yet some pittiful fellowes (that have faces like fire-drakes, but wittes colde as Whet-stones, and more blunt) not Poets indeede, but ballad-makers, rub out there, and write Infernals: Marrie players swarme there as they do here, whose occupation being smelt out, by the *Cacodæmon*, or head officer of the Countrie, to bee lucrative, he purposes to make up a company, and to be / chiefe sharer himselfe ... (Grosart, vol. II, pp. 98–9)

Dissentient writing thus operates as a way for discovering social truth. As such the autonomous writer or true poet cannot be tolerated because he threatens the central figure of authority, none other than 'the *Colonel of Conjurers*' himself. Dekker's use of the term 'conjury' is significant. Though magic was officially considered a mechanism of the Devil, in its configuration here, it could also inflect deeply sublimated attitudes of dissidence towards God. As Stachniewski indicates, 'the attraction of magic was that it was the most extravagant symbol of escape from the impotence Calvinism imposed.'[50] Stachniewski sees magic as a hollow force precisely because it could never be a theological possibility. Dekker's illusion of the diabolical conjurer, one whose 'Circle' implies both a closed society and rhetoric, seems to make this point apparent. Juxtaposing the poet's 'libells', the force of his manifesto, against the fear-producing circuit of 'the *Colonel of Conjurers*' appears as a validation of writing against conjury. 'I will call upon no ... conjurer', he contends, in emphasizing the 'will' in his writing, for 'conjurers, thou knowst, are fellow and fellow-like with *Monsieur Malediction*' (Grosart, vol. II, p. 102). But conjury is precisely what Dekker does claim for his writing! With a degree of authorial prestidigitation (demanded, it seems, by the exigencies of the marketplace) he rewrote *Newes from Hell* under the banner of *A Knight's Conjuring*. More precisely he considered 'Conjurations' an effect of words, especially as they were the inspiration and source of *Newes from Hell*; 'for with the conjuring of my pen, al Hell shall breake loose'. Ambition and autonomy: that which Faustus claimed for magic, Dekker claims for writing. According to Stachniewski, this would carry the same risk of tripping over the Calvinistic double-bind; 'that by embracing devil-dependent magic he simultaneously confirms ... the metaphysical belief-system he wants to transcend.'[51] But a belief-system which operates through the totalizing apparatus of such double-binds depends more on socio-political rhetoric than it does on the metaphysics of faith. Dekker's convoluted and pan-social descriptions of Hell make it the poet's duty to

write 'libells' against such conjury, to expose it as propaganda. Do
the rhetorical tricks which accompany the ideological force of Hell
become less convincing if we see their sleight of hand? In Dekker's
relentless 'discovery' of Hell it appears so. Rather than rationalizing
with an authority which depends upon the reinscription of voices
tipped against it, why not mire that voice in its imaginative contradictions, in the inherent confusion of its languages?

Dekker also targeted the managers of the theatre. As players
swarm to Hell, their chief exploiter appears to be the 'head officer
of the Countrie', who for lucrative purposes makes 'up a company',
and becomes 'chiefe sharer himselfe'. Sharers and administrators of
the theatre were the principal recipients of its 'lucrative' business,
not the writers. Not surprisingly, Dekker saw the management and
control of theatrical companies replicated in the administration of
Hell. Dekker knew that the problems he faced as a writer were en-
trenched and systematic. Bringing those structures into play as a
hellish *'Empire'* indicates his anger and frustration. Of course, it was
a critique which had to be muted because the managers of the
writing industry, men like Philip Henslowe and Edward Alleyn,
were often those who bailed him out of debt and prison when that
industry failed to reward him adequately. Such a double-bind was
certainly not lost on the financially embarrassed Dekker.

In Dekker's eulogy to his inspiration and friend, Nashe, hyperbole becomes the hallmark of the disrespectful writer.

> And thou, into whose soule (if ever there were a *Pithagorean
> Metempsuchosis*) the raptures of that fierie and inconfinable Italian
> spirit were bounteously and boundlesly infused, thou sometimes
> Secretary to *Pierce Pennylesse*, and Master of his requests,
> in/genious, ingenuous, fluent, facetious, T. *Nash*: from whose
> aboundant pen, hony flow'd to thy friends, and mortall Aconite
> to thy enemies: thou that madest the Doctor a flat Dunce, and
> beat'st him at two tall sundry Weapons, Poetrie, and Oratorie:
> Sharpest Satyre, Luculent Poet, Elegant Orator, get leave for thy
> Ghost to come from her abiding, and dwell with me a while, till
> she hath carows'd to me in her owne wonted ful measures of wit,
> that my plump braynes may swell, and burst into bitter
> Invectives against the Lieutenant of Limbo, if he casheere *Pierce
> Pennylesse* with dead pay.[52] (Grosart, vol. II, pp. 102–3)

This section of *Newes from Hell* was not included when he rewrote it
as *A Knight's Conjuring*, probably because of the references to

Nashe's activities in the Marprelate controversy and his concomitant argument with Gabriel Harvey ('Doctor Dunce'). Like his
earlier allusion to Tamberlaine, invoking Nashe produced a deliberate statement about the autonomy of the literary voice in conflict
with forces that would deny it. Among the stimulants to the
Nashe–Harvey altercation, as Hutson argues, was the question of
access, control, and dissemination of writing: 'publication of unau-
thorized fiction was being regarded by the government as a threat
... to its own religious and political authority.'[53] Nashe was suspected, and accused, of the non-conformist tendencies of 'singular-
ity' or 'individualism'. Harvey's 'own exemplary conformity' was
rooted in the belief that literature could and should be solely the
agent of authority, and therefore, there could be 'no authenticity
without governmental patronage'.[54] Nashe was deemed disruptive
precisely because of his anti-logocratic use of the word and rhetoric.
Most noticeably, this sense of dissentient wordplay was tied to 'acts
of individualism [which] it seems could not be tolerated if the
printed word were to be the instrument of divine and civil authority within the state'.[55] Not surprisingly this produced some anxieties for the authorities especially because, as Hutson states further,
some 'writers aimed directly at individuals in power.'[56] In a serious-
comic way Dekker invokes Nashe to harness the thrill of attacking
powerful individuals as he pluckily confronts 'the Lieutenant of
Limbo.' In mocking him he captures the anti-authoritarian plea-
sures of satirical writing: with 'bitter Invective' the reader could
deal 'mortall Aconite' to his enemies. Print gave powerful expression to the fantasies of those socially discontented and often included fantasies of violence and revenge upon the privileged as
they were, in considerable detail, stripped, degraded, and punished
in Hell for the delectation of the reader. It was often a sadistic and
masochistic spectacle. Whatever else can be said, Nashe could be
revered for that which he was condemned; that is, his writing style
– Lucianic, Rabelaisian, ironic, all loaded with the sceptical characteristics which upset Harvey because they were 'too licentious in
the imaginative sense'.[57] Such a literary imagination was, in
Hutson's analysis of Harvey's reaction, 'too fantastic, too comic',
one in which 'sacrificing the credibility of the author to the plea-
sures of his impertinent wordplay' diminished any 'credit for the
writer'.[58] My point is that in his tribute to Nashe, one which bears
witness and responds to the manner of his victory over Harvey,
Dekker recognizes a literature which in its style and form was

specifically designed to undercut authority by radically tarnishing it. Referring to himself as 'sometimes Secretary to *Pierce Pennilesse*', Dekker invites us to read *Newes from Hell* through the frame of Nashe's socio-literary stylistics (Grosart, vol. II, 103). That means we are asked to see the 'inconfinable' qualities with which his writing is 'boundlesly infused', to see the 'ingenious, ingenuous, fluent, and facetious', as a Lucianic and satirical form of the imagination with which to beat diabolical disciplines in whatever shape they came. Expanding on this theme, Nashe's 'Ghost' becomes, in Dekker's bizarre appeal, a darkly licentious muse who can only liberate the abusive words from the author by metaphorically rupturing the very source of their production. With words he did battle the constraining machinations of the Devil, partly because it would be impossible to confront the authority directly. Under the intense pressures of anger, failed aspiration, lack of social entitlement, and financial frustration, some type of expressive outlet was necessary. In many ways the ludicrous image of a writer's brain exploding as it attempted to address the tension produced by those feelings seems an appropriately grotesque literary moment.

## III   GOD'S PLAGUE AND THE *THESPIAN* BOWLE

What is a Church? & What is a Theatre? ... can they Exist Separate?[59]

Inspire us therefore how to tell the *Horror* of a *Plague*, the *Hell*.[60]

In Dekker's time, London could be divided into two sorts of people: those who could afford to leave during the outbreaks of plague and those who could not. Dekker was one of the latter. Not only did the poor bear the brunt of the epidemics but they functioned as a gauge for those who liked to skip town. Surveys of plague deaths in the suburbs were kept in detail, and when the tolls reached certain levels many wealthy city-dwellers left for the country.[61] From the late sixteenth century onwards, plague had a considerable and almost continuous presence in the city and in one way or another occupied everyone's mind. During the period 1603–10, a crucial time in Dekker's career, London's theatres were closed for approximately sixty out of the possible ninety-six months due to the City authorities' reaction to plague.[62] From the beginning of 1603 to the end of 1604 a full nineteen months out of twenty-four, including the prime theatre-going summer months, were affected.[63] Even though he later developed a career as a pamphlet writer Dekker, perhaps more than any other writer, desperately needed the theatres to stay open. Quite simply, as Pendry says, 'work for the press was even less rewarding than work for the theatre'.[64] And for a writer teetering on the brink of bankruptcy, the significance of 'less' reward was often the difference between solvency and debt.

Dekker's earliest pamphlet was *The Wonderfull yeare* (1603). An off-beat tribute to Elizabeth, it deployed a variety of picaresque descriptions of London laid waste by plague. The horrific images of the effects of the disease were used as a kind of hymn, signifying the cosmic rupture which accompanied the sovereign's passing away. This eccentric work helped to secure for Dekker the joint authorship, with Jonson, of the ensuing royal eulogy of succession, *The Magnificent Entertainment*, the plague-delayed celebration of James' entry into the city. But it seems clear that his muse and political sympathies lay elsewhere, which is why he was never accepted as a courtly writer. Nevertheless, options were few for professional writers. Dekker lost, or failed to find, a suitable patron for another, later, piece of writing which focused on the plague – his apocalyptic *Newes from Graves-ende*, in which he reworked some of his theatrical rhetoric.[65] Certainly the vitriolic 'Epistle Dedicatory' which accompanied this pamphlet attests as much to genuine anxieties about poverty as it does to the lack of literary acknowledgment. Horror of loss due to plague thus provided feasible metaphors for personal crisis, while still retaining their symbolic force for depicting London as a literary dystopia.

Pendry writes of Dekker that 'the plague is to him above all a calamity that strikes at the community'.[66] Dekker saw plague as much about the values within a community as a threat from outside. For example, a strong sense of moral revisionism within London overshadows tracts like *The Seven deadly Sinnes of London* (1606) which, in seven coaches through the seven gates, were deemed responsible for 'Bringing the Plague with them' (Grosart, vol. II, p. 3). That the plague was brought to London was a common misperception, but when we get to the vices Dekker presents them as endemic to the city rather than imported. Dekker exploited the way in which plague and vice were conflated in the public mind. In *Newes from Graves-ende* attitudes to plague are made the measure of London's community and of the writer's role in its interpretation. Community, plague, and writing are rhetorically constructed as mutually interconnected forms for defining and shaping cultural meanings within the city. Working with its quasi-apocalyptic format, *Newes from Graves-ende* analyses 'the cause of the plague', 'the horror of the plague', and, somewhat desultorily, 'the cure of the plague'. Typically Dekkerian, *Newes from Graves-ende* is a pan-social mosaic more impressive for its use of images and spectacle than for its structural or narrative consistency. For Dekker closure of the theatres was nothing less than a tragedy. With its drama of plague-death, *Newes from Graves-ende* was both a response to, and a compensation for, that closure. He steeps his commentary with dramaturgical rhetoric such as 'Tragick', *'Thespian'*, 'Scene', 'Stage', and so on, and carefully makes the underlying action of the poetry represent a simultaneous elegy and requiem for all things theatrical.

In a recent investigation of the logistical and political effects of the plague on the Jacobean theatre, Leeds Barroll shows that, given the absence of microbiological techniques, contemporary understanding of the cause and spread of the disease was, at a pragmatic level, fairly sophisticated. Consequently the 'miasma theory', that rotten air was the source of infection, though medically fallacious, appears less far-fetched when one considers that the rats, the root source of plague, were likely to be evident in the areas of organic matter from where the smell emanated.[67] Furthermore, plague was more virulent during summer months when such odours were more likely to be pungent, and when informal social gatherings such as the theatre-going occurred. Infection, both functionally and phenomenologically, was understood at an empirical level even if the interpretation of such data was often hijacked for political purposes. It seems unclear, for example, at what point the authorities closed the theatres in terms of death rates, or patterns. Though variable, the rates were made contingent upon other considerations not connected with the plague, like so-called 'public order'.[68] Governmental concerns usually outweighed empirical evidence or any other forms of comprehending the disease. In spite of the strong conviction that plague spread through interpersonal contagion, Churches (operating symbolically and practically as an instrument of ideological cohesion) remained open while the theatres (less likely to operate as an instrument of government control) were closed. A complicating aspect of this argument is that the Church, or God, provided the other main alternative theory to the cause of

the plague. Yet this was a difficult and complex issue, and not necessarily one of rationality versus superstition, or faith versus
scientific atheism, as Barroll's commentary indicates:

Whether miasma was the basis of their thinking or not, the
London authorities were so convinced that plague was spread by
infection – not an obvious fact, really, before microscopes – that
they ignored some important religious tenets that one might
expect to have given them pause. In fact, it is crucial to theater
historians to realize that city fathers, without actually saying so,
turned their backs on the highly providential orientation to be
found in preludes to most treatises on plague. These remarks asserted the usual theme: God, in his infinite and knowable provi
dence, was, through plague, scourging humankind for sin,
warning the survivors to mend their ways and go about the main
business of attending to their salvation. But infection contra-
dicted any rational theory of God's punishing ways, because the
punishment seemed unselective. If plague was really infectious,
how did one explain that, after bubonic death had descended
as punishment upon some hapless sinner, it then leaped infec-
tiously, with seeming moral randomness, to possible innocent
persons coming into close physical proximity with said sinner. A
theory of infection made it easy to view God's punishment,
blindly seeking out both sinner and sinless, as random celestial
swatting … If those who argued for providence might reason
that providence was ample enough to embrace the choosing of
who would be infected, skeptics could respond that determined
avoidance of plague-infected persons often turned out to be a
gratifyingly easy way of fleeing God's avenging wrath.[69]

Of course, fleeing God's wrath was fraught with impossibilities. In
*A Rod for Runawais*, Dekker severely chastises those who try to
leave London in times of plague. He tried to snag them with the
double-bind that you cannot accept the need to flee from a wrathful
God without accepting that a wrathful God would be impossible to
flee from. Failing that argument he proffered that those who fled
rendered themselves unfit for civic rule or even to be part of a
Christian community. As usual, Dekker used social rather than theological terms through which to cast aspersions: 'We are warranted
by holy Scriptures to flie from *Persecution*, from the *Plague*, and
from the *Sword* that persues us: but you flye to save your selves,

and in that flight undoe others' (Wilson, p. 148). Here Dekker refers directly to the rich and able withdrawing their support from the community when it most needs them.

Of course, all humanity was technically damned, and disease metaphorized that state: Dekker noted, 'For every man within him feedes/A worme which this contagion breedes' (Wilson, p. 85). Clemency was not dependent on appeal, but alone through God's select mercy; though during the plague there seemed little of that, as Barroll indicates: 'plague was God's punishment for sin, and infection, a quaint, unproved theory, was an atheist's pipedream.'[70] Dekker's *Newes from Graves-ende* was an attempt to tease out some of these fraught issues, not least because the City Fathers, some of whom undoubtedly held strong providential beliefs, chose a miasma theory over orthodox religious views when deciding upon theatre closures. According to Gasper, 'in the Reformation era, religion and politics were inseparable, and many, such as Dekker, regarded their separation as not only difficult but undesirable.'[71] But in the late sixteenth and early seventeenth century reconciling the multiple valences of plague, theatre, and politics, proved difficult for both writer and politician. Maintaining a common belief exposed the epistemological and theological contradictions of the City Fathers' decision to close London's theatres for reasons of infection. Such a decision was not only tainted with the 'runawaies' problem (that is, seeking an impossible escape from God's judgement) but it also assumed that the theatre was anti-Christian or anti-God. As Dekker was one of the most conspicuous pro-City and Protestant writers, it was an issue which severely strained his writing.

In the beginning of *Newes from Graves-ende*, Dekker locates therapeutic writing in tense competition with 'Phisicke' as a way to interpret the plague: 'To *Sicknes,* and to *Queazie Tymes,*/We drinke a health in wholesome *Rymes,*/*Phisicke* we invoke thy aide,/Thou (that borne in heaven) art made/A lackey to the meanest creature …' (Wilson, p. 80). A mock-toast, it seems, captures the apparently therapeutic synergy between writing and plague. Theories of disease are invoked in jest only to be damned because they seem too easily manipulated; too shaped and pressured by words, or manufactured by diminished forms of art. The toast, also, lyrically embraces and ribs the conventions of an apocalyptic tradition so evidently bannered in the poem's title. He sharpens the appetite for paradoxical play by promising the impossible: news from 'the end of … *Graves*' (Wilson, p. 73). Dekker expands upon his distrust of

'Physicke' by referring to 'Phisitions' as those who 'learne the abstruse powers' of sucking 'from poysonous stinkinge weede/Preservatives, mans life to feede' (Wilson, p. 80). Physicians were thus deemed rotten with hubris. They pretended to be 'Mens Demi-gods' interfering in the mechanics of God's world; 'for none can work it [the continuation of life] but a God alone' (Wilson, p. 80). With professional irony he later asks those 'Phisitions' to 'Teach us how we may repaire/These Ruines of the rotten Aire' (Wilson, p. 81). For if 'the Aires pollution can/So Mortal strike' then why does one person die and not another (Wilson, p. 81). Failure to answer this question (however similar to God's 'random celestial swatting') becomes a 'Tragick song' (Wilson, p. 81). Such epistemological insecurity meant that physic itself could be called directly into disrepute:

> But (ô griefe) why do we accite
> The charmes of Phisick? whose numbd sprite
> Now quakes, and nothing dare, or can,
> Chekt by a more dread Magitian?
> Sick is Phisicks selfe to see
> Her *Aphorisms* prov'de a mockery
> For while shee's turning o're her bookes,
> And on her drugs and simple lookes
> Shee's run through her owne armed heart,
> (Th'infection flying above Art:)
>
> (Wilson, p. 80)

With tongue-in-cheek metaphors of the plague, Dekker allows disease to infect and finally kill 'Phisick' as the personified figure of science and medicine. Such humour cannot conceal the sense of anxiety which underlies the fact that Dekker, like most Londoners, witnessed the death of every fourth person in the 1603 bout of plague.[72] In apparent confusion, because it was never clear whether seeking medical attention was part of God's plan, Dekker offers grief and fear as emotions which obscured the understanding that 'Phisick' could not make sense of the plague's mystery. Still, the vexed question of a miasma theory as a cause of the plague is brought into discredit. Diagnosis by a 'Phisition' might be considered defiant pride when compared to that 'more dread Magitian', God.

Dekker assiduously spells out the inadequacies of '*Phisick*' to interpret the '*Queazie Tymes*'. He clears the way for a glossary of

'wholesome Rymes' as a preferment of his own peculiar art, enlist-
ing the force of grotesque metaphors to poeticize and dramatize the
plague. A 'thirstie soule' is invited to tap the health-drinking mead
with which the poem opened, and the self-promoting writer offers
a life-confirming elixir when taken as a 'full draught from the
Thespian bowle'. Dekker presents the spiritually hungry, not to
mention the mortally anxious, with its most vital source of nourishment, the theatre. It was a provocative gesture because the London
audience was being denied its 'full draught' by precisely the same
reason which spurred his professional need to turn 'limping Prose
... into more perfectly-halting Verse'; the 'Thespian bowle' was
closed (Wilson, pp. 82 and 79).[73] Plague became the medium which
necessarily shaped his work: 'To work which wonder, we will
write'; and write he does, giving the mechanics of writing a strange
gothic aura of death and dying. 'Penns' are 'puld' from the 'Owle'
('that bird of night'); 'Inck' is drawn from the 'teares of widowes';
'paper' from a 'winding sheete'; and lest we lose sight of dramaturgical metaphors, 'that the scene may shew more full,/The Standish
is a dead mans scull' (Wilson, p. 82). Writing is woven into the
grotesque aesthetics of disease and death via the logistics and
mechanisms of its production. This, he contends, allows him more
readily to diagnose the disease which 'Phisick' has misinterpreted.
Already a cosmic drama, '*The Horror of the Plague*' is played out
before the captive audience of the city: 'Acts full of Ruth' are seen
through 'sad Spectators eyes' (Wilson, p. 96). 'These are the
Tragedies, whose sight/With teares blot all the lynes we write,/The
Stage whereon the Scenes are plaide/Is a whole Kingdome ...', he
writes as each plague-stricken street became a queasy mise en
scène, every death a graphic tragedy (Wilson, p. 96). Closing the
theatres, in his account, truncated the spiritual and aesthetic life of
those who inhabit the city; if the plague was to blame, he feels, we
should know why.

*Newes from Graves-ende* opens with a section subtitled '*The cause of
the Plague*', and here Dekker seems to reaffirm his disproof of the
infection theory; 'Nor drops this venome, from that faire/And
christall bosome of the Aire' (Wilson, p. 82). If the 'Ayre' is so
general, so 'round about' and its 'poyson drop on all' then why
isn't the 'Sore being spread so generall?' he asks rhetorically as he
pointedly finishes 'Nor dare we so conclude' (Wilson, p. 83). He
states that to be 'sure there lyse/Some vengeance more than in
the skies' (Wilson, pp. 83–4). If 'Aire' is not vengeful, and can be

discounted, then we are invited to turn our attention to the conventions of a punitive God: 'That God in anger fills his hand/With Vengeance, throwing it in the land;/Sure tis some Capitall offence,/Some high, high Treason doth incense/Th'Eternall King, that thus we are/Arraign'd at Deaths most dreadfull barre ...' (Wilson, p. 86). Dekker invokes the typically stern Protestant God, one paradoxically moved to omnipotent anger because of Man's recalcitrance. According to the poem, part of that recalcitrance stems from the hubris of seeking a cure for the plague when divine judgement had already been made. Sinfield states this Calvinistic standard, '[that] no man can be thoroughly humbled until he knows that his salvation is utterly beyond his own powers, devices, endeavours, will, and works, and depends entirely on the choice, will, and work of another, namely, God alone.'[74] God knew and preordained the fate of every single human 'before the foundation of the world were laid' according to the official policy of article 17 of the Thirty-nine Articles of the Elizabethan Church in 1562. Though not openly denying predestination – although in his account the somewhat testy 'Eternall King' appeared to have a disconcertingly spontaneous, rather than predetermined, temper – Dekker chose to side-step the issue. Instead he offers an apparently more straightforward explanation. When he invokes the term 'Capitall offence', he indicates both the effrontery of certain types of City behaviour and its appropriate (capital) punishment, death (Wilson, p. 87). 'City-sin' was presented as the prima-facie case of treason against God. But who and what was being held accountable? 'The Courtiers pride, lust, and excesse,/The Church-mans painted holinesse;/The Lawyers grinding of the poore,/The Souldiers starving at the doore,/Ragd, leane, and pale through want of blood,/Sold cheape by him for Countries good' (Wilson, p. 86). God's anger, it seems, had very socially specific targets. Dekker charges the better-off with social negligence and moral failure. Once again neglect of those less well-off who had served their country, the soldiers, stands for something rotten in the state.

Aside from these acute jibes of social vengeance, Dekker ostensibly sought a valid claim for the determination and purpose of the plague. In so doing he exposed the narrow-minded doctrine which saw plays 'forbidden because of the plague'; a policy propagated by preachers like Thomas White who, with reductive a priori logic, argued that 'the cause of plagues is sin ... and the cause of sin are plays: therefore the cause of plagues are plays'.[75] Dekker interprets this argument as one rooted in ignorance and religious dogma. Why, he wonders, does each day see the plague 'act in more new Tragedies', killing some and not others? '... from whence/Comes this? youle say from *Providence*./Tis so, and that's the common Spell,/That leades our Ignorance, (blinde as hell)/And serves but as an excuse, to keepe/The soule from search of things more deepe ...' (Wilson, p. 85). The more Dekker delves into the cause of the plague, the more doubt he uncovers on the doctrine of predestination.[76] He seems to intimate a more flexible, humanistic, and sensitive, interpretation of the 'everlasting purpose of God'.[77] While appearing to accept the logic of providence, his tone suggests that it should not become a dogmatic version of the superstition which it was ostensibly designed to replace. He also appears to suggest that the universalizing thrust of providence, as a 'common Spell', functions as a form of false consciousness, a form of self-deception which bars the way to a greater understanding of God's purpose. He suggests that the plague is a cosmic drama from which man must seek to learn the meaning of God's sentencing. Dekker wavers between the rigid conventions of predestinarianism and a rhetoric which implies volition and flexibility on behalf of both Man and God. God's punishment could be selective and rational: 'Cease vexing heaven, and cease to die' (Wilson, p. 102). Other theories which were 'Against heavens everlasting King' were considered acts of desperation (Wilson, p. 100). But what was it that he felt was deeper than the 'common Spell', and where was the path from myopic 'Ignorance' to be found? Elsewhere Dekker had written that 'Much labour, Art, and Wit, make up a Play', and it was these qualities which could be aligned against ignorance, and crucially not against God but rather on his behalf.[78]

Although his writing follows the traditional Christian view that mankind had fallen, Dekker seems less certain that redemption was forever beyond the scope of human agency. This was not necessarily as heretical as it sounds, for the Reformed Church (that with which his militant Protestantism was linked) was riven with theological inconsistencies, and the question of redemption was one of them.[79] For Dekker, London functioned as the imaginative instrument through which humanity and God could bridge the 'vast and uncertain gulf between them.'[80] London – '*Europs* Iewell; *Englands* Iem:/Sister to great *Ierusalem*'; this 'Altar of *Ioue*', this 'throne of Kings', this 'Fownt, where milke and hony springs ... bout whose wast/The Thames is like a girdle cast' – was, for him, a privileged space worthy of God's redemption and grace (Wilson, p. 89). Only one thing stood in the way, a clean bill of health: 'Thou that (but health) canst nothing want,/Empresse of Cities, *Troynovant*' (Wilson, pp. 89–90). Plague enabled London to be 'A Nation new, and purified' (Wilson, p. 88). Disease was an instrument of social purification: 'plague's the Purge to cleanse a Cittie' (Wilson, p. 102). According to *Newes from Graves-ende*, plague was the 'medicine for a ryotous land', and could transform the 'bankrout bosome of our Realme/Which naked birthes did overwhelme', as it operated like a Malthusian-style wand, culling the excesses of city society (Wilson, p. 103). Those that 'from th'infected citie fly' renounced their moral rights and Christian duty, while those who grasped at 'bold fantastick Empiricks' and 'Phisickes crummes' should stop vexing heaven (Wilson, p. 102). Although Dekker may have been imitating the abusive or masochistic language of London's Puritans, social vengeance only partly explains what is going on here. The writer was seeking a covenant made 'Immortall by our prophecing pen' that mankind and 'heaven is friends againe' (Wilson, p. 103). In terms of Dekker's populist stance, these last words of *Newes from Graves-ende* are highly significant. They implicitly criticize the conception of an excessively remote and austere Calvinistic God, and make a call for more harmony between heaven and the city. They also suggest a détente with heaven, one which would stop 'This civill warre of Pestilence' (Wilson, p. 101). Dekker was definitely not seeking to invoke a Catholic-style, pre-Reformation version of 'co-operation between God and humanity'.[81] But his writing continually hints at the possible reconciliation of divine sovereignty with human freedom. Even a 'whore', for example, that overemployed reprobative paradigm, could become 'honest' in Dekker's investigative dramas. Although a Dutch heritage may account for Dekker's proto-Arminianism, his most significant influence was his London audience, who were also beginning to question the stark tenets of Calvinism. Yet, while acknowledging the pressures of social forces, he held firm to the idea that the individual was to be held accountable for the health of the community, the new Jerusalem: 'And that's the Soule: each one purge one,/And *Englands* free, the plague is gone' (Wilson, p. 102).

Theatre was called upon to speak for all kinds of loss, not least of which was mankind's loss of God and its way in the world. In his section 'The *Horror of the Plague*' drama becomes an extended metaphor for a lost Eden and a way to find the new Troy. Symbols of an Edenic-pastoral are depicted as withering and dying as his 'Countrie' does a disappearing act (Wilson, p. 89). This destruction was due to anti-theatrical sentiments: 'Her Revells and her May-meriments,/Turned all to Tragick dreeryments' (Wilson, p. 89). In both nostalgic and populist mood, Dekker indulges in a rare moment of *melancholic* irony. Sinfield has shown how tragedians were engaged in the 'rigours and limitations' of the paradoxes of Reformation Christian dogma.[82] For the most part Dekker eschewed the aristocratic crises of dislocation which characterized Grand Tragedy, preferring to deploy the genre further down the social scale and within the domestic sphere.

Nevertheless, he still drew upon the culturally residual forces in which tragedy was rooted. 'Tragick dreeryments' encoded social and divine dislocation; and lost 'Revells' and 'May-meriments' were dramatic forms which evoke times of festivity and harmony. Dekker was trying to censure those who have argued and legislated against folk drama and festivals without invoking and privileging the aristocracy who supported them. Again Dekker calls for the theatres to remain open; they must not be allowed to become dark and cheerless places. In this call to 'Revells' he not only makes an allusion to the traditions of entertainment from which London theatre developed, but he also tacitly asks Edmund Tylney (the contemporary Master of the Revels, who had a considerable degree of control over the theatre at this time) to allow the theatre what he considered was its rightful social space. More directly Dekker appealed to the city's authorities, in particular the City Fathers, who issued many ordinances to close the theatres because they saw them as a source of social disorder. To those who subscribed to infection theory, or theories of physic, he attempted to reveal the irrationality of their argument and the concomitant rationality of God's purpose. To those renowned for their anti-theatrical views, he indicated the instructive use which God had made of a cosmic drama like the plague. Drama was presented as the chief didactic instrument through which the city might learn to inherit its moral purpose and rightful place. About the same time as Dekker was writing *Newes from Graves-ende*, his fellow writer-actor, Thomas Heywood was also extolling the moral and social value of theatre in *An Apology for Actors*:

To proceed to the matter: First, playing is an ornament to the Citty, which strangers of all Nations, repairing hither, report of in their own Countries, beholding them here with some admiration: for what variety of entertainment can there be in any Citty of Christendome, more then in *London*?[83]

Heywood's rhetoric plays upon the national and metropolitan chauvinism of the Puritan City fathers who might like to see London as the premier 'Citty of Christendome'. But this was only possible if they perceived and endorsed playing as a proper Christian (Protestant) activity.[84] Following Heywood, Dekker argues that dramatic writing could lead the 'soule' away from the myopia of 'Ignorance' towards the kingdom of heaven with London as the City of God.

Dekker's challenge to those who held fantasies of purity was a crafty one: he harnessed the repressed sense of pleasure which structured their rejection of drama. In turn, this sensibility led them to close the theatres due to so-called 'problems of disorder'. Plague provided the ideal excuse for such a shutting-up because it was made to conflate ideas about disease, disorder, unseriousness, corruption and, perhaps worst of all, social commingling of all kinds. Dekker's writing reveals the latent gratification which attends the deployment of disease as punishment, and as social and moral cleansing. Taking, for example, a common target like 'the rich Glutton', one whose religious conviction is doubtful ('a goblet is his Saint'), even pagan ('For none's his God but *Bacchus*'), Dekker subjects him to the punitive apparatus of the plague as a rightful form of divine discipline (Wilson, p. 98). Punishment is grotesque:

> When he shall wake from wine, and view
> More then Tavern-tokens, new
> Stampt upon his brest and armes,
> In horrid throngs, and purple swarmes,
> Then will he loath his former shapes,
> When he shall see blew markes mock grapes,
> And hang in clusters on each veine,
> Like to wine-bubbles, or the graine
> Of staggering sinne, which now appeares
> In the December of his yeares …

(Wilson, p. 98)

Through staging textual hyperbole, and the dramatization of the gluttonous body, plague symptoms become a bizarre source of

delight as well as a theatre of punishment. Anyone who takes pleasure in this moral penalty for gluttony could not but help being implicated in the ludicrous spectacle. Punishers are co-opted as
spectators; and discipline becomes a grotesque ravishment. By
making each bubo, each token, each blemish, part of the dramatic,
rhetorical, performance Dekker sneaks behind anti-theatrical sensibilities. While condemning intemperance, each line celebrates
another 'full draught from the *Thespian* bowle'. In precise terms, the
body is being grotesquely celebrated for that which it is ostensibly
chastised. In spite of this conceit, Dekker combined his need for the
theatres to remain open with an elaborate display of the moral
value of writing. His vision of the social role of the writer included
writing against what he thought was 'Ignorance'. Even the genuine
terror of the plague he dressed up in dramatic form through
'wanton habits, riotous fashions/And all these Anticks drest in
hell,/To dance about the passing bell' (Wilson, p. 100). For him, the
plague bell signaled a kind of macabre and literary revelry.[85]
Dekker's latent argument with Puritan ideology is contradictory
and complex. Undoubtedly he was highly critical of their platform
of anti-theatricality even as he championed (often on the very stage
they condemned) the realm which they inhabited, the city.

## IV THE DIVELL'S IN IT

In different forms, offering the 'Divell in Print' was variously
popular during the early modern period. *Dr Faustus* had been a big
hit in the early 1590s, and continued to be played off and on
throughout the Elizabethan period.[86] In many ways Dekker's devils
in the Hell pamphlets owe a lot to Marlowe's pointed exposure of
Calvinistic beliefs, but with the advent of Jacobean city comedy it
was considered somewhat 'out a fashion to bring a Divell upon the
Stage' (Grosart, vol. II, p. 95). When Dekker eschewed his own
advice, a different kind of Devil from Marlowe's instrument of
terror emerged in *If It Be Not Good The Divel Is In It* (alternatively
titled *If This be not a Good Play, the Divell is in It*). The Devil now appeared to be more intimate, more familiar, more recognizable, but
what, we should ask, was at stake in this change of form?

*If This be not a Good Play* was closely connected to the Hell's-broke-
loose theme of Dekker's earlier pamphlets. As a parody of London's
commercial world, the play opens in Hell, where we witness a dis-

gruntled discussion by its inmates about an ongoing recession there. Hell's legendary ferryman, Charon, who in the pamphlets always needed repairs to his boat, is depicted as 'olde, craz'd, Stiffe, and lam'de'; and business is not what it used to be (*If This be Not a Good Play*, I.i.29). Not only does he demand more money for his service; he also complains about the diminishing quality of the souls he carries. Pluto, too, is concerned about the lazy devils in Hell who are failing to attract new clients. The reason for this lamentable state of affairs is made apparent in the observation that 'above us dwell/Divells braver and more subtill then in Hell' (I.i.75–6). To rectify this dilapidation of Hell three devils are sent to the City to play various roles, 'to tempt churles hither' (I.i.89).[87] 'Rufman' is told to 'take instantly a Courtiers shape'; 'Shackle-soule' dons 'A Friers grave habit'; and 'Grumball' is to walk 'In trebble-ruffes like a Merchant' (I.i.78–82). So, in order 'T'uphold Hells Kingdome' these three take on the more solid aspects of London's primary world. Put simply, then, the play's theme revolves around three sectors of the metropolitan establishment, in three sub-plot frames, who tangle with the beguiling forces of the Devil. According to Hunt, this scenario produces 'an almost pitiless indictment of the court, the church, and the world of money dealers, a play in which but one wrongdoer is allowed to repent, the rest perishing body and soul.'[88] With its various expositions of vice, malpractice in privileged positions of power, and ensuing retribution, it appears to be a conventionally updated morality tale made topical for a Jacobean audience. The play's targets are fairly familiar even if the space of their exposure, the decidedly theatrical conjunction of London and Hell, was offered anew to excite the audience. Yet a sense of fragmentation within the consistency and purpose of Hell has concerned many of the play's readers. With no small degree of literary and historical irony, scholarly criticism has tended to endorse the play's title. What has been perceived by critics as dramatic disjunction has led them, strangely echoing the managers of the Fortune, to dub the play a 'failure'.[89] Leaving aside what might constitute such a conclusion, it is remarkable that the issue around which critical conjecture operates appears to be the role of the devils. Larry Champion's remarks on the play are typical:

> The opening scene, then, establishes a perspective which the later actions contradicts ... the theme of human pawns caught in the web of devilish power is itself never developed; just when it

becomes obvious that the devils can indeed manipulate humans to their own advantage, that theme, too, disappears. The devils, more precisely, actively participate in the opening scenes ... By the middle of the play, however, their role has become entirely passive. The devils, in other words, do little more than initiate the complications in the three plot strands; human ingenuity, though ultimately no match for Hell, is sufficient to create chaos on earth.[90]

Inconsistencies and contradictions of the devils' roles marks the dysfunction of human agency and contributes to an insecurity of moral purpose, all of which becomes a reflection of a flawed dramatic integrity. Champion continues:

> The consequences of this fragmentation is that the play hovers between didactic morality and realistic intrigue, provoking fundamental confusion for the spectator – and for the critic – who variously perceives the plot satiric ... lighthearted intrigue ... dark or problematic, tragicomic, or even tragic.[91]

Although Champion picks up the complex shifts in diabolic functions which occur throughout the play, his analysis – that 'such a failure of perspective by a practiced professional playwright is the result of hasty revision required by Queen Anne's men' – falls far short of explaining the play's dramatic uncertainty.[92] The 'fundamental confusion' which arises through the play is not due to the playwright's failure but develops from the play's proximity to the theological and cultural faultlines which are stressed during the staging of Hell. Early Jacobean Protestantism was, after all, 'a belief in contradictories'.[93] Hell, and its theatre, was an interstitial space where those contradictories could be worked out. To read or assume otherwise means that the play sought to present a single, certain, voice or vision – one which attempted to gloss the points of contradiction and disjunction and failed. By hovering between 'didactic morality and realistic intrigue', the play documents a multiplicity of voices and perceptions which the conventional iconography of Hell strained to avoid.

Early modern representations of Hell were variously pressured by conflict between residual, dominant, and emergent, theological and ideological structures which developed out of the Reformation.[94] Not least of which, as we have seen, was rhetorical deployment of

Hell as an instrument for setting up institutions and maintaining certain types of authority, often through a state of terror. Yet, as Howard Dobin remarks, that particular voice of authority was profoundly fraught:

> Protestant politics created a schism between corporate authority and individual spiritual authority ... the internal contradiction was far more insidious. The self-contradiction of the English Reformation rested on the fact that this new order, itself created by voices of prophetic dissent against bankrupt and centralized authority, had to suppress all prophetic challenges to its own legitimacy. As prophetic opposition succeeds, it must deny its own antiauthoritarian impulses in order to adopt the priestly functions of containment and control. The forces that derived their legitimacy from their prophetic resistance to corporate authority had themselves become the institutional embodiment of that authority.[95]

Militant Protestants, and those like Dekker who sympathized with them, continually wrestled with this contradiction. Throughout his prophetic or anti-prophetic Hell pamphlets, Dekker's writing operated in the vast, conflictual, and ever-changing, space between bankrupt and legitimized authority. When negotiating pressures of patronage, censorship, and public opinion, the different voices of authority in Dekker's work often oscillated. This vocal ambiguity, most noticeable when encrusted with his [in]famous spirit of optimism, contributed to his reputation as one of the most irregular writers of the period. Yet it was as much a strategy of writerly self-protection as it was of perplexed dramatic obfuscation. By restaging some of the valences which ratified the Reformation it was possible to explore problems in the present while still, ostensibly, legitimizing the past. Broadly speaking, this meant validating the protesting voice as a way of erasing the contemporaneous schisms in authority and the contradictions of moral posturing. Dekker attempts this is in *If This be not a Good Play*. His Octavio unambiguously occupies a position of moral integrity and appears as a lone voice ever talking against corruption and the bankruptcy of centralized authority. According to Gasper, 'he is criticizing a whole system in which monarch, noblemen, and money-merchants all participate'.[96] Though Octavio functioned prophetically and 'essentially as the Good Angel', he also paradoxically put 'forward the doctrine of the divine right of kings'.[97] This obfuscates the voice of any radically dissentient Puritanism, potentially critical of the king, while providing a continuous critique of the abuses and corruption endemic to the crown-court system; as Octavio says, 'Woe to those dayes,/When to raise Upstarts, the poore CHURCH decayes' (III.iii.122–3). Invoking the dissidence of the past he effectively legitimizes the *status quo* of the present, even though the Church which he defends was precisely a product of Reform. For Gasper, *If This be not a Good Play* was sufficiently critical of established power that the extensive prologue and epilogue were written to 'make the play more politically acceptable' and serve to endorse the play's contradictory structure.[98] Although 'the King and his policies have been criticized throughout the play', Gasper argues, 'in the epilogue we see the devils tormenting Guy Fawkes and *Ravillac*, along with Bartervile and a "Puritane"' (all enemies of monarchy, one way or another) and, further, the 'epilogue was surely appended to the play in order to provide a safe and loyal (though rowdy) conclusion.'[99] Given the huge sense of rhetorical irony contained in the epilogue and prologue, they seem less obsequiously linked to the political establishment, as Gasper means it, than they were to the capricious demands of the theatrical establishment. For a hard-pressed writer like Dekker, political acceptability had many faces. The sop to the ruling class was, as Gasper indicates, the lampooning of a rag-bag of royal and high-church demons, and the denigration of Puritans. Staging the eternal punishment of regicidal bogey-men appeared to offer an easy palliative to those in authority, though just how 'safe and loyal' was the effect of their depiction in Hell is difficult to say. Like Dekker's other plays which have similarly boisterous conclusions, rowdiness had a habit of escaping the very hand which was trying to quell or grasp it.

Before analysing the meaning of that rowdiness, we need to explore further the topography of post-Reformation Hell, and the devils who inhabited it. In crystallizing Hell as the exclusive condition of everlasting torment, Calvinistic theology sought to assume control of various Reformation economies. In doing so it sought to relegate its ideological challenger, Purgatory, to a realm of superstition. In the theologically fraught 1590s there appeared a controversial pamphlet, before either Nashe's *Supplication* or Dekker's work, comically entitled *Tarlton's Newes Out Of Purgatorie* (London, 1590), which directly addressed the marginalization of Purgatory. Its prophetic voice took on the mockery of Purgatory:

and as soone as I heare the principles of your religion. I can say,
oh there is a Calvinist: what doe you make heaven and Hell
*Contraria immediata*, so contrarie, that there is no meane betwixt
them, but that either a mans soule must in post hast goe
presently to God, or else with a whirlewind and a vengeance goe
to the divell? yes, yes my good brother, there is *Quoddam tertium*
a third place that all our great grandmothers have talkt of, that
Dant hath so learnedly writ of, and that is Purgatorie. What syr
are we wiser then all our forefathers? and they not onely feared
that place in life, but found it after death: or els was there much
land and annuall pensions given in vaine to morrowmasse
priests for dirges, trentals and such like decretals of devotion,
whereby the soules in Purgatorie were sooner advanced into the
quiet estate of heaven. Nay more, how many Popes and holy
Bishops of Rome, whose cannons cannot erre, have taught us
what this Purgatorie is? ... and if anie upstart Protestant denie ...
I could not but smile at the mad merrie doctrine of my friend
*Richard*.[100]

Though the Catholic Church is the overt target of *Tarlton's Newes*,
it really opens a window on Protestant beliefs and anxieties. It attempts to restructure cultural memory, and to absorb and re-
evaluate social tradition. The narrator appears reluctant to defame
his ancestors, many of whom are almost within living memory; nor
does he wish to slur past figures of learning and authority, like
Dante. Discrediting Purgatory is its main point of focus, because it
was around this concept that a vast Catholic clerical and ideological
apparatus had developed. The worldly petitioning for souls, according to the writer, underscored the whole corrupt priestly
edifice. Mocking tradition is carefully confined to denigrating
Catholic practices rather than its secular practitioners: it was a be-
smirchment of the shepherd, not the flock. The voice of prophecy is
given the task of eradicating any third space in the hereafter. Only a
binary belief system could have the theological vigour, psychological impact, rhetorical force, and cultural dynamism, to be able to
reinterpret religious belief and simultaneously degrade its powerful predecessor. Purgatory was tarnished with irrationality and attacked as a realm of ignorance and superstition. Many Protestants,
including Dekker, found it easier to satirize Catholicism rather than
attempt the more difficult task of presenting an uncontradictory
and coherent version of Protestanism. The tradition of mockery,

manifest in the figure of the charismatic folk-hero Richard Tarlton, is invoked to perform its, or his, own self-mockery. Ironically, Tarlton appears to emanate from Purgatory, a place now deemed to be non-existent.

After the Reformation, the panoply of terror which had hitherto been so vividly ensconced in Purgatory was refashioned into harsher images of *everlasting* torment. Because the ideological capture of Hell was crucial to the principles of Calvinistic theology, its representation had to be less symbolically and topographically located, and more permanently emplaced as an exclusive world of irrevocable misery. '*Quoddam tertium*', that 'third place', had to be devalued while the heat was being turned up in Hell! This was achieved by shrinking the palpable realms of good and evil, with 'no meane betwixte them', and siting their universal battle within the individual soul. Upon defeat or victory the soul was either utterly vanquished, and therefore terminally excluded, or absolute bliss was attained. Apocalyptic discourse reinforced these concepts by attempting to eliminate any theological grey areas concerning the topography of the afterlife. Installing such sharp lines of demarcation within people's minds produced an incredible amount of personal stress. For many Protestants there appeared to be no theological alternative if the Catholic belief system, which potentially offered grace for all, was to be nullified. Only an absolutely rigid exclusionary system would be capable of overthrowing the attractions of Catholicism and the various props offered by superstition. Hell simultaneously narrowed its symbolic focus and expanded its reach and purpose. At the level of overarching magnificence, mighty Satan, the 'Devil', the '*Grand Sophy of the Whore of Babylon*', the anti-Christ, could represent the ultimate source of Catholic power; on another more mundane level, all kinds of devils could embody everyday superstitions and the manifestations of epistemological doubt, as well as the dark shadows of cosmological power. In their representation of the Devil and devils, Calvinists consolidated their attempt to monopolize the theological word. Hell symbolized exclusion from God, rather than being a realm where the protracted rehabilitation of souls took place. In the afterlife, the Devil's activities were effectively undermined as his role became reduced to one who merely chastised the soul to the measure of its crimes. This often left the Devil in an ironic position. Having ascribed to him either immense oppositional power, as anti-Christ, or endowed him with the trappings of pagan magic, it then became possible, and necessary, to orchestrate his downfall, elimination, or repression. Pamphlets charting this decline were common in the latter sixteenth century and were, as Payne Collier argues, 'a virulent attack upon the Roman Catholics in an early stage of the Reformation'.[101] *The Wyll of the Devyll, And Last Testament* was, for example, a mock-legal will which bequeathed the nefarious and immoral goods and services formerly held by the Devil to those who, already it seems, now hold them (usurers got all the money, doubtful vintners acquired the rotten wines, and so on). In this mockery, the temporal world had become the world of the Devil. Aside from the conventions of social satire and the savage attacks upon the putative trappings and power of the Catholic Church, *The Wyll* creates an image of Christ the Protestant dissenter, one who has 'a stubburne, styffe, rebellious hert ... to withstand and resist', as he is placed alongside the imagined death of the foe he is resisting.[102] The graceless comic tone and rough-hewn irony of *The Wyll* prefigured not only the later more jocular comedies like *If This be not a Good Play* and its successors (such as Jonson's *The Devil is an Ass*), but also contributed to the forces which made the Devil a standing stage-joke upon which those comedies depended.

Middleton's *The Black Book* (1604) also presents the Devil as a cultural repository for the anti-Protestant evils of the world. In bringing 'Hell ... here upon the earth' Middleton's 'Lucifer' is a downgraded version, one who is 'sick in soul' (Bullen, vol. VIII, pp. 8 and 19). It seems that everywhere the Devil was, euphemistically, passing away. *The Black Book* satirizes this demise and purports to include 'The last Will and Testament of Lawrence Lucifer, the old wealthy bachelor of Limbo, alias Dick Devil-barn, the griping farmer of Kent' (Bullen, vol. VIII, p. 33). It was a diabolical mockery which located all the familiar targets now associated with, and ascribed to, the Devil. *Lawrence Lucifer* also stood as a symbol of social decay through an allusion to urban corruption and rural hardship. Although *Lucifer* manages to bequeath to an earthly realm all his other nefarious accoutrements, he could find no appropriate place, person, or heir, for 'Limbo', a kind of Purgatory. Middleton, Dekker, and Jonson all drew upon the legacy of the social demise of the Devil. According to Peter Womack, the Devil, in Jonson's *The Devil is an Ass*, comes across as 'the despondent owner of a declining family business'.[103] Similarly, Dekker's *If This be not a Good Play* opens with an argument among the devils over the decline of their

diabolical enterprises as Hell resonated with a feeling of deterioration and dilapidation. The Devil's imaginative and theatrical
appearence on the streets of London corresponded with a decline
in his symbolic status.

At the heart of *If This be not a Good Play*, central to its 'didactic
morality', is an openly comical display of dramatic form. In each of
the play's three sub-dramas an actor plays a devil who in turn
adopts a well-known social role to discover the workings of vice in
the city. Such a ploy stylizes theatricality and offers a multiplicity
of voices and lines of communication. At the moment when the
drama appears to conflict with the avowed intentions of the author
it fulfils the promise held in the title. If the task of Reformation
theology was to repress and instrumentalize the imagination, to
monopolize through the image of Hell, then the play remobilizes
the fetters of the imaginative process by using the very images
which conceptualization of Hell had forced into existence.
Calvinistic authority needed to reduce the symbolic force of Hell's
images into a single, monotheistic meaning, to make it immediately
and simply allegorical. Dekker's play sought to release Hell from
any one-dimensionality so 'that house of divels' becomes the stage
device by which 'to set forth our Revels' (*If This be Not a Good Play*,
V.iii.129–30). In a literal rendition of hellish 'Torments in-utterable'
and 'Terrors incomprehensible', the play's last scene physically
stages the machinery and technology of Hell (V.iv.2–3).[104] Hands
are burned off, molten gold is poured down a sinner's throat, and
all manner of deprivations, stabbings, tauntings and tortures are
put on display. These were the spectacular mechanisms of the now
familiar disciplinary apparatus which seems to haunt the period,
and the means by which the terrified subject was meant to be held
enthralled. To some extent, though, such a dramatic moment
would require the physical and symbolic to be held in suspension.
Difficult to achieve with certainty anytime, this tension was particularly unstable in the deliberately grotesque and farcical scene set
by the play. Theatrical spectacle could dislodge as readily as it
transfixed the apparatus of terror: demonic spirits might be farci-
cally exorcised as much as they are frighteningly installed. The
elaborate mechanisms of the theatre – stage-props, trapdoors, cos-
tumes, fire, and so on – conspired against setting a sober frame of
subjection. As the devils leap 'in great joy' and laugh their 'ha ha
ha's' many times throughout the scene, it is difficult to imagine the
audience always being caught on the other, serious, side of this

laughter. Could the subject laugh and be terrorized at the same moment? In laughing at or with the devils, and Hell's horrible bogey men with their theatrical tortures, the audience were inevitably laughing at themselves as potential reprobates; or that part of themselves in which the spirit of reprobation was instilled. Such laughter was a direct slap, or rather custard-pie, in the face of theological coercion. Just as the many who paid to see the spectacle of the mad being mad in Bedlam, what the audiences of Dekker's Hell saw were parodic images of themselves flouting the forces which made them feel helpless. In the play's Hell we encounter the soul of Guy Faulx; a figure apparently born to be displayed as a public enemy. He cries out that he is mad (angry and unstable) only to be met with peals of maniacal laughter from all those around him. Although this scene borrows from official attitudes and popular anti-Catholic sentiments, it seems unclear at a structural level just how effectively this kind of theatre could operate in the service of authority.

A number of cultural bogey men – 'Ravillac', 'Guy Fawkes', 'A Prodigal', and 'A Puritan' – were put on stage by Dekker so that they could be seen encountering their impending punishment. Located in Hell for anti-state activities, *Ravillac* and Guy Fawkes immediately show their defiance: 'I am *Ravillac*, that laughs at tortures, spurnes at death, defies all mercy: Jybbets, racks, fires, pincers, scalding oyle, wilde-horses, I spit in the face of all' (V.iv.151–3). We witness the drama of an unrepentant will as it confronts its theological match, the terror of Hell. Like Faustus' ambition, *Ravillac*'s autonomy appears futile; yet he still bears that heroic dissident quality even, and especially, when facing torture. *Ravillac* belligerently grabs an illicit sense of immortality through his own bravado and action: 'Fames tonges shall thunder out *Ravillacs* name, extoll it, eternise it, Chronicle it! Canonise it!'; a sentiment which his presence in the play endorses (V.iv.155–7). His hubristic self-publication complicates the idea that Hell enforced abjection as he instates his own eternal fame. Like many of the stage's tragic hero-villains, Guy Fawkes, too, appears magnificently wicked as he starts out on the road to infamy. We see him as a brazen and powerful desperado, one whose actions so nearly brought a 'realme' to 'doomesday' (V.iv.198). Though he too is finally, and defiantly, seen to be punished in Hell, we seem to remember his attempt more than we celebrate his failure. Even today, Guy Fawkes is the one remembered on 5 November, rather than parliament or James I.[105]

If *Ravillac* and Fawkes invoke the secret thrills of a condemna-
tory admiration, then Dekker's other hellish protagonist, the
Prodigall, appears designed to elicit both sympathy and compassion. These qualities would have been inappropriate if we consider Hell as an absolutely unredemptive medium of discipline.
Nevertheless, it falls to the Prodigall to ask one of the fundamental
questions of divine justice, manifest in the context and purpose of
Hell, and address it to a seemingly merciless God: 'Why for a few
sinnes that are long ere past,/Must I feele torments ever last?/Ever,
ever.' (V.iv.25–7). 'Ever', 'ever', 'ever'; he plaintively saturates his
eternal indictment with a sense of infinite and unassailable injustice. Dekker's Prodigall uncovers one of the cornerstones of contemporary Christian structures of belief: what justified eternal
damnation? A vexing question for many, it was one which Dekker
was to ask of and for himself. In the play, Dekker contrives to get
that question asked in the very place designed to suppress noncon-
formism and contain dissent. Underlining this paradox, the
Prodigall's interrogation precipitates a (theo)logical impossibility,
a *debate* in Hell. Unveiling yet another vexing question at the heart
of Christian belief *Ravillac* responds by asking 'Why is the
divell,/(If man be borne good) suffred to make him evill?'
(V.iv.29–30). Far from quelling doubt, Hell appears as the place
where one irritating theological problem is piled on to another.
With prudence Dekker distanced himself from charges of heresy by
placing discontent, and awkward questions, firmly in the mouths
of doubters already damned. Yet such unanswered questions, just
through being asked, inevitably qualified certain views of the
wisdom and purpose of divine authority.

Next on stage came the devils who carried with them the problematic of whether they work on behalf of that divine authority or
in antithesis to it, and whether they still encoded elements of superstition and Catholicism? Full of unbridled and unholy joy, Dekker's
devils appear as deeply comic or unserious figures, grotesque
beings or demented clowns who continuously laughed and cackled
as they went about their business. In Hell, it seems, perverse pleasure is licensed in order to uphold authority. Sounding like a cross
between Zeal-of-the-land-Busy and Falstaff, Pluto notes in the last
line of the play that 'Soules are Hells Subjects, and their grones our
mirth' (*If This be Not a Good Play*, V.iv.297). Within this world of
groaning mirth and hellish revels appeared an overwhelming
threat to Pluto's 'Empyre'. It was not some awesome theological
caveat or sanction but something deemed far more powerful, a

figure of anti-pleasure, a figure of discipline, an 'Arch-great Puritane' (V.iv.266). Pluto realizes all this the moment the 'Puritan' appears at the gates of Hell with a strident insistence to be admitted. Making a political disturbance (perhaps invoking Puritan claims at Hampton Court), the Puritane arrived with, as the stage directions indicate, '*A confused noyse to come pressing in*'. Once in, he spouts the same kind of brimstone-laden rhetoric which condemned so many to the place where he now stands. With a good measure of irony he claims that 'Tis a burning zeale must consume the wicked, and therefore/I will not be kept out, but will chastise and correct the foule/Fiend' (V.iv.262–4). Due to the stereotypical hypocrisy associated with Puritans – that 'All the brethren and sisters [are] crooked' – he finds himself in Hell (V iv.279). And because of their militant activities, designed to purify the main body of the Church, the Puritan admits the error of this challenge; 'I pulld a whole church down upon my back' (V.iv.284). Anarchy appears on the threshold when a whole 'wicked assembly' of Puritans try to gain access to Hell. Voicing their anxiety about this assault, the devils note that 'he will pull all Hell downe too [and] Theile confound our kingdome, If they get but a footing' (V.iv.285–7). That the devils might lose control of Hell to a bunch of Puritans is a delicious farce which embarrasses any claim to theological monopoly. The inflexible and monological voice which defined the terrors of Hell so absolutely appears as its greatest threat, able to bring the punitive proceedings upon which that rhetoric depended to a halt. 'Sessions is deferd', it is universally declared, 'Because of Puritanes, Hell cannot be cleerd' (V.iv.289–90). With considerable cultural irony, not to mention dramatic expedience, the devils decide to expel the Puritan and his brethren from Hell; to 'Thrust him out at Hell gates' into the very state of limbo in which he and they disbelieved so vehemently (V.iv.286).

## V  THEN CRUELTY KNITS A SNARE

*For what else is a prison but the very next doore to hel?*

Thomas Dekker (Grosart, vol. II, p. 340)

Dekker's theatricalized Hell raised problems which are intrinsic to the issue of punishment as a spectacle. As Foucault indicates, audiences who gathered for the punitive public spectacles in the period did not 'simply witness the sufferings of the condemned [but] often heard the victim who had nothing more to lose curse judges, the laws, the government and religion'.[106] Even when ritualized and authorized, as Roger Sales argues, 'each part of this official script was in danger of producing meanings which could subvert the chastening, deterrent effects of the theatre of Hell'.[107] Often at odds with its purpose, 'the great spectacle of punishment ran the risk of being rejected by the very people to whom it was addressed'.[108] This rowdiness and potential unruliness necessitated a move to surveillance as a more effective disciplinary apparatus. According to Sales, the 'main purpose of Foucault's account is to contrast the public spectacle of punishment with a more modern orthodoxy concerning the need to keep criminals under constant surveillance, [but this] polarization between spectacle and surveillance is in danger of underestimating their co-existence in the early modern period.'[109] The function of imprisonment, then, was a complex issue, and one in which Dekker, with appalling irony, became completely entangled.

Dekker's inability to sell *If This be not a Good Play* precipitated his most serious financial crisis which, in turn, led to the writer's debt and his subsequent imprisonment for seven years. With the appropriate dramatic metaphor, Hunt states that this period of incarceration 'began the real tragedy of his life'.[110] Undoubtedly this experience and its associated psycho-sociological effects leaned heavily on Dekker's last, and darkest, vision of Hell, *Dekker his Dreame* (London 1620). Any act of imprisonment inevitably brings into focus latent social relations; particularly those between the state, authority, and the individual. The duration and severity of Dekker's imprisonment for debt was symptomatic of the penal system's inability to cope with the problems created by a burgeoning metropolitan society and its concomitant increase in the operation of paid labour (wages) and the function of credit. As the city expanded and modernized its financial infrastructure, these changes impacted upon a penal system which had changed little since medieval times. Both the bureaucracy of the law and its institution became stressed and overloaded. Dekker's extended incarceration should be considered a *de facto* punishment for debt rather than a judicial sanction. Prison at this time was still a place where technically the subject awaited, rather than received, punishment. Only a royal patent or the complete disbursement of debts could bring a discharge for the hapless prisoner. Dekker's lengthy prison term was due to the untimeliness of his debt, which occurred during a fifteen-year period when James acquiesced to pressure by creditors who insisted on harsh treatment of debtors.[111] Consequently, the king proceeded with a moratorium of any relieving patents following the death of Elizabeth. This royal sanction precipitated much social concern, as this contemporary observer reveals:

> London's jails were filled [with] the Bodies of those persons whose imprisonmente canne noe waie avail their Creditors, but rather is an hinderance to the Satisfaction of their Debts, for that, during the tyme of their Restrainte, they are in no wise able to goe aboute or attende their lawfull Busynes, but must of force consume themselves and little they have miserably in prison.[112]

If the goal of jail was the disbursement of debt then it appeared to be counter-productive for the collection of outstanding money. In its criticism, this commentary glosses the coercive effects which the spectacle of debtors languishing in jail induced. Incarceration was not aimed at financial recuperation but directed towards protecting the existing value of money and underwriting the value of debt itself. While the meaning of trust and bonds were being renegotiated in the new commercial world of interest and credit, with its speculation upon present and future social resources and labour, the 'Bodies of those persons' imprisoned remained more tangible guarantors of the face-value of money and stabilizing the function of debt. Creditors gambled on their chance to obtain the return on their money by denying debtors the ability of conducting their 'lawfull Busynes', in return, through the prisoners' pledge, they acquired greater security for their commodities and interest. Punishment of this kind could not adequately address the real and growing problem which was, as Dekker's case reveals, about an increase in the availability of, and desire for, credit and the diminishing means to pay for it. When combined with the problems of a legal system not designed to deal with large numbers of debtors, these factors overwhelmed and overcrowded London's jails. Debt was one of the city's social problems which was often read in terms of moral uncertainty and religious anxiety. The image of the jailed debtor, with no hope of release, easily encoded ideas about the reprobate with no hope of salvation.

Questions about the nature of trust and guilt were central to the new economies of discipline within the city. As the external constraints of social behaviour like shame withered in the atmosphere

of the impersonal and faceless city, the notion of trust, and how it
could be upheld and determined, became a crucial factor in the development of metropolitan identity. Some kind of customary regulation of the developing business community was becoming
increasingly necessary, and trust appeared as the appropriate pre-
requisite for commercial activity. The need to internalize a disciplinary apparatus became more pressing. Guilt, for example,
appeared to be an especially effective tool for social order in an
atomistic society like early modern London where the citizen was
meant to police himself.[113] Not surprisingly, then, there was considerable public interest in the idea and operation of trust, credit,
and debt. Inflecting the interest of those in society who had and lent
money appeared the popularized figure of the politic bankrupt; a
character who deliberately acquired credit and then 'maliciously'
avoided the subsequent debt. The concept of politic bankruptism
was, in effect, highly politic in that it made the debtor both scape-
goat and target for the growing pains of London's commercial development. In Dekker's revision of an old formula, *The Seven deadly
Sinnes of London*, 'Politick Bankruptisme' appears as the primary sin
for the new times. Though *The Seven deadly Sinnes of London* encompasses a wide range of anxieties in London, its main concern is the
breakdown of bonds of trust which accompanied arrival in the city.
'Lying' is the city's second deadly sin, about which it is said:
'*Oathes* are *Crutches*, upon which *Lyes* ... go' (Grosart, vol. II, p. 34).
If the witness to truth was absent or compromised, this could precipitate lack of probity, deception, and social degradation: 'Little
oathes are able to beare up great lyes: but great Lyes are able to
beate down great *Families*' (Grosart, vol. II, pp. 34–5). He expresses
a deep social concern about what actually backs social and linguistic value, and what now functions as social cement; especially if it
is, as he fears, the protean force of 'Magick Golde'. Language no
longer appeared to be honestly viable: as Feste says so acutely in
*Twelfth Night*, 'words are very rascals, since bonds disgraced them'
(III.i.20–1). Without the metaphysics of grace, words simply could
not be trusted. The smallest misdemeanor or lie was therefore
deemed capable of undermining the whole edifice of truth. Minor
transgressions in faith, trust, and language, were made responsible
for the wider problems in the business and financial worlds and
were punished accordingly, often with a severity which far outweighed the apparent size of the 'crime'.

Against the flow of this reasoning, Dekker asks: 'what ... gives a
whole City the *Lye*?' as he targets the agents of exploitation rather

than their scapegoats (Grosart, vol. II, p. 35). Usurers, brokers, and extortioners, were, for him, culpable because they exploited the interest which accrued on money. In *The Honest Whore, part II*, the moral hero of the play, Orlando, is unequivocally suspicious of interest: 'No, no, no, sir, no; I cannot abide to have money ingender: fye upon this silver Lechery, fye ...', he says in response to Matheo's speculation about acquiring 'ten *percentum, per annum*' (II.i.92–3). Like Feste in *Twelfth Night*, Orlando opines that sexual promiscuity and financial immorality are two sides of the same coin.

Obviously, Dekker was far from being a sophisticated financial economist even though he was an avid critic of the social consequences of shifts in economic policy. Chief among his concerns were those trapped unjustly in jail. In his massive contribution to 'Jacobean Prison Literature', Dekker is often presented as a social conservative, as Shaw explains:

> It is evident that Dekker did not oppose the law, which entitled a creditor to restrain his debtor in jail as security, while and until the latter's estate was liquidated to defray the debt; he only decried the abuse of the law by unreasonably vindictive creditors.[114]

However, Shaw misreads Dekker's position. Creditors, as Dekker saw it, did not so much abuse the law as enforce one which was, or had become in the changed legal and fiscal climate, abusive. He rarely took the authorities head-on, but his writing always offered an image of the system's casualties as a suggestion of its endemic failure. Dekker's compassion is directed towards the community and its responsibilities. For him the law could not be an abstraction removed from its social consequences or effects. Deciding what was reasonable was a matter of social pressures and interests, and that then becomes a measure of the law and society. What if, as Dekker knew all too well, there was no estate to liquidate to pay off any debt? Criticism of the law, most noticeable in the matter of debt, was usually couched in moral terms. For 'Dekker morality is largely a function of money', Pendry determines, 'Virtue is the proper use, and vice the improper use, of money.'[115] Condemnation of the creditor, or the more villainous term 'usurer', focused on the immorality of their greed in pursuing the poor creditor for their own personal gain. In spite of his somewhat anachronistic language, Dekker was attempting to change the way people perceived debt in seventeenth-century London.

In Dekker's topography 'Cruelty', London's seventh sin, was symptomatic of the city's punitive institutions:

There are in London within these buildings, round about touch
her sides, & stand within her reach, *Thirteene strong houses of
sorrow*, where the prisoner hath his heart wasting away sometimes a whole prentiship of yeres in cares. They are most of them
built of Freestone, but none are free within them: cold are their
imbracements: unwholsom is their cheare: dispairful their lodgings: uncomfortable the societies, miserable their inhabitants: O
what a deal of wretchedness can make shift to lye in a little
roome! if those 13. houses were built together, how rich wold
Griefe be, having such large enclosures? Doth crueltie challenge a
freemans roome in the City because of these places? no, the poli-
ticke body of the Republicke wold be infected, if such houses as
these were not maintained, to keep up those that are unsound.
(Grosart, vol. II, pp. 69–70)

We can read here a deep ambivalence about the function of the
penal system and the value of imprisonment. Although drawing
upon Calvinistic rhetoric condemning the reprobate, he invites his
readers' compassion and asks them to share the social responsibility of what the process and burden of imprisonment brings. If the
prisoner is a paradigm of the reprobate, then implicitly humanity
itself is also tragically diminished. Cold and impenetrable walls
stand despairingly between the inmates or 'inhabitants' and social
redemption. 'Cruelty' thus appears as a ruthless force wasting
human and social resources and would therefore be antithetical to
freedom. Advocating a different way of seeing the city, Dekker asks
what kind of community is constituted through such strong houses
of sorrow. Withholding access to certain rights inevitably means
privileging and defining those rights. When Dekker asks if such ir-
redeemable prison treatment challenges a 'freemans roome in the
City', he leaves us wondering whether such cruel treatment is the
price or penalty of freedom. If the cost of protecting the body politic
damages it, then it might not be worth paying: the cure might be
worse than the disease.

Dekker shared a widespread and growing concern that the condition of prison itself imposed undue and unjust hardship upon the
prisoner. During the period in which he produced his so-called
'prison literature' there was a spate of legislation: 'For better order
and government in the several Counters of this City of London, and
more charitable usage of the prisoners'.[116] But such Acts and
Articles mainly addressed the problem of the public's awareness of

the poor treatment of prisoners in the jail; rarely did they effect real reforms. Given the prevalence of plague, disease, starvation, and the considerable 'want and infection' which characterized the experience of a Jacobean prison, life expectancy while in confinement was likely to be very short.[117] It was a deplorable situation, and many Londoners were well aware of the consequences of incarceration.[118] Imprisonment for debt therefore often carried a *de facto* death penalty. This was yet another attribute of Dekker's assessment of 'Crueltie': 'You have another cruelty in keeping men in prison so long, til sicknes & death deale mildely with them ...' (Grosart, vol. II, p. 72). Dekker was not alone in criticizing this practice. In a deliberate conflation of secular and divine legislation 'a draft Bill to Parliament prepared by debtors went so far as to claim that it was an *offence against the law of God*, the law of Nature, Equity, civil law, common law and Christianity to make a man pay for debt with his life.'[119]

Not surprisingly, common references to prison intersected with colloquial language about Hell. Dungeons were called 'limbo' or 'limboes'; prison officers at Newgate were called the 'Black Dog' after Cerberus the mythical gatekeeper of the underworld; and the worse place in prison, the deepest dungeon, was often called the 'hole', or 'hell-hole'. Another popular term was 'Counter Hell', or 'Compter Hell', which referred to debtor's prison. Even the customary, though not technically legal, bribe which had to be paid to crooked jailers for release, 1d, was the same as Charon's infamous one-way fee for ferrying the soul to Hell. In Dekker's expansive rhetoric:

what else is a prison but the very next doore to hel? It is a mans grave, wherein he walkes alive: it is a sea wherein he is alwaies shipwrackt: it is a lodging built out of the world: it is a wildernes where all that wander up and downe grow wilde, and all that come into it are devoured. It is an unsatiable gulfe, a feadomlesse whirlepul, an everlasting scaffold on which men go dayly to execution. It is the cave where horror dwels, it is a bed of terror: no, no, it stands not next doore to hell but it is hell it selfe: for soules lye languishing and cannot dye. The keepers of it are churlish and so are Divills, the officers of it are tormentors, and what are torments? goeth not a man therfore toward hell when hee is leade to Prison? (Grosart, vol. II, pp. 340–1)

This description is full of anguish, anger, and frustration; and the deplorable abuse of prisoners captures the social abuses underwritten by the language of Hell. Such a theatre of punishment is one in which we catch, as Sales says, 'a glimpse of the everlasting torments associated with Hell' complete with the comprehension that 'death offered no release from punishment'.[120] As Dekker put it, 'These transitory, poore Terrestriall terrors,/Serv'd but as Heralds to sound forth Horrors/Of woes Eternall' (Grosart, vol. III, p. 17). God's law and secular law benefited from their imaginative proximity. In terms of their function, however, 'officers' of the state could become synonymous with the devils, perhaps even drawing their power from Satan. Instability of meaning bred concern among the authorities, particularly in relation to the 'scaffold' upon which many went 'dayly to execution'. To alleviate problems of authority and diabolical agency 'it was customary for the condemned person to forgive the executioner for the brutalities he was about to inflict', argues Sales, as 'this was meant to weaken the parallel that could be drawn between his activities and the Devil'.[121] Dekker's descriptions did not elide that connection between 'keepers' and 'Divells'. The purpose of this was not so much to criticize the authorities directly by representing them as being in collusion with Satan, but rather to separate and condemn the diabolical activities of the keepers or jailers sufficiently for those in authority to be embarrassed into taking a more humanely responsible position.

A couple of years after writing *If This be not a Good Play* Dekker faced the very consequences of incarceration which he had so vividly presented in his Hell-prison writings when he was consigned to prison for non-payment of debts. That which he had previously decried as 'a bed of terror' became, 'the bed on which seven years' he 'lay Dreaming' for a large chunk of his adult life (Grosart, vol. III, p. 7). Released from this sentence in 1620 he immediately wrote *Dekker his Dreame* which was, not surprisingly, his most anguished and troubled work on Hell. With its hitherto rare appearance of the author's name, the title exemplifies both his own personal sense of suffering and the significant role which the fear of Hell played in the imagination. It is a deeply personal account in which the author appears at the centre of the narrative. Imprisonment had profound and traumatic consequences upon his physiology: he claimed that his 'Haire turn'd white/More through the Ghastly Objects of this Night,/Then through the Snow of age' (Grosart, vol. III, p. 60). In his *Dreame* Dekker attempts to draw upon an inner language to articulate himself, to use it as a crucial resource in order to reveal, to utter, the 'In-utterable Horrors' he found there. In that attempt he delved into his unconscious; 'More did I behold thus Sleeping, then ever I could before, when my eies were wide open' (Grosart, vol. III, p. 11). He opens the 'Epistle Dedicatorie' to his *Dreame* with the thought that *'Bookes are Pilots in such voyages'* of (self) discovery, of exploring one's psychological interior; *'would mine were but one point of the Compasse'* (Grosart, vol. III, p. 8). Traces of the self-monitoring, self-admonishing, self-guiding, writings of many a seventeenth-century Puritan overshadow his *Dreame*. Written from a Jacobean death row, the 'Booke' is steeped in doctrinal problems and contradictions associated with Calvinistic ideology. Both prison and Hell, it seems, demanded a degree of subjective erasure which renders Dekker's bitter and personal inquiry anomalous. The author openly presents himself as a conformist, as he appears suitably abject before heaven's might. Having tasted enough of paradise to ensure the pain of its loss he 'went to the Star-Chamber of Heaven' before being 'throwne (after all this Happinesse) into a sea Infernall, and forced to swim through Torrents of unquenchable fire' (Grosart, vol. III, pp. 11–12). The majority of mankind could expect no less. Unlike his previous excursions into Hell, *Dekker his Dreame* proclaimed itself to be rigidly orthodox. Any expression of the deep sense of play we saw earlier was eradicated or considerably muted.

It is possible to see *Dekker his Dreame* as the only piece of his writing overwhelmingly sustained by the despair which governs Stachnieswki's principles of 'the persecutory imagination'. For most of the tract the writer lies metaphorically and literally prostrate and contrite before a stern, merciless, Calvinistic God. In this position he writes with 'the weake *Pen* of a silly man' rather than with his previously bold 'conjuring pen' (Grosart, vol. III, p. 16). The images of Hell which had once been full of 'Paper-monsters' had now become too starkly terrifying (Grosart, vol. II, p. 129). Gone are the grotesque allusions and the intrinsic sense of drama, to be replaced by the dour and weighty evidence of Testamental authority.

Now, albeit by the lawes of God we both beleeve, and are bound to acknowledge Him onely to bee supreme Lord and Judge both of Heaven, Earth, and Hell, yet sithence those former figured Names (drawn from Poeticall Invention) carry in them a Morall and Instructive Meaning, they are not altogether to be rejected: and the rather because in Picturing forth so Terrible an Object as the Kingdome of hell, and Tortures of the Damned, I strive to shaddow the Horrors of them, and so set them off with heightening both of Profit and Delectation. (Grosart, vol. III, p. 37)

Gone, too, is the writer who nudged and winked at the audience (even when moralizing) only to be replaced by a finger-wagging proselyte. Along with the Biblical quotes which appear ubiquitously in the margins throughout the text, these stern citations express a single authority, one which cajoles dissentient voice or voices. Even Dekker's imaginative use of classical terms, something in which he had previously revelled, now seem reined in, explicated, truncated, shorn of their textual play. Dekker was symbolically thrashed! Compared to the writer who had previously vaunted his muse, in his *Dreame* he seems soggy and sermonic. Written in parentheses, his 'Poeticall Invention' now appears isolated as he tragically recants his belief in his muse. Through these pages, the majority of the book, we witness the broken spirit of the writer overwhelmed by the effects of seven years in prison.

Although for the most part the iron grip of despair sets the tone, occasionally, in his *Dreame*, descriptions of Hell escape the 'mind forg'd manacles' of simplistic 'Morall and Instructive Meaning'. The playful tormenting devils, though, are mostly absent leaving his *Dreame* Hell bare but for the machinery and technology of terror. Upon this barren landscape Dekker concentrates on the grand theme of judgement. Invoking the court where Dekker was tried, his *Dreame* offers the reader a stark apocalyptic vision; 'To summon the whole world to stand to th' Barre', 'at this Grand Assize', 'The Judge being set, in open Court', 'Eternal Files' are opened and 'Heaven's Lord Chiefe-Justice' passes 'Sentence' (Grosart, vol. II, pp. 17, 24, 25, 27). At the world's end Dekker unleashes the sternest, most distant and vengeful, 'God' he can imagine. In the face of this God, 'Out-casts' were meant to be utterly abject through torment; 'they to dust be grinded ... seeing themselves inforc'd to stand the Doome/They gnash'd their teeth, and curs'd their mothers wombe' (Grosart, vol. III, p. 29). Being human was a terrible curse as judgement and punishment merge at the instant of complete eradication of the subject. Hopelessly frustrated about his intolerable position, Dekker wrote with impotent rage through images of a savage social revenge:

They who on earth were reard (Colossus-high)
Spurn'd Kingdomes, trod on Thrones, and did defie
Omnipotence it self, into base graves
Tombling: prow'd Monarches here tooke place with Slaves
And like to broken statues down were throwne,
Trampled (but in scorne) not look'd upon.
Their cries, nor yellings did the Judge regard,
For all the doores of Mercy up were bard;
Justice and Wrath in wrinkles knit his forehead ...

(Grosart, vol. III, p. 30)

Dekker felt condemned forever by the unheeding judge of an unyielding legal system. As one of those being indefinitely imprisoned, Dekker waited *each and every day* for a royal Patent to free
him while all around him his fellow prisoners died. With ironic
writerly conceit, and some awkward syntax, Dekker puts a helpless poet behind bars in the pun on 'bard'. Much of his *Dreame* was
an exposition of the anguish and helplessness which was faced by
those who could imagine that they 'got to th' Court where Soules
were Sentenced' (Grosart, vol. III, p. 36) and 'who there enter ne're
come forth againe,/Being lock'd-up Ever' (Grosart, vol. III, p. 37).
  Towards the end of the poem there appears a lone dissenting and
questioning voice:

One/Soule, (me thought), boyling in sulphurous flame
Curs'd God, and on his Rigor did exclame;
Rail'd at him for Injustice, and thus Cri'd,
If for my Sin thy Son was Crucified,
Why am I hell'd in Execution
In this Damned Jayle, ever to be Undone?
If Hee layd down his life to set me Cleere
From all my Debts, why am I Dungeon'd Here?
Why for a life no longer then a span,
Am I Everlasting damned Man? ...
Why/then for Sin but of a minutes date
Must I for Ever be a Reprobate?

(Grosart, vol. III, pp. 55–6)

A small spark of the old Dekker fires this outburst as the narrator openly criticizes the Christian tradition of retribution without redemption. Not only does the questioner insist upon the pronoun 'I' when accusing God, but he does so in a place where personal expression was meant to be impossible. As he invokes the founding principles of Christianity, this lone voice asks whether compassion and persecution can rightfully coexist in such a system of justice. As he continues his interrogation, albeit unheard, the speaker's minute sense of autonomy appears to be at odds with the overt meaning of the poem. Basic Calvinistic tenets assumed that comprehending God's will was absolutely beyond the scope and purpose of mankind. Attempting to do so practically and theologically confirmed one as a reprobate. Closed belief system, or effective double-bind, it was around these issues that, later in the seventeenth century, Protestantism was forced to change. According to Hill:

> God's elect were a minority, and the mass of men predestined to eternal damnation ... But in order to encourage their congregations and save them from despair, they had also taught that anyone who seriously worried about his salvation probably already had sparks of divine grace at work in him. It was a short but momentous step – and to Calvinist ministers a monstrous step – to proclaim that all men were equally eligible to receive divine grace.[122]

Much of the underlying appeal of Dekker's work was directed towards taking that step. His reprobates exhibit an aura of injustice rather than their designated role as the rightfully condemned. Ruefully punning on his condition one such condemned man asks of his infernal gaolers 'why am I Hell'd'? In answer he is given the party line which demands complete and unquestioning obedience by 'a Voice (tun'd to an Angels Sound)' (Grosart, vol. III, p. 58). This bitter-sweet voiced angel utterly trashes the reprobates' dissentient spirit: 'What was thy whole life but a Mutinous Warre/'Gainst thy Creator Every Sense did Jarre/From his Obedience' (Grosart, vol. III, pp. 58–9). Every organ, every sense, every act of conscious living was quite simply an affront to God. Although total obedience was mandatory it offered no guarantees, eternal or otherwise. Far from bringing the designated and expected acquiescence, the angel's commands spark a riot in Hell whereby the reprobates' cries finally overcome his dictatorial voice: 'On was he going, but to drowne this Voice/All Hell broke loose, and then were heard no Noyse/But Ululations, Shrikings, Horred Soundings/Of Ratling-Chaynes' (Grosart, vol. III, p. 59). Was that chain-rattling meant to invoke the many instances of prison riots, protests, and revolts, which occurred during this period?[123] Did the ensuing 'Noyse' indicate that the prisoners might be breaking loose or were they being hopelessly recontained? The poem remains ambiguous and more or less ends with this rowdy conclusion. Dekker pushed the Calvinistic doctrine of absolutes to the point where, at least in human terms, the chains had to be rattled. And if the purpose of ideological chains is that they remain hidden, keeping their prisoners quiescent, then it must have been a sound which rattled the authorities.

## VI  CONCLUSION: DEKKER'S WRITING DYSTOPIA

Come, I think hell's a fable.[124]

Dekker was a writer of dystopic prose fiction. Dystopia could simply refer to an ill-place like disease-ridden London; but it could also mean a place of cultural maladjustment, a space where dystopic writing re-perceives the world askew in order to discover the foundations of latent social conflict. Imagining a dystopic world creates an eccentric or opposite dimension, one which casts a shadow on any utopic or idealistic social vision. As Romantic comedy retreated following Elizabeth's decline, many writers reviewed the mechanics of love and sex through the dark side of urbanization. Theatre-goers and book-buyers looked for different forms of writing which addressed the stress and needs of city life. Upon this socio-literary climacteric topical drama like city comedy was borne. With a few exceptions Dekker, unlike his partner Middleton, eschewed the cynical tales of sex, money, and men about town, which became the hallmark of a new style drama, later dubbed Jacobean city comedy. Instead, Dekker turned to writing London's dystopic worlds; the asylum, prison, poverty, the underworld, and, of course, Hell. Albeit with a good deal of camp enthusiasm, he unfolded the sombre social visions through which those locations were constructed, and the way in which they, in turn, inhabited the cultural imagination. Inside his writing of those worlds it is possible to detect two distinctive elements of dystopianism. Though sometimes difficult to tease apart, and often in conflict with one another, the conjunction and interaction of these two strands do much to give Dekker's work its special ambivalent texture and contradictory interpolation of critique and conservatism.

There is a form of dystopianism which is deeply pessimistic because it originates from confrontation with forces apparently beyond any human or social control. Humanity's Fall from a utopic Eden, the very structuring condition of mankind's malcontentment, is a prime exemplar of a fixed social myth. This means, as Frye reminds us, that the world is, and always will be, an ongoing ill-place.[125] Such principles underscored many negative images operating within early modern culture; and which found considerable purchase in the contemporary mind. Reading through these complex structures of feeling Keith Thomas notes that 'at the beginning of the seventeenth century the prevailing orthodoxy in England was profoundly anti-utopian.'[126] It was a mood which charged the feelings of the malcontent, as well as the socially disenfranchised, and gave tragedy a radical edge. Stachniewski's notion of despair, as we have seen, appears to be deeply rooted in the soil of this pessimism. Although many pessimistic dystopia are overshadowed by post-Lapsarian concepts they neither needed to be nor were confined to the notion of a post-Edenic state. Whatever the origins, such dystopia define any way of seeing the world as permanently and ineluctably afflicted. Depicting the world as intrinsically dystopic tends to render any impulse to change futile and inept, especially at a local level. Such forms of dystopianism may be charged with a reactionary aesthetic and non-progressive political practices.

In contrast to these conservatizing forces, there is a second form of dystopianism which operates on a different, though sometimes connected, plane. If a culture's dystopic elements are presented as being determined by social, historical, or human forces then they would not only facilitate change, but insist upon it. If the underlying causes which make society an ill-place are literally revealed, openly scrutinized, then the reader may be encouraged to seek or imagine alternative ideas and actions. If the dark visions of torment are unfolded, disclosed, exposed, and revealed in juxtaposition and conjunction with the source of that discontentment, then progressive spaces may be created and imagined – and, sometimes, located.[127]

Undoubtedly, dystopian fiction charted the fragmentation of residual feudal structures and the way in which they bound social identity. Any dominant world view (be it feudalism, Hell, or capitalism) which perceives itself as built on essentially unchangeable ontological concepts is vulnerable to scrutiny and interrogation by dystopic fiction. Even through the bleakest representation of a specific *status quo* the most energetic call for reconception and change could still be made. In *Radical Tragedy*, Dollimore, *pace* Stachniewski, describes how the genre of tragedy incorporated the inscription of 'a subversive discourse within an orthodox one'.[128] Dekker's topical dystopia, like the prison-Hell theme, followed similar patterns. In response to the conflicting demands placed upon his work, he often ambiguously combined both dystopic functions; reformist and reactionary. Hell, for example, was ineluctably tied to a certain ontological pessimism, yet within it Dekker managed to weave many dystopic elements which called for society to do and think things differently. Often he presented prison as a dystopically moribund place where illness and injustice tangled horribly, and where the hapless prisoner bore sole responsibility for the sickness of society. In the strangely claustrophobic turbulence which characterized the transition from Elizabethan to Jacobean society, Dekker found his readers receptive to the entertainments of a progressive dystopic literature. As a medium that both criticized and recognized the forces which structured it, his dystopic fiction appealed to a wide audience in part because it avoided having to specify any narrow class or social interest. Such literature held a grudge against the centres of power, not its margins, so it did not have to define itself against other critical views. Nor was it burdened by the idealism and stasis endemic to utopia. Utopian impulses were, in many instances, considered a primer for social reform. Seventeenth-century educator, Samuel Hartlib, noted that 'No wise man ... will lay his old habitation waste till he know what to erect instead therof; hence it is that a new model is commonly first prepared before the old one be removed'.[129] While Hartlib suggests the progress which utopic thoughts might encourage, even he begins with notion that the wrongs of the old world are a prelude to this. Utopia can be a static place where nothing changes because it does not need to. By inflecting the energy of discontent, dystopic images attempted to overcome social inertia. Moreover they allowed you to work within the very system being criticized, which is why dystopic fiction usually functions as a tactic rather than a goal. Every dystopic vision in some way already imagines, if only in absence, a well-world – another place where things are better than the here and now. Later, we can see that the radical Utopian movements of the mid-seventeenth century such as the Diggers and Levellers were, arguably, motivated by such a rationalization of social discontent rather than the straightforward realization of a utopic fantasy.

But why do I use the specific image of dystopia in relation to Dekker's work as opposed to any other form of fictive defamiliarization? Why is his prose framed by the structural particularities of time and place which writing dystopia performs? For one thing, dystopic fiction operates most effectively when rifts in temporal conception accompany shifts in the nature of social space. The massive emigration from country to city which made London what it was meant that each and every day the rhythms and sensibilities of rural life broke down and into the socio-economic patterns of the metropolitan life which absorbed them. Dystopic images flashed across those complex moments of rupture in time and space producing in writing like Dekker's a peculiar mixture of the topical and the idiosyncratic. Grotesque aesthetics were, for example, reconfigured through the spacial and temporal refraction of city topography to become something quite different. Once tied to a utopian understanding of the collective social body, now the individuated body bore the truncated marks of the grotesque and could be read in terms of personal fear, disgust, and caricature. Dekker's dystopic images restructured grotesque idioms as both uncannily nostalgic and frighteningly contemporary. As the immigrant crossed the threshold of the city she or he inhabited a different sense of time along with a new space. The ethos and practice of the city elongated time; drawing it out of its continuity with people and the land into the linear forms which the new work rhythms of labour and production demanded. This jarred, if not broke, the notion of cyclical time, thereby rupturing any residual sense of a bucolic utopia. So nostalgia acquired a new meaning in the city and was exploited considerably by writers like Dekker. In many ways nostalgia is irrelevant to grotesque: because the latter's forms display a temporal immediacy and universality, growing as they do from an inevitable sense of renewal, rebirth, and revolution.[130] Within linear time the past is always recognized as an echo, derived from but irrevocably lost to the present. In that moment grotesque loses its ability to express the rhythms and qualities of revivification, becoming more tractable to the representation of decadence, death, and loss. Writing across these different temporal forms, the linear and the cyclical, Dekker, ironically, sentimental-ized a nostalgia for the grotesque in a way that Nashe, say, could not. His earlier work, like *Old Fortunatus*, was steeped in nostalgia, but comfortingly organic visions of society were to collapse slowly under the pressures of metropolitan society. In *The Shoemakers' Holiday* Dekker deals with a number of metropolitan tensions: ideo-logical conflict between the established Court and the growing claims of the City; the violent dissentient energies of London's 'prentices; and the urban predominance of the richer guilds, which did not include shoemakers.[131] These tensions become variously glossed or resolved in the play: the aristocratic heir apparent, Lacy, marries Rose, the Lord Mayor's daughter, thereby integrating and uniting Court and City; the pent-up frustrations of the 'prentices which were prone to cause riots become dissipated into the shoe-makers' holiday; and Simon Eyre establishes the honour of the shoemakers, and our recognition of the 'Gentle Craft', as the whole play concludes with a harmonious 'banquet' in which everyone, in-cluding the king, is invited. But the utopic impulses of the feast cannot wash away the dystopic aftertaste which the story of Ralph and Jane leaves. These lovers exist always on the verge of tragedy. Once Ralph is packed off to the 'bitter wars in France', Jane does not receive the promised support from Eyre's household (though its unclear whether this is negligence or accident) and begins a life of poverty where she is encouraged to sell herself (IV.i.74). Dekker, who was keenly aware of the plight of soldiers, brings Ralph home lame. Like many ex-soldiers without 'limbs and lands', Ralph needed, but did not get, support from the state for which he had fought. Elizabethan governments especially paid only lip service towards many of their discharged soldiers. According to J. W. Fortescue:

> Elizabeth was not friendly to soldiers, and hated to be troubled with obligations towards men who had faithfully served her. An Act had been passed in 1593 throwing the relief of crippled or destitute soldiers on their parishes, and she could not see what more they could want.[132]

Many parishes, especially in London, were hard-pressed dealing with the increased numbers of vagrants – often the very people who were targeted for conscription in the first place. Luckily Ralph only needs his hands to work, and luckily he finds his Jane against the odds, but such fortune exposes rather than obscures the problems which the working poor faced in London. From *The Shoemakers' Holiday* on, Dekker began producing urban images of savage sentimentality and ironic pathos. The bathetic figures which occupied his dystopic literature, those on the brink of society (madman, prostitute, rogue, soldier, devil), appeared along the faultlines of time and place.

One of Dekker's most incisive uses of dystopic fiction occurs in his prophetic *Worke for Armourers*, subtitled *The Peace is Broken*. Conflict appears to be an endemic problem for the City, as the narrator admits that *'Open warres* [are] *likely to happin* this yeare 1609' (Grosart, vol. IV, p. 87). Unable to attend the theatre, due to plague, the narrator now seems free to imagine the City divided into 'Two Nations', the rich and the poor.[133] Through the tension of two disparate literary forms, allegory and caricature, he constructs a vividly dystopic world in which the two armies of 'Money' and 'Poverty' are camped on the threshold of a destructive battle, and seem about to pitch the City into anarchy. If the social trends and governmental irregularities which have produced the army of poverty go unchecked then a catastrophic civil war will follow. According to Clark, this nihilistic state is just averted:

> The battle itself never takes place. The troops of Poverty beseige the City, and during the siege both sides become so enfeebled that they finally agree to a perpetuall truce. Poverty's men are to be ever ready to fight for Money, and Money to help Poverty, and a Utopian law is enacted whereby Fortune is to be cured of her blindness, so that 'she maight see those upon whom shee bestowes her blessings.' But when the siege is raised there is only one conclusion possible, a return to the status quo ...[134]

Such a *détente*, however, simply flaunts its own sense of inadequacy. Returning to the *status quo* will not contain or resolve the dystopic elements which have been raised prior to the hostile stalemate. *'Poverties* subjects should be ever in a readinesse', we are told, 'to fight for *Money*', though its never quite clear whether he means on behalf of or to attain 'Money' (Grosart, vol. IV, p. 165). 'Poverties' wrath appears as a darkly ambiguous and menacing social force, potentially liable to acquire a life and motive of its own. Further on Dekker depicts 'Violence' who, like 'Crueltie', operates as a prime councellor to 'Money', a figure who 'hath borne many great offices' (Grosart, vol. IV, p. 131). Although 'Violence' is presented as a force which has worked on behalf of 'Money' rather than 'Poverty', its allegiance is by no means secure. Money, it seems, could well be overthrown by the forces which uphold it. A ceasefire is not the end of hostilities. The conflictual energies which underscored such a rebellion remain in place until the notion of 'commonwealth' which drives Dekker's story lives up to its promise and potential. To endorse this solution, Dekker pointedly invokes the history of insurrection; 'but a number of *Jack-Strawes* being among them, and opening whole Cades of councell in a cause so dangerous, they were all turned to dry powder' (Grosart, vol. IV, p. 110). The powers that be are reminded that political flashpoints are likely to explode in the faces of the negligent authorities who fired them. One of these flashpoints, to which the title alludes, was the problem of malcontented and underpaid discharged soldiers: 'military service induced a restlessness and criminality that every country found it difficult to reabsorb.'[135] London was especially affected, not least because the forces which drove many jobless and homeless people to the city – a factor which made London such a popular 'recruiting' ground – was also the reason why they returned there. Implicit criticism of the Crown and the country can be read in the City Fathers' complaints: when troops discharged from France under the Treaty of Boulogne arrived in the city the mayor and aldermen complained:

> There be such a number of soldiers at this present within this city that unless speedy order be taken to rid and bestow them into the country, great danger will thereby ensue, for we are perfectly informed by such as heard some speak that their report is this: that they cannot work, and if they cannot obtain a living [a livelihood] at the King's hands in consideration that they have long served the King's Highness and the King his father, they will appoint themselves in several companies in London come out of several lanes and streets in London and meet together in some one place in the said city and thereupon set upon the citizens and their houses and take such booties and spoil ... they can lay hand upon and ... that if it shall fortune them not to be ordered somewhat after their expectation, that then they will turn all England upside down at their pleasures.[136]

Bourgeois wealth, it seems, is threatened by something not of its own making, as the blame is laid upon the King as much as on the dissident soldiers. Once again the disenfranchised got caught between the policies of the Crown and the interests of the City. Evidently there was a real fear that discharged soldiers might fight, in an organized way, for their *own interests*! Even the most glorious *'Golden age'* might find itself mired in sedition if it continued to ignore 'Poverty'.

*Worke for Armourers* reveals both the forces which underpin social polarization and the language used to obscure its effects. If, for example, the rich are rich because they have exploited the poor, the poor are exploited further when they are made to represent a state of moral turpitude and potential insurrection. Thus the poor are condemned for being poor and for threatening those who made them so. Dystopic fiction exaggerates the condition of the world, polarizing it so that the structural relationship between rich and poor can be seen more clearly as one of exploitation and privilege, as antagonistic rather than inevitable. For Dekker, this meant taking the worst nightmare of the dominant group to the brink of its nightmarish possibility; to see, for example, the poor laying siege to their city of wealth, to threaten the very thing the rich held so dear. Though these images often unleashed political and social reprisals, which Dekker anticipates in *Worke for Armourers*, his vision qualifies, taints, and changes the social perception of wealth and its justification in a society with so many poor. Whether this dystopic fiction calms or stirs its reader is debatable. Certainly the price rises of the early seventeenth century created an army of 'Poverties people' when 'corne skipt from foure to ten shillings a bushell, from ten to twelve shillings' (Grosart, vol. IV, p. 150); but as *Worke for Armourers* makes clear, although inflation sparked the considerable unrest and riots of the period it really added fuel to a fire already burning.

Dekker's prose fiction achieved its popularity because it sought to caricaturize the city in ways which made it seem both newly familiar and audaciously strange. Not surprisingly, like the city itself, this could be reassuring and alarming. In spite of his urban dystopia, the London which he vaunted was not depicted as an intrinsically ill place; it was unfinished rather than pre-programmed to fail. Yet he rarely presented a clear, concise, or whole, vision of contemporary London, preferring to write in and of its many contradictory places. Of course, within the context of early seven-

teenth-century politics, disclosing the knowledge that contradictions exist would in itself be a potentially powerful impetus for
improvement.

I began this chapter by exploring the relationship between Nashe
and Dekker, and it seems appropriate to return to this comparison.
In 'Nashe, Rhetoric, and Satire', Rhodes demonstrates that Nashe's
verbal excess, his rhetorical flamboyance, his stylistic opulence, was
an attempt at making linguistic violence a form by which he could
escape his situation both socially and as a writer. But the world he
could not change eventually overwhelmed him and wiped him out.
Not surprisingly, his dystopic fiction was rooted in an almost inex-
pressible disappointment. Whilst Dekker borrowed some of
Nashe's energy, his prosaic fiction did not confront the inexorable
forces of change in the same way, rather it went with them. Dekker
took off the frills, grounded the metaphors, and channelled his exuberance into a less bitter form of social candour. And this registers
the most significant difference between them, as Rhodes says in
referring to his *Worke for Armourers*:

> Dekker's pamphlet illustrates the increasing social awareness of
> the Jacobean period, but it also illustrates how the plain style can
> be effective in making radical points. A few years earlier Dekker
> had been imitating Nashe; the move away from Nashe is a move
> towards effective social criticism.[137]

Just how effective this move was is difficult to say, but we can see
that Dekker's satirical fiction was located on the cusp of a dis-
affected rhetorical violence and the acuity of a straight-talking
social criticism. This gave Dekker's work the constituency and
content which Nashe's 'unredeemed rhetoric' deliberately eschewed.[138] It also created a tension in his writing which at times
locates him as champion of the oppressed, a proponent of a City-
bourgeois, even Puritan, ethos, as well as (occasionally) a watery-
eyed sentimentalist for a (feudal) world always and forever lost. If
we are to read Dekker as a social critic, and I think we must, then
we need to understand the complex tension between a literature of
progressive optimism and its pessimistic dystopical frame.

# Notes

## INTRODUCTION: 'OUR SCENE IS LONDON'

1. Ben Jonson, *The Alchemist* edited by Douglas Brown (London: The New Mermaids, 1966) prologue, pp. 5–9.
2. A. L. Beier and Roger Finlay (eds), *London 1500–1700: The Making of the Metropolis* (London and New York, 1986) p. 3.
3. Ibid., p. 11.
4. Ibid., pp. 12–13.
5. E. A. Wrigley, 'A Simple Model of London's Importance in Changing English Society and Economy 1650–1750', *Past & Present*, no. 37 (July 1967) pp. 44–70.
6. By 'city' I mean the area within and without the walls of the old medieval city (excluding Westminster), including the suburbs, Liberties, Southwark, and Holborn to the Strand; and the socio-economic modes and practices, both licit and illicit, which took place there. The 'City' (when capitalized), also known as the City of London, strictly and legally defines the place, approximately one square mile, 'within the walls'; that is the walls of the medieval city. The City also functions as a metonym for all the political, administrative, and governmental aspects of the City, including institutions such as the Guildhall, the major companies, and the Royal Exchange; in other words 'the City' stands for the higher functions of civic life. When capitalized the 'Court' specifies the immediate socio-political functionaries who served the monarch (sometimes 'Westminster' is used as a metonym for the Court–Crown axis). The 'court', on the other hand, encompasses the wider ethos and culture of the aristocracy and upper class. Clearly these terms are highly fluid and often overlap at many ideological and topographical points (for example, the court could have a presence in the city). 'Metropolis', then, meaning mother of cities or mother city, is the nexus of all these various elements along with the special relations which their incorporation produced.
7. Beier and Finlay, *London 1500–1700*, p. 5.
8. Jonathan Raban, *Soft City*, first published 1974 (London, 1984), pp. 69–70.
9. Jean-Christophe Agnew, *The Market and the Theater in Anglo-American Thought, 1550–1750* (Cambridge, 1986), see ch. 3 'Artificial Persons', pp. 101–48.
10. Ibid., p. 112.
11. See Peter Womack, *Ben Jonson* (Oxford, 1986), especially ch. 2, 'Characters', pp. 31–75.
12. Dekker wrote only one masque, and that was never performed at Court. It was co-written with John Ford for the Cockpit Theatre. For a full account see Julia Gasper, *The Dragon and the Dove: The Plays of*

202

*Thomas Dekker* (Oxford and New York, 1990), especially ch. 7, '*The Sun's Darling*: An Apocalyptic Masque', pp. 190–217.

13. Marie Thérèse Jones-Davies, *Un Peintre de la Vie Londonienne: Thomas Dekker (circa 1572–1632)* (Paris, 1958, 2 vols.) p. 21.

14. See Raymond Williams, *The Country and the City* (London, 1973) p. 158. Although Williams is referring to the writing of Dickens, his sense of the writer and urban medium being mutually inflected is certainly applicable to the work of Dekker. Given their ambiguous social position, their fraught roles as professional writers, their metropolitan material, and their popularity, there is a remarkable parallel between Dekker and Dickens; but that is another story.

15. · Ibid.

16. For a list of Dekker's plays, both lost and extant, with his collaborators, see George R. Price, *Thomas Dekker* (New York, 1969) pp. 171–6.

17. Ring-around-the-roses (sometimes 'rosy') is an incredibly enduring folk ditty which probably dates back to the Black Death of the fourteenth century. There are some different versions; the one I sang in the playground went thus: Ring-a-ring of roses,/A pocket full of posies,/A-tishoo, a-tishoo,/We all fall down,/Dead! The commonest variant has the words 'ashes, ashes' replacing the third line; most likely referring to the cremation of the plague's victim. The first line refers to certain skin manifestations, petechiae or ecchymoses, which ominously predict the onset of bubonic plague. See Graham Twigg, *The Black Death: a Biological Reappraisal* (London, 1984): 'It is believed that the words of the old nursery rhyme "ring-a ring of roses" referred to the livid spots on the body, which were due to subcutaneous haemorrhages, when these occurred around the waist' (p. 19). Belief in the miasma theory underlies the second line, because flowers, or anything sweet-smelling, were thought to ward off the effects of 'bad air'. The third and fourth lines most probably refer to the pneumonic version of plague (rather than its bubonic version which was spread by rat fleas). See Robert S. Gottfried, *The Black Death: Natural and Human Disaster in Medieval Europe* (New York, 1983):

> Pneumonic plague is unique in that it can be transmitted from person to person ... After the two-to-three day incubation period, there is a rapid fall in body temperature, followed by a severe cough and consolidation in the lungs ... Neurological difficulties and coma follow infection, with death coming in 95% to 100% of the cases. (p. 8)

Small wonder, then, that they all fall down dead. Apart from the ghastly economy of the rhyme, it seems that over the years the oral tradition has combined the effects of both bubonic and pneumonic plague.

18. See Chapter 4, where I examine Dekker's criticism of the wealthy who fled London during times of plague; and the supposed impossibility of fleeing the wrath of an omnipotent God.

19. Raymond Williams, *Marxism and Literature* (Oxford and New York, 1977) p. 132.

20. Mary Douglas, *Purity and Danger: An Analysis of the Concepts of Pollution and Taboo*, first published 1966 (London and Boston, 1984) p. 4.
21. See Robert Darnton, *The Great Cat Massacre and Other Episodes in French Cultural History* (New York, 1985) p. 124.
22. William Shakespeare, *Timon of Athens* (IV.iii.43). Shakespeare's Bastard, in *King John*, gives a vivid description of exchange:

> That smooth-fac'd gentleman, tickling commodity,
> Commodity, the bias of the world,
> The world, who of itself is peised well,
> Made to run even upon even ground,
> Till this advantage, this vile drawing bias,
> This sway of motion, this commodity,
> Makes it take head from all indifferency,
> From all direction, purpose, course, intent:
> And this same bias, this commodity,
> This bawd, this broker, this all-changing word ...

> (*King John*, II.i.574–82)

23. Stephen Greenblatt, *Renaissance Self-fashioning: From More to Shakespeare* (Chicago, 1980) p. 5.
24. Peter Stallybrass and Allon White, *The Politics and Poetics of Transgression* (Ithaca, 1986).
25. Ibid., pp. 2–3.
26. Julia Gasper, *The Dragon and the Dove: The Plays of Thomas Dekker* (Oxford and New York, 1990) p. 22. For an extended account of Dekker as a Puritan writer see Anne M. Haselkorn, *Prostitution in Elizabethan and Jacobean Comedy* (Troy, 1983).
27. Gasper, *The Dragon and the Dove*, p. 2.
28. George Price, *Thomas Dekker* (New York, 1969) p. 144.
29. Terry Eagleton, *Ideology: An Introduction* (London and New York, 1991) p. 113.
30. John Stachniewski, *The Persecutory Imagination: English Puritanism and the Literature of Religious Despair* (Oxford and New York, 1991) p. 2.
31. Christopher Hill, *Society and Puritanism in Pre-Revolutionary England* (Harmondsworth, 1964). pp. 19 and 22.
32. Ibid., p. 27.
33. Patrick Collinson, 'The Puritan Character: Polemics and Polarities in Early Seventeenth-Century English Culture', a paper presented at a Clark Library Seminar, 25 April 1987 (Los Angeles, 1989) p. 28.
34. Ibid., p. 27.
35. Ibid., p. 28.
36. For the social and political effects of the drive towards purity, including its wide-reaching consequences for understanding gender relations, see Klaus Theweleit, *Male Fantasies*, 2 vols: vol. i, *Women, Floods, Bodies, History*, trans. Stephen Conway in collaboration with Erica Carter and Chris Turner; vol. ii, *Male Bodies: Psychoanalyzing the White Terror*, trans. Stephen Conway in collaboration with Erica Carter and Chris Turner (Minneapolis, 1987 and 1989).

37. Collinson, 'The Puritan Character', p. 20.
38. Ibid., p. 22. The drive towards individualizing social experience was a central part of Puritanism's structure of feeling, hence Collinson's economic title.
39. Hill, *Society and Puritanism*, p. 16.
40. *The Complete Works of William Hazlitt*, ed. by P. P. Howe, after the edition of A. R. Waller and Arnold Glover, 21 vols (1930–4), vol. VI, pp. 234–5.

## 1   BEDLAM AND BRIDEWELL

1. Michel Foucault, *Madness and Civilization: A History of Insanity in the Age of Reason*, trans. Richard Howard (New York, 1965) p. 61.
2. *John Howes' MS., 1582*, (London, 1904 rep.) p. 22.
3. A compact account of such changes is available in A. L. Beier and Roger Finlay (eds), *London 1500–1700: The Making of the Metropolis* (London and New York, 1986): see also Norman G. Brett-James, *The Growth of Stuart London* (London, 1935); C. G. A. Clay, *Economic Expansion and Social Change: England 1500–1700* (Cambridge and New York, 1984); Roger Finlay, *Population and Metropolis: The Demography of London, 1580–1650* (Cambridge and New York, 1981); Emrys Jones, 'London in the Early Seventeenth Century: An Ecological Approach', *London Journal*, vol. 6, no. 2 (1980) pp. 123–33; E. A. Wrigley, 'A Simple Model of London's Importance in Changing English Society and Economy 1650–1750', *Past and Present*, no. 37 (July 1967), pp. 44–70.
4. On the growth in mental illness due to debt and other cultural factors, see Michael MacDonald, *Mystical Bedlam: Madness, Anxiety, and Healing in Seventeenth-Century England* (Cambridge, 1981); Jonathan Dollimore, *Radical Tragedy: Religion, Ideology and Power in the Drama of Shakespeare and his Contemporaries* (Brighton, 1984). There was also the breakup and appropriation of monastic property after the Reformation, with the ensuing diminution of trust funds and gifts upon which Bedlam depended. For a broader cultural view see William J. Bouwsma, 'Anxiety and the Formation of Early Modern Culture', in Barbara C. Malament (ed.), *After the Reformation: Essays in Honour of J. H. Hexter* (Philadelphia, 1980) pp. 215–46.
5. John Stow, *A Survey of London*, ed. Charles Lethbridge Kingsford, reprinted from the text of 1603, first published 1908, 2 vols (Oxford, 1971).
6. Revd. E. G. O'Donoghue, *The Story of Bethlehem Hospital From its Foundation in 1247* (London, 1914) p. 112.
7. The appointment of doctors was newsworthy at the time of the production of *The Honest Whore, part I*. Hilkiah Crooke 'was appointed in 1604 physician to James' (O'Donoghue, *The Story of Bethlehem Hospital*, p. 157), the same year in which a 'crooked' doctor poisoning the king's enemies is featured. James later placed Crooke in charge of Bedlam. Middleton also picked up on the topicality of nefarious doctors. His character 'Alibius', the jealous doctor/keeper of the

madfolk in *The Changeling*, was, according to O'Donoghue, based on Hilkiah Crooke (O'Donoghue, *The Story of Bethlehem Hospital*, p. 158). An earlier play by Middleton, *The Family of Love*, also featured a devious doctor, one Dr Glister.

8. Patricia Allderidge, 'Management and Mismanagement at Bedlam, 1547–1633', in Charles Webster (ed.), *Health, Medicine and Mortality in the Sixteenth Century* (Cambridge, 1986) pp. 141–64. See also George Rosen, *Madness in Society* (London, 1968); in particular he notes that 'During the sixteenth century there appears a slowly growing tendency to place the mentally deranged in special institutions' (Rosen, p. 142). The purpose behind this tendency provides the scope of Foucault's seminal study on the institutionalization of the insane. To a considerable degree these practices of confinement were influenced by the social policies of the City's Protestant reformers. Although the civil authorities had assumed some responsibility for matters of health and welfare before the sixteenth century, there was a growing feeling that there ought to be an effective organization of all agencies of public assistance, and that all facilities and resources (hospitals, domiciliary relief and the like) should be united in the hands of municipal or national authorities (p. 142). In London the control of the hospitals registered and effected a shift in the centre of gravity of administrative power in favour of the City.

9. O'Donoghue, *Bridewell Hospital*, vol. II, p. 25 (full citation in n. 11 below).

10. The play's upper-class plot centres around the Duke's attempt to prevent his daughter from marrying the son of a rival family; while in a draper's shop in the city, the draper, a man of indefatigable patience, infuriates all those around him. Both plot strands come together, and are played out, in Bedlam where their respective authority is found wanting.

11. Revd E. G. O'Donoghue, *Bridewell Hospital, Palace, Prison, Schools*, 2 vols: vol. I, *from the Earliest Times to the End of the Reign of Elizabeth* (London, 1923); vol. II, *from the Death of Elizabeth to Modern Times 1603–1929* (London, 1929). A. J. Copeland, *Bridewell Royal Hospital* (London, 1888); *John Howes MS.* (London, 1582).

12. See the biography of William Fleetwood in ch. 19 of Charles, M. Clode (ed.), *The Early History of the Guild of Merchants Taylors*, 2 vols: vol. I, *The History*, vol. II, *The Lives* (London, 1888) vol. II, p. 283.

13. Clode, *The Early History*, vol. II, p. 290.

14. Zygmunt Bauman, *Legislators and Interpreters: On Modernity, Postmodernity and Intellectuals* (Ithaca, 1987):

> 'The new socially accepted definition of the poor was focused on the moral opprobrium attached to an inability to earn one's living. It was not so much the ennobling impact of work which counted, as the fact that working always implied having a master, belonging to a community, and otherwise remaining in sight and hence under control. Being out of work, on the other hand, [meant] escaping social control – staying 'socially invisible'. It was the elusiveness of the masterless men's social identity that was most frightening. The

poor were denounced as staying deliberately out of work The main danger, however lay not so much in the immanent moral abomination of poverty, as in the resulting danger emanating from the state of rootlessness. (pp. 41–2)

15. Clode, *The Early History*, vol. II, p. 290.
16. *John Howes*, p. 3.
17. E. D. Pendry, *Elizabethan Prisons and Prisons Scenes*, 2 vols, for Dr. James Hogg (ed.), *Elizabethan & Renaissance Studies* (Salzburg, 1974) vol. I, p. 48.
18. See Chapter 2, which shows how whipping was used to demarcate both the contours of the city and the boundaries of its premier citizens.
19. Pendry, *Prisons*, p. 47.
20. See Pendry, *Prisons*, pp. 46–53. The worst of the excesses included the infliction of over 100 lashes continuously; and the use of wire in the whips to ensure the flesh was cut open. Chapter 2 contains a detailed account of the use of whipping as a punishment for prostitution. Terrifyingly, the effect of cutting open the tormented body was precisely what was desired by those orchestrating these savage acts.
21. Pendry, *Prisons*, p. 48.
22. Others, too, were not protected under Habeas Corpus, including foreigners and Catholics.
23. Bridewell's notoriety as a place of vicious sanctions was increased by the knowledge that many 'prisoners were sent there with the sole purpose of extracting confessions from them by torture.' Pendry, *Prisons*, p. 49. See also, Ian W. Archer, *The Pursuit of Stability: Social Relations in Elizabethan London* (Cambridge and New York, 1991) pp. 204–60.
24. *Measure for Measure's* courtroom scene, for example, depicts the adjudicator Angelo relatively unconcerned with accurate or judicial testimony. His goal is the arbitrary quality of punishment! He finally hopes that the court 'find good cause to whip them all' (*Measure for Measure*, II.i.136) as he leaves before knowing whether his hopes are fulfilled. From Clode's account of Fleetwood, including the epithet 'The Honest Recorder', there are many instances which parallel the characters of both Angelo, in Shakespeare's *Measure for Measure*, and Candido, the 'Honest Madman' in both parts of *The Honest Whore*. Fleetwood's capacity for swift dispensation of the law, including sessions in the morning and afternoon (see Clode, *The Early History*, pp. 280–1), comes from his conviction that those brought before him must already be morally compromised, either through poverty or for just being there in court. Therefore, he felt that the role of a good magistrate was to decide upon the punishment, rather than assess guilt or innocence. Vagrants and prostitutes were, by the nature of the charges against them, already guilty in his eyes. His working schedule dispensing this kind of 'justice', 'according to his deserts' (Clode, p. 289) was as extensive as he was indefatigable: 'I have not leisure to eat my meat – I am so called upon' he says (p. 290). Like Angelo, Fleetwood dispenses justice more speedily when the sovereign leaves town:

Fleetwood attributes his success in dealing with crime to the absence of Elizabeth's Court, which had left London to escape the plague. [in Fleetwood's words] 'The only cause that this reformation taketh so good effect here about London is that when by order we have either justly executed the laws or performed the Councils commandment, we are wont to have a great men's letter, or lady's ring, or some other token from such other inferior persons as will devise one untruth or another to accuse us of if we prefer not their unlawful request, the Court is far off, here we are not troubled with letters, neither for the reprieve of the prisoners nor for sparing that fray maker'. (p. 285)

Brought in to carry out the letter of the law in the monarch's absence, Fleetwood, like Angelo, was free of the encumbrances, as he saw them, of courtly interference. According to Fleetwood, crime was controllable by the blanket administration of a precise law. Even Fleetwood's sympathetic biographer recognizes that although he dealt with social 'problems' 'by the strong arm of the law' he could not 'find [in Fleetwood] any traces of charitable and benevolent agencies' (p. 297). Fleetwood was despised by many, but he was more than tolerated as part of Elizabeth's government because of his tireless anti-papist work, which was ostensibly needed to 'ward off the consequences of the Bishop of Rome's recent sentence of excommunication against Elizabeth' (p. 275). My contention that Angelo was partly modelled on Fleetwood is further supported by the fact that his wife was named 'Mariana'; similar to Angelo's wife in *Measure for Measure*.

25. See J. R. Hale, *War and Society in Renaissance Europe 1450–1620* (New York, 1985), especially ch. 2 'The military reformation: techniques and organization', pp. 46–74; and C. G. Cruickshank, *Elizabeth's Army* (London, 1946) pp. 137–8.
26. Cruickshank, *Elizabeth's Army*, p. 9.
27. According to Hale: 'Through the recruiting procedure, armies got vagrants; men forced onto the roads by enclosures, population increase, rising prices – factors they could not adapt to. And because jobless men on the move were popularly thought of as potential criminals, crime became associated with the army service they were too weak to avoid. For many, begging was afar preferable to military service; that is how they caught the eye of the local authorities and were rounded off to war' (Hale, *War and Society*, p. 89).
28. Ibid., p. 40.
29. Ibid.
30. Ibid., p. 24.
31. William Shakespeare, *Henry IV, part I* (V.iii.35–8).
32. Ibid., IV.ii.70. Through Falstaff we get many glimpses at the conscription practices of mustering an army. Captains, like Falstaff, made extra money by taking bribes from anyone wealthy enough to buy their way out of service.
33. Hale, *War and Society*, p. 86.

34. Ibid., pp. 100–1.
35. O'Donoghue, *Bridewell Hospital*, vol. I, p. 190.
36. Dekker structures the sub-plot of *The Honest Whore, part II* around several pieces of stolen cloth (such material also forms the basis of Orlando's sting operation).
37. Pendry, *Prisons*, p. 49. The term 'whore' is a pejorative rather than a practical one. It is an ascribed name, and to use it reproduces the attitudes of those who see people in those terms. Where possible, I have tried to avoid using the term except when quoting or alluding to other speakers/writers.
38. O'Donoghue, *Bridewell Hospital*, vol. I, p. 191. He further explains that some of the women were charged with disorderly conduct after having been wined and dined.
39. Much of the period's Coney Catching literature was rooted in this contradiction. They were often depicted as having a skills hierarchy which echoed values and practices within the city, sometimes their socio-economic structure was likened, albeit parodically, to guilds or companies. Othertimes they were represented as mirroring legitimate military organizations, a 'Motley Crue' as it were.
40. Apart from nail-making and spinning, which are both mentioned in the plays, the other labour included carding, hemp-beating, corn-grinding using a huge man-powered treadmill, baking, clothworking, and all manner of other menial cleaning and labouring tasks.
41. Whipping was not confined to punishment yards in Bridewell. From the 1590s onwards the authorities' systematic attack on the unaccommodated and poor meant that the corner of almost every main street had a whipping post with exhibitions of punishment carried out daily. As Dekker noted elsewhere: 'you have whipping posts in your streetes for the Vagabond' (Grosart, vol. II, p. 70).
42. *Greevous Grones for the Poore* (London, 1621), sig. B2: 'Excellently was that on-set given in the making of sundry Statutes; for the releefe of the Impotent, and setting the ydle on Worke: but if we consider how Negligence hath overthrowne that Famous Worke; wee shall finde, how Selfe-Love is settled farre in everie mans heart, and that we so hotly hunt after private Gaine, that wee freezing coldly, seeke not any Publicke Profite'.
43. Allderidge, 'Management and Mismanagement', p. 147.
44. Ibid., p. 153.
45. John Gerard, the Elizabethan autobiographer, cited in Pendry, *Prisons*, p. 53. Like many of his contemporaries, including Dekker and Middleton, Gerard considered that the treatment of prisoners was inhumane.
46. *Greevous Grones*, pp. 13–14.
47. *Howes*, Intro., p. v. Howes' indictments were more directly levelled at the residual values of a feudal aristocracy, the 'Norman Yoke'. Ultimately he wished to strengthen the City's resolve in the application of its draconian Bridewell policies.
48. Foucault stresses the relationship between poverty and madness throughout his seminal study, *Madness and Civilization*; see esp. pp. 38–84.

49. In *Northward Hoe* (co-written with John Webster) Mayberry asks Full-moone, a keeper at Bedlam, 'may we see some a your mad-folkes' (*NH*, IV.iii.36). Like the Duke in *The Honest Whore, part I,* who says 'Lets all goe see the madmen' (*HWI*, V. ii. 10).

50. Michael MacDonald, 'Popular Beliefs About Mental Disorder in Early Modern England', in *Heilberufe und Kranke im 17. und 18. Jahrhundert Die Quellen – und Forschungssituation,* Müstersche Beiträge zur Geschichte und Theorie der Medizin, nr. 18, herausgegeben von K. E. Rothschuh und R. Toellner (Münster, 1982) pp. 148–73 (p. 154).

51. Ibid., p. 121.

52. Robert Rentoul Reed Jr, *Bedlam of the Jacobean Stage,* first published 1952 (New York, 1970).

> Spectacle, then, regardless of the degree to which the satire tended to enlarge its scope, was both the chief motive and the chief characteristic of most of the mad-folk scenes if the popularity of Bethlehem Hospital was a direct influence upon the reproduction of mad folk upon the stage this was so primarily because the grotesque and unexpected behaviour of Bedlamites, particularly when elaborated upon, typified the theatrical extravagance that the Jacobean audience seems to have unflaggingly demanded of its playwrights. (p. 64)

53. Ibid., p. 13.

54. Among those who have commented on Foucault's work are Vieda Skultans, *English Madness: Ideas on Insanity 1580–1890* (London and Boston, 1979), where she says that the 'elementary question which he poses – and which, I feel, he fails to answer – is why was madness set apart and feared?' (p. 12); Roy Porter, *A Social History of Madness: The World Through the Eyes of the Insane* (New York, 1988), who follows Foucault in seeing the victory of 'Reason' in its dialogue with madness. The ensuing 'shutting up' of difficult and dangerous people was called 'the Great Confinement' by Foucault. The most trenchant critic of Foucault's periodization and questionable historicism is H. C. Eric Midelfort, 'Madness and Civilization in Early Modern Europe: A Reappraisal of Michel Foucault', in Barbara C. Malament (ed.) *After the Reformation.* See also Michael MacDonald, *Mystical Bedlam,* which gives a lucid and meticulous account of a seventeenth-century physician, Richard Napier, and the patients he treated.

55. Foucault, *Madness and Civilization,* pp. 38–64.

56. MacDonald, *Mystical Bedlam,* p. 147.

57. Ibid.

58. Foucault, *Madness and Civilization,* p. 36.

59. Carol Thomas Neely, ' "Documents of Madness": Reading Madness and Gender in Shakespeare's Tragedies and Early Modern Culture', in *Shakespeare Quarterly,* vol. 42, no. 3 (Fall 1991) pp. 315–39 (p. 318).

60. In disarming the spectators Dekker accurately portrays Bedlam's administrative practice. There had been a number of serious incidents at Bedlam involving injury to spectators by inmates who had snatched

weapons from them. This reveals the practice of not just looking at the madfolk but actively intermingling with them.

61. It has been suggested that Dekker and other writers were merely responding to the competition for spectators between the theatre and the institution (see Reed, *Bedlam*, p. 38). Such a reading, I feel, develops from an unsophisticated perception of the relationship between writing, the writer, and society, not to mention between theatre and audience.

62. It was common to call dispossessed or 'mad' people Tom O'Bedlam or Bess O'Bedlam after the institution. Occasionally distracted people were called 'Abraham Men' after one of the wards in Bedlam. As now, Bedlam appeared to be a metonym for madness in general.

63. A. L. Beier, *Masterless Men: The Vagrancy Problem in England 1560–1640* (London and New York, 1985) p. 116.

64. A simple analogue was often drawn: in O'Donoghue's words 'generally speaking (the road or the prison was the only hospital for mental illness'; O'Donoghue, *Bethlehem Hospital*, p. 134.

65. 'The country gives me proof and precedent/Of Bedlam beggars '(*King Lear*, II.iii.13–14).

66. That England was full of madmen was a popular theme; one enjoyed for example by the First Clown in his conversation with Hamlet (V.i. 140–8).

67. See especially Bouwsma, 'Anxiety and the Formation of Early Modern Culture'; Dollimore, *Radical Tragedy*; Stephen L. Collins, *From Divine Cosmos To Sovereign State* (Oxford and New York, 1989).

68. Foucault, *Madness and Civilization*, p. 64.

69. Neil Rhodes, *Elizabethan Grotesque* (London, 1980), p. 43.

70. Ibid., p. 44.

71. Mikhail Bakhtin, *Rabelais and His World*, trans. Hélène Iswolsky (Cambridge Mass., 1968).

72. Rhodes, *Elizabethan Grotesque*, p. 46.

73. Porter, *A Social History of Madness*, p. 30.

74. According to Neely, 'Shakespeare's language of madness is characterized by fragmentation, obsession, and repetition, and most importantly what I would call "quotation", which might instead be called "bracketing" or "italicization" '(p. 323). Although Neely captures the decentredness of the voices of the mad (evident in Dekker and Middleton's depiction) along with a sense of alienation associated with the institution, her insight does not really allow for the farcical, grotesque, or even theatrical, dimensions of madness.

75. MacDonald, *Mystical Bedlam*, p. 140.

76. Ibid., pp. 151 and 162.

77. Skultans, *English Madness*, p. 19.

78. Ibid.

79. Robert Burton, *Anatomy of Melancholy* (London, 1985), cited in MacDonald, *Mystical Bedlam*, p. 34.

80. It would not be true to say, as Knights does, that 'all classes were affected by it': L. C. Knights, *Drama and Society in the Age of Jonson* (London, 1968) p. 315.

81. Joy Wiltenburg, 'Madness and Society in the Street Ballads of Early Modern England', *Journal of Popular Culture*, vol. 21, no. 4 (Spring 1988) pp. 101–27 (p. 113).

82. One of the Acts of Treason in Elizabeth's time stated:

> That yf any person or persons whatsoever durying the naturall Lyfe of our moste gracious Sovereigne Ladye Quene Elizabeth shall within the Realme or without, compasse imagyn invent devyse or intend the Deathe or Destruccon or any bodely harme shalbe taken and deemed & declared by the aucthoritie to be High Treason (13 Eli Iz. c.1 [1572]).

In *The Wonderfull yeare* (1603), Dekker was one of the first writers to eulogize her death. He wrote about her being 'dead at *White Hall*', though he also relates how she will be '*living at White Hall in Heaven*' (Grosart, vol. I, p. 94). Dekker is also aware of the effect that the change in monarch had on the courtier class: 'by this time King James is proclaimed: now does fresh blood leape into the cheekes of the Courtier' (Grosart, vol. I, 99). Although Dekker uses the metaphor of Stuart blood as a life-giving force, behind it lies the sense that a new monarch merely invigorates an old system of courtly competition rather than inaugurating anything different.

83. Opening of stage instructions to *The Honest Whore, part I*. For a perceptive study of wooing as a discourse of power see Arthur F. Marotti, ' "Love is Not Love": Elizabethan Sonnet Sequences and the Social Order', in *English Literary History*, vol. 49, no. 2 (Summer 1982) pp. 396–428.

84. Leonard Tennenhouse, 'Representing Power: *Measure for Measure* in its Time', in Stephen Greenblatt (ed.), *The Power of Forms in the English Renaissance* (Norman, 1982), pp. 139–56 (p. 149).

85. See the Sieve Portrait in Roy Strong, *The Cult of Elizabeth: Elizabethan Portraiture and Pageantry* (London, 1977) p. 11.

86. Likewise, Ophelia is tragically overwhelmed by the passions which Hamlet projects onto her. I develop these patterns further in Chapter 2.

87. In the 1570s there was a campaign by hard-line Puritan governors of Bridewell to punish clients as well as prostitutes. This declined as the investigations kept touching those close to the centres of power. The effort, though, reveals that the City men engaged in the 'Reformation of manners' were attempting to seize the initiative on defining social morality: see Archer, *The Pursuit of Stability*, p. 249.

88. See Ben Jonson's *Bartholomew Fair* (II.v.) where Ursula is goaded into a display of bawdy 'Bartholomew wit' in the presence of a disguised Justice Overdo. Part of the design of these scenes is to mock and embarrass his interpretation of the law.

89. The connection between *Measure for Measure* and the *Honest Whore* plays has long been noted. Most recently Larry S. Champion, *Thomas Dekker and the Traditions of English Drama*, American University Studies, series IV, English Language and Literature, vol. 27 (New

## Notes

213

York, 1985) remarks on 'the similarities between *Measure for Measure* and *2 The Honest Whore*' (p. 52): also Cyrus Hoy, *Introduction, Notes, and Commentaries to the texts in 'The Dramatic Works of Thomas Dekker'* edited by Fredson Bowers, 4 vols (Cambridge, 1979) vol. II, pp. 68–127: 'the principle influence in *2 The Honest Whore* is Shakespeare's. The Play has been closely modeled on both the structural and the thematic design of *Measure for Measure*' (p. 71). I would argue that it is precisely because of this affinity Dekker's play should be considered as a parody of *Measure for Measure*; not least because the integrity of the Nun, Isabella, is matched by that of the ex-prostitute, Bellafront, and because of the many other (inverted) parallels between the plays' (see n. 127). That Dekker could write a parody of this kind suggests that the sub-genre of 'disguised Duke plays' had run its course. *The Honest Whore, part II* was the last recognizable version.

90. Dekker is probably being vulgar and disrespectful here in his choice of name. When Bridewell was a palace, Henry VIII stayed there with Queen Catherine while the constitutional crisis about their potential marriage was being discussed in nearby Blackfriars. It is quite possible that in the public mind, not to mention tavern gossip, Bridewell was already associated with the shady doings of the establishment and governmental crisis.

91. Leah Lydia Otis, *Prostitution in Medieval Society: The History of an Urban Institution in Languedoc* (Chicago, 1985) pp. 41–2.

92. See Ben Jonson's Epigram 7, *On the New Hot-House*, in *Ben Jonson*, ed. Ian Donaldson (Oxford, The Oxford Authors, 1985) p. 224. Not only did brothels change their name and location, but prostitution itself became topographically more mobile with the increase in coach traffic. The era of male clients 'cruising' for streetwalkers had begun.

93. See Alexander Leggatt, *English Drama: Shakespeare to the Restoration* (London and New York, 1988). Leggatt says, 'the actual institutions of Dekker's London, Bedlam and Bridewell, can do nothing with society's misfits but lock them up. Dekker can write for effect, and can write sentimentally; but he can also use the fringe areas of his plays to suggest that the world is more intractable than conventional theatre allows.' (p. 173) Dekker's writing also allows us to see that incarceration shaped social attitudes and definitions by who constituted misfits. His depiction of Bedlam must figure as an indictment of a society which has failed them.

94. Fathers denying lovers because of family and kindred rivalry was a mainstay of earlier comedies; the story also invokes Shakespeare's *Romeo and Juliet*.

95. Leonard Tennenhouse, *Power on Display: The Politics of Shakespeare's Genres* (New York and London, 1986). These theatrical devices are part of what Tennenhouse calls the 'new strategies for authorizing monarchy' in 'the face of a new political challenge' (pp. 156 and 159).

96. Whilst Bedlam was almost exclusively an asylum by Dekker's times a chuch still remained there, it being a vestige of its former function as past of the priority of St Mary Bethlehem.

97. For a detailed account of the term and use of 'disguised duke' in the context of Shakespeare's *Measure for Measure*, see Rosalind Miles, *The*

*Problem of Measure for Measure: A Historical Investigation* (New York, 1975), pp. 125–96.

98. Tennenhouse, *Power on Display*, pp. 159 and 155.
99. See Kenneth R. Andrews, *Trade, Plunder and Settlement: Maritime enterprise and the genesis of the British Empire, 1480–1630* (Cambridge, 1984); ch. 11, 'The Sea War 1585–1603', pp. 223–55. While many businessmen in the city suffered from acts of piracy, and were against it, a group of rich and powerful 'professional owner-captains' were operating as privateers throughout and beyond the sea war with Spain. For some 'leading merchants', privateering was considered 'commerce by other means' and extended 'the drive for luxury imports' (p. 251). Like the deal which makes Eyre both rich and a mayor in *The Shoemakers' Holiday*, Dekker alludes to the way in which some merchants obtain their wealth through shady deals and/or illegitimate acts.
100. See Beier, *Masterless Men*.
101. E. K. Chambers, *The Elizabethan Stage*, 4 vols (Oxford, 1923), 4 vols, vol. IV, pp. 336–7.
102. The 'Counterfeit Crank' was an apocryphal figure who found his way into a good deal of the pamphlet literature of the late sixteenth and early seventeenth centuries. Dekker's literary sources consisted mainly of Thomas Harman and Robert Greene. One of Harman's stories concerns the tale of Nicholas Jennings, an 'upright man' who disguised himself as a Bedlamite in order to facilitate his begging, at which he made a good living (Conan Doyle later borrowed the same story when he wrote *The Man with the Twisted Lip*). These tales were connected with the authorities' attempts to discredit the extent of poverty and begging. There is little evidence of anyone making any real money from begging, although it is easy to see how rumours that they were appealed to the prejudices of those in work earning little money, or employers wishing to keep wages low by exploiting unemployment. Both Dekker and Middleton draw a firm connection between the dispossession of the means for existence and madness. See Beier, *Masterless Men*, pp. 112–19.
103. Of course, acting itself is a continuous feigning which is why there existed a legal ordinance to exclude the patronized 'Players of Enterludes belonginge to any Baron of this Realme': Chambers, *The Elizabethan Stage*, vol. IV, p. 337.
104. Debt was a common preoccupation of those who sought treatment for mental instability. In part it was due to the stress produced via a perceived loss of social standing. MacDonald mentions this throughout *Mystical Bedlam*.
105. *Royal Proclamations of King James I, 1603–1625*, ed. James F. Larkin and Paul L. Hughes (New Haven and London, 1969) no. 15, p. 30.
106. Andrews, *Trade, Plunder and Settlement*, p. 247.
107. Larkin and Hughes, *Royal Proclamations*, no. 28, pp. 53–4.
108. Ibid.
109. It is not unlikely that it was London's City oligarchs, its merchant capitalists and their financial backers, who stood to lose most from these acts of piracy. Both Dekker and Middleton were connected to this

social group via their writing. Other significant figures such as John
Stow and William Fleetwood were members of the Merchant Taylors
Company, who undoubtedly felt the effects of losses at sea due to
piracy.

110. In making this 'citizen' stand for the incarceration of the poor the play
opens up the irony that 'mass poverty' provided the means for 'cheap
manning' of trade ships and had 'promoted the growth of privateering, though it created problems for owners' (Andrews, *Trade, Plunder
and Settlement*, p. 247).

111. Stow, edited by Kingsford, vol. II p. 197.

112. Wiltenburg, *Madness and Society*, p. 122.

113. *London's Tempe*, 99–100.

114. *A Gramscian Reader: Selected Writings 1916–1935*, ed. David Forgacs
(London, 1988), on Hegemony and moral and intellectual leadership,
especially pp. 189–221 and 249–50; also *Antonio Gramsci, Selections
from the Prison Notebooks*, ed. Quintin Hoare and Geoffrey Nowell
Smith (New York, 1971).

115. For a sample, see Jonathan Goldberg, *James I and the Politics of
Literature: Jonson, Shakespeare, Donne and Their Contemporaries*
(Baltimore, 1983); Tennenhouse, *Power on Display*; Jonathan Dollimore,
'Transgression and Surveillance in Measure for Measure' in Jonathan
Dollimore and Alan Sinfield (eds), *Political Shakespeare: New Essays in
Cultural Materialism* (Manchester, 1985) pp. 72–87.

116. Yet *The Shoemakers' Holiday* also appears to offer Dekker's most overt
criticism of conscription. Through the figure of Ralph we see how disruptive service could be to city life, to the workshop, and how tragic it
could be for those who could not afford to pay off the mustering captains. As Hale says, 'governments wanted the very men whose labour
provided a prime base for urban comfort and profit' (*War and Society*,
p. 76). Eyre claims that he will get Ralph 'discharged' because he is 'a
man of the best presence' (I.i.119 and 125), but has no success. The
play is, however, careful to make the city folk, especially Eyre's work-
shop/household, appear patriotic, but only after Ralph is told by the
gentleman, Captain Lacy, that 'he must go' 'because [as Ralph real-
izes] there is no remedy' (I.i.184 and 203). Ralph's master and co-
workers support his entry into service, giving him some money
because of the strong likelihood that he will not receive much in pay.

117. This is not to say that Simon Eyre is a pro-carnivalesque figure,
because in his appropriation of the Feast for narrow political claims
he inevitably diminishes the spirit of Carnival.

118. We have to recognize, however, that plays like *The Honest Whore, parts
I* and *II* and *Measure for Measure* deal with the City's governmental
conflict with Westminster. As Fleetwood says, 'My singular good
Lord, My Lord William of Winchester was wonte to say, "When the
Court is furthest from London then is there best justice done in all
England" I heard as great a personage in office and authority as ever
was and yet living say the same wordes' (Clode, *The Early History*, vol.
II, p. 286).

119. Ibid.

120. Max Weber, *The Protestant Ethic and the Spirit of Capitalism*, trans. Talcott Parsons, first published 1930 (New York, 1958) p. 167.
121. See Eric Roll, *A History of Economic Thought*, first published 1938 (London, 1973), especially pp. 40–85. Candido's impetus to go to any lengths to sell his goods is a fundamental principle of 'commercial capitalism': 'In the period in which commerce was the dominating force of economic development the circulation of goods was the essence of economic activity' (p. 64). If we take this as part of a hegemonizing strategy, we can see that selling a pennyworth of lawne to aristocratic customers is an ideological victory. Whatever the price paid in damaged goods selling is the crucial factor. At the heart of Candido's ethos, as Roll might say, was a 'fear of goods' unsold (p. 65). Candido discloses that 'the attitude to selling, the fear of goods, the desire to accumulate treasure, and the opposition to usury' are, as Roll says, 'the essential qualities of the economic thought of the time' (pp. 68–9).
122. Part of the play's comedy depends upon the audiences' knowledge that certain Puritan protagonists had been imprisoned in Bridewell, the most interesting case being the ubiquitous Fleetwood, London's infamous Recorder and Puritan zealot, who was incarcerated there for a time. Upon release he stoically recounted that Bridewell was a 'place where a man might quietly be acquainted with God' (O'Donoghue, *Bridewell*, p. 201). This sanctimonious posture was deliciously satirized in Dekker's play.
123. MacDonald, *Mystical Bedlam*, p. 158.
124. Dekker seems to have enjoyed savaging Candido, a figure who could be easily identified with those City Fathers who both refused to patronize him and who continued to interrupt his chief source of employment when they closed down the theatres.
125. Ironically for Candido and his ilk their 'patience' paid off as they continued their campaign against popular theatre and other festive gatherings like 'bone-fires' and Maypole dancing.
126. This is precisely the position adopted by London's Puritan recorder, William Fleetwood, when he found himself imprisoned in the Fleet for his ideological rigidity. See William Fleetwood (1535–1594) in *Dictionary of National Biography*, and Clode, *The Early History*, vol. II, pp. 271–97.
127. In effect, Bellafront reverses the role of Isabella in *Measure for Measure*. Shakespeare's play depicts a pure woman, a novice nun, being coerced into an act of prostitution in order to discredit Angelo's government of the City.
128. Bellafront's reprobative 'profession' and her ensuing self-redemption also appears to be Dekker and Middleton's cryptic and ironic critique of Calvinistic principles; that Grace was beyond reach of an individual's effort, no matter how they tried.
129. Roy Baumeister, *Identity: Cultural Change and the Struggle for Self* (Oxford and New York, 1986) p. 44.
130. Here then the notion of 'relying on one's own judgement and feelings' is propagated at a moment in history when the ego is extremely uncertain of the reliability of its own judgement and feelings. Just

when people had begun to wonder whether their feelings could claim any basis in reality and to fear that emotions were nothing more than insubstantial conceits, one such emotion – trust – moved into the centre of male–female relationships. Klaus Theweleit, *Male Fantasies: Women, Floods, Bodies, History*, trans. by Stephen Conway in collaboration with Erica Carter and Chris Turner (Minneapolis, 1987) p. 330.

131. Richard Horwich, 'Wives, Courtesans, and the Economics of Love in Jacobean City Comedy', in *Drama in the Renaissance*, ed. Clifford Davidson, C. J. Giankaris, and John H. Stroupe (New York, 1986) pp. 255–73 (p. 264).

132. Ibid., p. 267.

133. Jonathan Dollimore, 'Shakespeare, Cultural Materialism, Feminism and Marxist Humanism', *New Literary History*, vol. 21, no. 3 (Spring 1990) pp. 471–93. Dollimore, referring to his earlier 'Transgression and Surveillance in *Measure for Measure*' in *Political Shakespeare*, says 'In the essay on *Measure for Measure* I remarked on the silence of the prostitutes. Although everything in the play presupposes them, not one of the prostitutes speaks. This absence, this silence, is one of the most revealing indications of the extent of their powerlessness and exploitation' (p. 475). My point is that Dekker's parody of *Measure for Measure* addresses and indicts Shakespeare for the same reason. In *The Honest Whore, part II* the prostitutes are provided with a certain bawdy autonomy, active presence, and mocking loquacity. In the final scenes, the Duke looks far less comfortable in *The Honest Whore, part II* than he does in *Measure for Measure*. While I would not claim that the prostitutes in *The Honest Whore, part II* have a great deal of power or are not exploited, they do appear noisily in the longest and last scene of the play.

134. Jean Christophe-Agnew, *Worlds Apart: The Market and the Theater in Anglo-American Thought 1550–1750* (Cambridge, 1986) p. 100.

135. 'Man in business is but a theatrical person': John Hall, quoted in Agnew, *Worlds Apart*, p. 97.

136. See Agnew, *Worlds Apart*, especially ch. 3 on 'Artificial Persons', pp. 101–48.

137. Horwich, 'Wives, Courtesans', p. 267.

138. Leggatt, *English Drama*, p. 173. He also recognizes that the 'critical edge' in Dekker's theatrical methods is 'to suggest that the world is more intractable than conventional theatre allows' (p. 173). This assumes, however, that the purpose of Dekker's theatre is one of inadequate mimesis.

139. Steven Rappaport, *Worlds Within Worlds: Structures of Life in Sixteenth-Century London* (Cambridge and New York, 1989). Rappaport's revisionist account provides a detailed elaboration of the complex layering of local government within the City, and its ability to cope with the rapid demographic expansion. While his account does give a valuable antidote to the perception of impending chaos which haunts certain literary criticism and history concerning the period, he does tend to see the City's 'problems' (or lack of them) through the lens of those in authority, rather than from the point of view of those who bore the brunt of governmental responses to those problems. A more valuable account of order/disorder in the City can be found in Ian

Archer, *The Pursuit of Stability*. As his title implies, Archer explores some of the reactive aspects of governmental dynamics of the period.
140. Agnew, *Worlds Apart*, p. 66.

## 2 PROSTITUTION AND DEKKER

1. John Berger and Jean Mohr, *A Seventh Man: Migrant Workers in Europe* (New York, 1975) pp. 82 and 86.
2. Ian Archer, *The Pursuit of Stability: Social Relations in Elizabethan London* (Cambridge and New York, 1991) p. 207.
3. Ibid., p. 211.
4. See A. L. Beier, *Masterless Men: The Vagrancy Problem in England 1560–1640* (London and New York, 1985) p. 78.
5. *Measure for Measure* (I.ii.75–7). Overdo is referring to the war with Spain, and the plagues which hit the city so hard in the late Elizabethan period. Overdo's reference to the 'gallows' is most likely a satirical allusion to the loss of upper-class clients who were allegedly caught up in treason and plots against her. Lucio may well be a parody, necessarily cryptic, of these incidents.
6. Upon their return, discharged soldiers had no more of a place in society than before they were conscripted. Those who had a trade often came back crippled and could not take it up again. Not surprisingly many, like Shakespeare's Pistol, when musing on their future decided 'Well, bawd will I turn' (*Henry V*, V.i.89). Characters like Black Will and Shakebag, in *Arden of Faversham*, were discharged soldiers. Army training, such as it was, the effects of war, and governmental neglect, provided London with an endless supply of small time pimps and enforcers.
7. In *The Shoemakers' Holiday* Ralph's co-worker, Firk, says to Lacy 'Truly, master cormorant, you shall do God good service to let Ralph and his wife stay together. She's a new-married woman; if you take her husband away from her a-night, you undo her; she may beg in the daytime, for he's as good a workman at a prick and an awl as any is in our trade.' (I.i.139–143). Living up to his name, Firk's bawdy language implies that Ralph is as good at making shoes as he is at sex, and that without her husband's service Jane will wander. For all his sexist prejudices, Firk gives us an idea of the bleak future which Jane faces: begging or prostitution. And whilst the play cranks out a happy reconciliation when Ralph returns crippled from the war, we are left in no doubt about what might, and usually, happened to women like Jane.
8. When faced with such personal devastation many went to extraordinary lengths to avoid the vicissitudes which conscription imposed. For example: 'The earl of Lindsey, raising troops in his lieutenancy of Lincolnshire, was confronted with the wife of a pressed man, who presented him with one of her husband's toes, wrapped in a handkerchief. He had deliberately maimed himself in order to provide graphic proof that he would not march North to face the Scots'; see Victor L.

Slater, 'The Lord Lieutenancy on the Eve of the Civil Wars: The Impressment of George Plowwright', *Historical Journal*, vol. 29, no. 2 (1986) pp. 279–96 (p. 291).

9. Roger B. Manning, *Village Revolts: Social Protest and Popular Disturbances in England, 1509–1640* (Oxford and New York, 1988) p. 193.

10. As prostitutes in *The Honest Whore, part I* and *Michaelmas Term* both Bellafront and the Country Wench are separated from their fathers. The search for reconciliation and reunion between father and daughter forms an important strand in the plays. It was undoubtedly an attempt to tap strong feelings of dislocation, familial disruption, and urban alienation.

11. Anne M. Haselkorn, *Prostitution in Elizabethan and Jacobean Comedy* (Troy, 1983) p. 13.

12. Ibid.

13. James Howell, cited in Lawrence Manley (ed.), *London in the Age of Shakespeare: an Anthology* (London, 1986) p. 47.

14. Archer, *The Pursuit of Stability*, p. 212.

15. Most noticeably: Archer, *The Pursuit of Stability*; Steven Rappaport, *Worlds Within Worlds: Structures of Life in Sixteenth-Century London* (Cambridge and New York, 1989); and Jeremy Boulton, *Neighbourhood and Society: A London Suburb in the Seventeenth Century* (Cambridge: New York, 1987). There appears to be a growing trend among some historians of the period to see the government of London as relatively stable and able to cope with its enormous social pressures, with an effective role for parish government, and the guild authorities.

16. Two notable, though different, studies which attend to this are Stephen Mullaney, *The Place of the Stage: License, Play, and Power in Renaissance England* (Chicago, 1988) and Jean-Christophe Agnew, *Worlds Apart: The Market and the Theatre in Anglo-American Thought, 1550–1750* (Cambridge, 1988). Mullaney's account leans heavily on Foucault to activate the sense of the Liberties or suburbs operating as the City's 'margins':

> More generally, the margins of the city were places where forms of moral incontinence and pollution were granted license to exist beyond the bounds of a community they had, by their incontinence, already exceeded. Social and civic margins, the Liberties also served as margins in a textual sense: as a place reserved for heterogeneous and overdetermined cultural phenomena and for divergent points of view – for commentary upon and even contradiction of the main body of the text, in this instance the body politic itself. (p. ix)

The main problem with this argument is that it is dependent upon so textualizing the city that we lose all sense of it as a location of social interaction. Thus the stage becomes somewhat misplaced, as it becomes stripped of that which most dramatically characterizes it, social and human interaction. Furthermore, the semio-textualization tends to reproduce the dominant discursive languages of the City which tendentiously 'saw' the margins as incontinent and polluted, precisely because that is what they needed to see there. Agnew's study is more concerned with the socio-economic underpinnings which changed the dynamics of the market/trading system on the edge of the city, and which produced the many protean forms and linguistic fluidity which accompanied that change. Although I find Agnew's analysis more grounded, both analyses, perhaps, whether as a semiotic riot or a deregulated dynamism, see the suburbs as a more disorderly or romantic realm than has previously been the case.

17. Ruth Mazzeo Karras, 'The Regulation of Brothels in Later Medieval England', in *Signs: Journal of Women in Culture and Society*, vol. 14, no. 2 (1989) pp. 399–433 (p. 414).

18. *Thomas Nashe, The Unfortunate Traveller and Other Works*, ed. J. B. Steane (Harmondsworth, 1972) p. 483.

19. Agnew, *The Pursuit of Stability*, p. 50.

20. As the title of Agnew's book suggests, the market is as much a concept as a material practice or place. This is precisely the point which this chapter develops. It means accounting for both the historians view of London as being far more governable than the literature suggests, and for the literary critics who see in the literature evidence of containment strategies to cope with London's seemingly ungovernable precincts.

21. A. L .Beier and Roger Finlay (eds), *London 1500–1700: The Making of the Metropolis* (London and New York, 1986) p. 43. More generally, see ch. 1, 'Population Growth and Suburban Expansion', pp. 37–59.

22. Karen Newman, 'City Talk: Women and Commodification in Jonson's *Epicoene*', *English Literary History*, vol. 56, no. 3 (Fall 1989). pp. 503–19 (p. 503). Newman's basic argument is that in a sexualized way women metonymically bore the language and practice of commodity relations as commerce developed in the city.

23 Francis Lenton, *Characterismi: Or Lentons Leasures* (London, 1631), cited in Lawrence Manley, *London in the Age of Shakespeare: An Anthology* (London, 1986) pp. 32–8.

24. Dekker replicates this commonplace assumption in *The Shoemakers' Holiday*. In Act IV, Scene i, Jane is depicted '*in a seamster's shop*' as Hammon tries to buy her. Seamstress was often a euphemism for prostitute in early modern London.

25. *Hic Mulier: Or The Man-Woman: Being a Medicine to cure the Coltish Disease of the Staggers in the Masculine-Femininies of our Times* (London, 1620), sig. B3. 'Nothing' was, of course, slang for female genitals at this time..

26. For an account of the integrated relationship between marriage, the marketplace, love, and comedy, see Richard Horwich, 'Wives, Courtesans, and the Economics of Love in Jacobean Comedy', in Clifford Davidson, C. J. Giankaris and John H. Stroupe (eds), *Drama in the Renaissance* (New York, 1986) pp. 255–73.

27. The word 'Livers' here is carefully chosen, not only for its meaning connecting it to a livelihood but also because it alludes to London's official liveried companies who dominated social and political life in the City.

28. Donald Lupton, *London and The Country Carbonadoed and Quartered into Severall Characters* (London, 1632), sig. G6.

29. James I, cited in Christopher Hill, *The Century of Revolution 1603–1714*, first published 1961 (Wokingham, 1980) p. 64. Clearly what troubled the authorities was not the styles themselves but the (unofficial) autonomy which they represented. On a technical note, the hats were wide because they often carried their baskets, their 'shops' on their heads.
30. A citizen became a Freeman after having fulfilled the requirements of his guild (apprenticeship and so on). He was then allowed to trade as a master, and open up a shop, under the jurisdiction and protection of the guild.
31. Officially becoming a citizen meant being sworn in as a Freeman of the City of London at the Guildhall. In practice, it was a privilege which could only be accorded to half of London's population. As Rappaport says, 'There may have been no legal impediment preventing a woman from obtaining the freedom, but in reality very few became citizens' (Steve Rappaport, *Worlds Within Worlds: Structures of Life in Sixteenth Century London*, p. 36).
32. James Howell, *Londonopolis* (London, 1657), cited in Manley, *London in the Age of Shakespeare*, pp. 47–8.
33. For an elaboration of the city conceptualized as a predatory medium see Gail Kern Paster, *The Idea of the City in the Age of Shakespeare* (Athens, 1985); see especially ch. 6, 'Parasites and Sub-parasites: The City as Predator in Jonson and Middleton', pp. 150–77. Paster's account, however, tends to see the texts merely reflecting metropolitan anxieties about the city as a 'man-devouring' matrix.
34. Manley, *London in the Age of Shakespeare*, p. 196.
35. Ibid.
36. Richard Johnson, *Look On Me, London* (London, 1613) in *Illustrations of Early English Popular Literature*, ed. by J. Payne Collier, 4 vols (New York: Benjamin Blom, 1966) vol. III, p. 23.
37. Lawrence Manley, 'From Matron to Monster: Tudor–Stuart London and the Languages of Urban Description', in Heather Dubrow and Richard Strier (eds), *The Historical Renaissance*, (Chicago, 1988) pp. 347–74 (p. 348).
38. Manley, 'Matron to Monster', p. 349.
39. Ibid.
40. Ibid.
41. Manley, in seeing Defoe as the explicator of the 'dynamism that deforms London into monstrous shape' (p. 366), concludes:

> The experience of London's monstrosity had long been a powerful current in such Tudor–Stuart genres as satire and city comedy. But the exclusion of this perspective for so long from prose description is testimony both to the power of generic distinctions and to the ideological force of conceptual models through which London retained a compelling and familiar humanized identity. The city lost this identity only as its portraitists discovered theirs. (p. 367)

My argument perceives that monstrosity already locatable in the prose of writers like Dekker and Nashe. Any chronological discrepancy is accounted for by a difference in perception as to what might be considered monstrous. Defoe's prose descriptions tame the energetic resources of the city in a way that Dekker and others cannot (consider, for example, their different attitudes to prostitution). Both Dekker and his prostitute characters are more locatable within the medium of the 'monstrous' because, unlike Defoe, the function of his writing does less to set up distance between writer and reader and that which is being written about (or described). So, though I question the argument about firm generic distinctions, Manley's point about the relationship between urban writer and identity is well taken.

42. For an analysis of the role of 'willful' women resisting the bourgeoisie's compression of women's cultural space see Margaret George, 'From "Goodwife" to "Mistress": The Transformation of the Female in Bourgeois Culture', *Science and Society*, vol. 37 (1973) pp. 152–77.

43. *HIC MULIER*, sig. A3.

44. Lupton, *London and the Country Carbonadoed*, p. 1.

45. Ibid., p. 2.

46. Ibid.

47. See Coppélia Kahn, *Man's Estate: Masculine Identity in Shakespeare* (Berkeley, 1981). Drawn from the work of Nancy Chodorow, Kahn's psychoanalytical readings of Shakespeare, particularly those depending upon 'the polarization of social roles and behaviour into masculine independence, power, and repression of feeling as opposed to feminine dependence, weakness, and tenderness' (p. 11) have an important impact on how the city was imagined. However, I argue that those gender distinctions must be read through a much wider matrix of social, topographical, and other cultural forms.

48. London's canting nomenclature was 'Rome-ville', from which Freevill's name is adapted. Marston obviously wants to express some tension between the unofficial and official identities in the City.

49. Robert Darnton, *The Great Cat Massacre and other Episodes in French Cultural History* (New York, 1985) pp. 107–8.

50. Richard Johnson, in Payne Collier, *Illustrations of Early English Popular Literature*, p. 18.

51. *Hic Mulier*, sig. C1.

52. Edward Jorden, *A Briefe Discourse of a Disease Called the Suffocation of the Mother* (London, 1603), STC 14790, G3.; also cited in Neely, 'Documents of Madness', p. 337.

53. Thomas Hall, *The Loathesomnesse of Long Haire* (London, 1654), p. 47.

54. M. M. Knappen, *Two Elizabethan Puritan Diaries by Richard Rogers and Samuel Ward* (Chicago: American Society of Church History, 1933) p. 66.

55. Ibid., p. 96.

56. Ibid., p. 66.

57. Ibid., p. 57.

58. Agnew uses Marx's vivid phrase 'Circulation ... sweats money from every pore', p. 42.

59. *Thomas Nashe* (ed. Steane) p. 483. Ursula's body in Jonson's *Bartholomew Fair* is thematized in the same way; as Quarlous says 'She's able to give a man the sweating sickness with looking on her' (II.v.103–4).

60. Knappen, *Two Elizabethan Puritan Diaries*, p. 94.

61. Angelo exemplifies this in *Measure for Measure*:

> Can it be
> That Modesty may more betray our sense
> Than woman's lightness? Having waste ground enough
> Shall we desire to raze the sanctuary
> And pitch our evils there?...

II.ii.168–72

Angelo perceives prostitutes or impure women through the topographical metaphor 'waste ground'. They function to keep women like Isabella pure, but mostly they are there to keep men pure. He sees his own lust through appropriately scatological metaphors. For him, any contact brings the risk of defiling himself and Isabella. For more on defecation as an evil passion, see the analysis of Nehemiah Wallington at the end of this chapter. It is significant that Angelo uses savage metaphors of territorialization as a way of recording the development of his own problematic desires.

62. Saint Jerome, cited by James A. Brundage, 'Prostitution in the Medieval Canon Law', in *Signs: Journal of Women in Culture and Society*, vol. 1, no. 4 (1976) pp. 825–45 (p. 827).

63. See *Proverbs*, 23:27: 'For a whore is a deep ditch; and a strange woman is a narrow pit.'

64. One of the few occasions where the client has been made the subject of scrutiny in the attempts to control prostitution occurred in the 1570s when the City authorities attempted to prosecute the prostitutes' clients as well. But too many rich and powerful men kept getting caught. Even here, as Archer (*The Pursuit of Stability*, pp. 231–3) shows, the civic authorities' attempts to bring the client into the law's field of vision were tied to the City's power battle with the Court.

65. Karras, 'The Regulation of Brothels', p. 426.

66. Thomas Norton, *Instructions to the Lord Mayor of London, 1574–5: Whereby he is to govern himself and the City*, in J. Payne Collier (ed.), *Illustrations of Old English Literature*, 4 vols (New York: Benjamin Blom, 1866), vol. III, pp. 1–23. It was commonplace from the early days of guild corporation to imagine the Mayor as governor of 'the corporate and politique bodie of her Citie of London' (p. 1). These metaphors became more dynamic as the city's tensions grew with its expansion. The ideology of self-discipline became politically highly charged.

67. Knappen, *Two Elizabethan Puritan Diaries*, p. 62.

68. This is the subtitle/frontispiece of Richard Johnson's pamphlet *Look on Me, London* (London, 1613).

69. Charles M. Clode, *The Early History of the Guild of Merchants Taylors*, 2 vols (London, 1888) vol. II, pp. 281, 283 and 288.

70. Ibid., p. 290.

71. Ibid.

72. Johnson, in Collier, *Illustrations of Early English Popular Literature*, p. iii.

73. *Analytical Index to the Series of Records known as the Remembrancia preserved among the Archives of the City of London A.D. 1579–1664*, ed. by E. B. McKerrow (London, 1878) pp. 358–9. Dated 8 July 1614, the entry

has been attributed to Thomas Myddleton or Thomas Hayes. For the connection between these remarks and the character of Justice Overdo, see C. S. Alden (ed.), *Bartholomew Fair by Ben Jonson*, Yale Studies in English, XXV (New York, 1904) p. 163; and E. A. Horsman (ed.), *Bartholomew Fair, Ben Jonson*, The Revels Plays (Manchester, 1960) p. xviii. However, the *Dictionary of National Biography* ascribes the *Remembrancia* entry to Thomas Myddleton. According to A. B. Beaven, *The Aldermen of the City of London, Henry VIII–1908*, 2 vols (London, 1908–13) the two mayors (both knighted on 26 July 1603) that year were Myddleton and Hayes; but as the changeover occurs around Michaelmas (see vol. I, p. xxxviii) it seems most likely that the reference is to the former, Sir Thomas Myddleton.

74. Johnson, in Collier, *Illustrations of Early English Popular Literature*, p. 16.
75. Archer, *The Pursuit of Stability*, p. 236.
76. William Averell, *A mervailous combat of contrarieties* (London, 1588), C2. Also cited in Sandra Clark, *The Elizabethan Pamphleteers: Popular Moralist Pamphlets 1580–1640* (Rutherford, 1983) p. 143.
77. Thomas White, *A Sermon Preached at Pawles Crosse on Sunday the Thirde of November 1577 in Time of Plague* (London, 1578) p. 93. Cited in Archer, *The Pursuit of Stability*, p. 255.
78. Archer, *The Pursuit of Stability*, p. 254.
79. *Thomas Platter's Travels in England in 1599*, trans. by Clare Williams (London, 1937). pp. 174–5, cited in Wallace Shugg, 'Prostitution in Shakespeare's London', in *Shakespeare Studies*, vol. 10 (1977) pp. 291–313 (p. 305).
80. Paul S. Seaver, *Wallington's World: A Puritan Artisan in Seventeenth-Century London* (Stanford, 1985). p. 183.
81. Ibid., p. 26.
82. Ibid.
83. Ibid.
84. Ibid., p. 27.
85. Ibid.
86. Ibid., p. 26.
87. Peter Stallybrass and Allon White, *The Politics and Poetics of Transgression* (London, 1986) p. 183.
88. Seaver, *Wallington's World*, p. 26.
89. Richard Johnson, in Collier, *Illustration of Early English Popular Literatures*, p. 18.
90. From the famous dictum of Thomas Aquinas, 'Prostitution in the towns is like the cesspool in the palace: take away the cesspool and the palace will become an unclean and evil-smelling place' (*De Reg. Principium. Opusc.* 20, IV, 14), cited in Fernando Henriques, *Prostitution in Europe and the New World* (London, 1963) p. 45.
91. *Thomas Dekker, Selected Writings*, ed. E. D. Pendry, The Stratford-Upon-Avon Library, no. 4 (London, 1967) p. 321.
92. For example, the Rogers and Ward Diaries and those of Nehemiah Wallington; *The Diary of Michael Wigglesworth 1653–1657*, ed. by E. S. Morgan (New York, 1965); see also Theodore de Welles, 'Sex and Sexual Attitudes in Seventeenth-Century England: The Evidence from

Puritan Diaries', *Renaissance and Reformation*, vol. 24, no. 1 (Winter 1988) pp. 45–64. De Welles relates how, for a Puritan, keeping a diary was an important facet of a 'disciplined, systematic self-interrogation' (p. 48). And, as Roy Baumeister says, 'The endless inner struggles of the Puritans are preserved for us in the unprecedented number of diaries they wrote; these reveal the Puritans' confrontation with the possibility of self-deception' (*Identity: Cultural Change and the Struggle for Self* [New York, 1986] p. 48).

93. *The Works of Gabriel Harvey*, ed. by A. B. Grosart, The Huth Library, 3 vols (London, 1869) 'I prostitute my pen in hope of gaine' said the Puritan sympathizer Harvey (vol. III, p. 31). Harvey, who held a deep suspicion of writing, was an assiduous organizer and annotator of his own writing, and a proponent of standardized spelling. After the linguistic mud-slinging of the Marprelate controversy he gave up writing.

94. Lyndal Roper, 'Discipline and Respectability: Prostitution and the Reformation in Augsburg', in *History Workshop Journal*, XIX (1985) pp. 3–28 (p. 20).

95. Archer, *The Pursuit of Stability*, p. 232.

96. Elizabeth Wilson, 'The Invisible Flâneur', *New Left Review*, no. 191 (Jan./Feb. 1992) pp. 90–110 (p. 98). Although referring to a much later period, Wilson charts a significant connection between the flâneur and the prostitute. Quoting Benjamin, she relates that 'Prostitution opens up the possibility of a mythical communion with the masses' (p. 106). We can see the terrible consequences of that 'mythical communion' in our earlier period.

97. David Morse, *England's Time of Crisis: From Shakespeare to Milton* (Basingstoke, 1989) p. 38.

98. In *The Honest Whore, part I*, Bellafront's interaction with the courtiers reveals how money symbolized City–Court friction and tension. When Castruchio says 'What an asse is that Lord, to borrow money of a Citizen', Bellafront replies, 'Nay, Gods my pitty, what an asse is that Citizen to lend mony to a Lord' (II.i.114–116). For Middleton, sex was also a source of competition and conflict between the City and the Court. In *Michaelmas Term*, for example, Quomodo puts the courtier's fascination with city-women succinctly: 'There are means and waies enow to hooke in Gentry,/Besides our deadlye enmitye which thus stands:/They're busye 'bout our wives, We 'bout their Lands' (*Michaelmas Term*, I.i.110–112).

99. Archer, *The Pursuit of Stability*, p. 213.

100. Of the more lurid examples, see E. J. Burford, *Bawds and Lodgings: A History of Bankside Brothels, c. 100–1675* (London, 1976); and E. J. Burford, *Wits, Wenchers and Wantons: London's Low Life; Covent garden in the Eighteenth Century* (London, 1986).

101. Morse, see ch. 4, which he begins, 'If there was any one place that could be confidently singled out as the focus of iniquity in the kingdom that place was London. The sheer size of London made it an unprecedented and altogether overwhelming phenomenon' (p. 37.) This fairly typical argument seems to replicate the perception of the city's rulers and occupants which I am investigating.

226 *Notes*

102. It is a significant historical irony that those who had once perpetrated a policy of 'lac'd correction' should then hand the whip and other instruments of correction to those whom they had once punished so assiduously. As the disciplinarian came to internalize and fantasize about his own self-discipline the market, ironically, allowed him to purchase that service. The 'dominatrix' (one who whips or 'punishes' her clients) has been one of the roles demanded of prostitute's trade since, at least, the nineteenth century. The story of prostitution continues!

103. Jean E. Howard, 'Crossdressing, the Theatre, and Gender Struggle in Early Modern England', *Shakespeare Quarterly*, vol. 39, no. 4 (Winter 1988), pp. 418–40.

104. Rudolf M. Dekker and Lotte C. van de Pol, *The Tradition of Female Transvestism in Early Modern Europe*, trans. by Judy Macure and Lotte C. van de Pol (Basingstoke, 1989) pp. 11 and 8.

105. Moll seems to excite as much interest now as she did for her contemporaries. Along with Jean Howard's fine article, see Margo Hendricks, 'A Painter's Eye: Gender and Middleton and Dekker's The Roaring Girl, *Women's Studies*, vol. 18 (1990) pp. 191–203; Patrick Cheney, 'Moll Cutpurse as Hermaphrodite in Dekker and Middleton's The Roaring Girl', *Renaissance and Reformation*, new series vol. 7, no. 2 (May 1983) pp. 120–135; Frederick O. Waagé, 'Meg and Moll: Two Renaissance London Heroines', *Journal of Popular Culture*, vol. 20, no. 1 (Summer 1986) pp. 105–17; Sandra Clark, 'Hic Mulier, Haec Vir, and the Controversy over Masculine Women', *Studies in Philology*, vol. 82, No. 2 (Spring, 1985) pp. 157–83; Patricia Gartenberg, 'An Elizabethan Wonder Woman: The Life and Fortunes of Long Meg of Westminster', *Journal of Popular Culture*, vol. 17, no. 3 (Winter 1983) pp. 49–59; Ellen Galford, *Moll Cutpurse, Her True History* (Edinburgh, 1984); Laura Levine, 'Men in Women's Clothing: Anti-theatricality and Effeminization from 1579 to 1642', *Criticism*, vol. 28, no. 2 (Spring 1986), pp. 121–43; Simon Shepherd, *Amazons and Warrior Women: Varieties of Feminism in Seventeenth-Century Drama* (New York, 1981); Jonathan Dollimore, 'Subjectivity, Sexuality, and Transgression: The Jacobean Connection', *Renaissance Drama*, new series vol. 17 (1986) pp. 53–81; Jonathan Dollimore, 'Shakespeare, Cultural Materialism, Feminism and Marxist Humanism', in *New Literary History*, vol. 21, no. 3 (Spring 1990) pp. 471–93; Mary Beth Rose, 'Women in Men's Clothing: Apparel and Social Stability in The Roaring Girl', in *English Literary Renaissance*, vol. 14, no. 3 (Autumn 1984) pp. 367–91. In very different ways all these critics show how Moll, through cross-dressing and ambiguous gender behaviour, flouts, subverts, colludes with, and transgresses, the dominant culture. But in doing so she allows for the reinscription, containment, and upholding of conventional practices and cultural norms. Rather than re-tilling this obviously fertile ground I am interested in how she could become a figure, then and now, around which those issues continually revolve.

106. Jack Dapper refers directly to Moll's symbolic heritage when he asks 'was it your Meg of Westminster's courage that rescued me?' (*The Roaring Girl*, V.i.2–3).

107. See *Four Tudor Comedies*, ed. by William Tydeman (Harmondsworth, 1984) which includes *Gammer Gurton's Nedle* by William Stevenson and *Mother Bombie* by John Lyly.
108. *Pasquils Jests with The Merriments of Mother Bunch* (London, 1629), A2.
109. Ibid., A3.
110. Chapter IV examines Dekker's *Worke for Armourers* (London, 1609), written about the same time as *The Roaring Girl*, which depicts London divided into two great armies; money versus poverty.
111. Howard, 'Cross-dressing', p. 437. Howard's article skilfully charts the relationship between cross-dressing and the theatre, which is why I see the audience's role in relation to both Moll and the play as crucial to any understanding of her as a figure who negotiates city–suburb and social stress.
112. Howard, 'Crossdressing', p. 420. As Howard makes clear, crossdressing women were charged with prostitution rather than sexual perversion. Women's continence, either sexually or vocally, was the primary source of anxiety for the authorities, hence the dramatic significance of a transvestite roaring girl.
113. Thomas Middleton and Thomas Dekker, *The Roaring Girl*, edited by Andor Gomme (London, 1976), p. xxx.
114. The promiscuity which accompanies linguistic and semiotic insecurity is explored by Feste in Shakespeare's *Twelfth Night*. As Viola says 'they that dally nicely with words may quickly make them wanton.' To which the clown replies, 'I would therefore my sister had no name ... her name's a word, and to dally with that word might make my sister wanton' (III.i.14–20).

## 3 LONDON'S LANGUAGES OF FASHION

1. Usually anti-English attacks through fashion targeted Continental styles worn by London's courtiers. Here, in a tacit allusion to an ironically preferred 'plain Englishness', Dekker employs some common slurs against other national groups: Scottish 'tightness' and Irish 'indolence'.
2. Jonson originally wrote this in Latin which is an elite (and dead) language, thereby increasing its removal from the colloquial, the vulgar, the ordinary and the potentially riotous. On Latin as authoritative word in this context, see Peter Womack, *Ben Jonson* (Oxford and New York, 1986) pp. 78–87.
3. Dekker's joke about Adam and the apple is a lot more playful than Middleton's more contemporary allusion to 'arch-traitor'.
4. It also produces a sense of inconsistency in Dekker's writing, for which many critics chide him.
5. *OED* records both meanings of 'bombast': 'cotton-wool used as padding or stuffing for clothes' and 'inflated or turgid language'.
6. Dekker spent most of his life in debt to more than his tailor: see George R. Price *Thomas Dekker* (New York, 1969) pp. 17–33; Mary

Leland Hunt, *Thomas Dekker: A Study* (New York, 1911) p. 148; R. A. Foakes and R. T. Trickert (eds), *Henslowe's Diary* (Cambridge, 1961) passim; Walter W. Greg, *Henslowe's Diary*, Part II: *Commentary* (London 1908) pp. 256–60.

7. Christopher Breward, *The Culture of Fashion* (Manchester and New York, 1995) p. 44.

8. Diana de Marly, *Fashion for Men: An Illustrated History* (New York, 1985) p. 37. See also Valerie Cummings, *A Visual History of Costume: The Seventeenth Century* (London, 1987) p. 29.

9. Breward, *The Culture of Fashion*, p. 51.

10. Ibid., p. 42.

11. Mikhail Bakhtin, *Rabelais and His World*, trans. by Hélène Iswolsky (Boston, 1968; Indiana, 1984) p. 27.

12. Ibid., p. 19.

13. Although Baroque offers rich and curving forms with elaborate ornamentation (often linking the body and the world) essentially it seeks an overall balance of disparate parts which the grotesque does not.

14. Breward, *The Culture of Fashion*, p. 42.

15. Ibid., see ch. 2, 'Renaissance: The Rhetoric of Power', pp. 41–74.

16. Ibid., p. 50.

17. Pickadillys were almost certainly made in Piccadilly (London, SW1), and gave the place its name. The neckwear derived its name from Peccadillo, meaning 'a trifling offence' (*OED*).

18. On the 'lower bodily stratum', see Bakhtin, *Rabelais*, pp. 368–426.

19. See *To Penshurst* in *Ben Jonson*, ed. by Ian Donaldson, The Oxford Authors (Oxford and New York, 1985) pp. 282–5.

20. The upper body was shaped like a triangle with each shoulder and the navel being the points; the lower half of the body mirrored this as if the woman was a shaped like a giant X.

21. Breward, *The Culture of Fashion*, p. 41.

22. Ibid., p. 182.

23. Ibid., p. 51.

24. Ibid., p. 49.

25. de Marley, *Fashion for Men*, p. 37.

26. Margaret Pelling, 'Appearance and Reality: barber-surgeons, the body and disease', in A. L. Beier and Roger Finlay (eds), *London 1500–1700, The Making of the Metropolis* (London and New York, 1986) pp. 82–112 (p. 89).

27. Breward, *The Culture of Fashion*, p. 90.

28. Ibid., p. 52.

29. Ibid., p. 67.

30. Ibid.

31. The fear/fantasy of being devoured by the people, I would argue, is powerfully connected to grotesque. There are many references in late medieval and early modern writing, from the *Book of Margery Kempe* to Ben Jonson's *Sejanus*, where there are images of being chopped up and put in the pot or being torn to pieces by an angry crowd, where absorption by the body of the people indicates the end of an individual existence.

32. Pelling, 'Appearance and Reality', p. 90.

33. Ibid.
34. Neil Rhodes, *The Elizabethan Grotesque* (London, 1980) p. 62.
35. In Chapter 4, I develop more fully the relationship between Nashe and Dekker, and their differing styles of writing within the metropolis. Ultimately, Nashe could not or would not adapt to the new writing which the London market required.
36. Rhodes, *The Elizabethan Grotesque*, p. 62.
37. Frederich Dedekind, *Grobianus*, trans. by Roger Bull, first published in Frankfurt in 1594, translated into English by R. F., entered in the Stationer's Register, 15 December 1602 and later 21 May 1604, later published in London as *The School of Slovenry* in 1605. Basically the book consists of various descriptions of scatological, emetic, and excremental functions written on a statue like an early form of graffiti.
38. For Breward this relaxed look indicated a kind of romanticism and/or pastoralism: 'The loosening of the male doublet, usually depicted worn unbuttoned over a shirt and sleeves embroidered with intricate flower motifs, together with the adoption of longer hair and a soft lawn falling collar edged with lace, presented a deliberate nostalgic, chivalrous and pastoral effect that coincided with whimsical trends in court music literature and drama' (*The Culture of Fashion*, p. 52). Certainly the titles of Shakespeare's romantic comedies allude to this sense of whimsy, though this affect was not about the superficial evocation of loss; it signalled deep-seated changes in aristocratic identity.
39. In *The Revenger's Tragedy*, for example, Cyril Tourneur's Vindice is a hyperbolical malcontent. Significantly, he achieves his 'revenge' upon a court system, one which he can neither inhabit or abandon, by adopting various courtly styles.
40. For a lively account of English fashion 'problems' see William Harrison in *Holinshed's Chronicles*, ed. by Henry Ellis, 6 vols (London, 1807–8) vol. I, pp. 289–90. English adoption of foreign fashions was extensive and often mocked (see Breward, *The Culture of Fashion*, ch. 2) and even Elizabeth, during the war with Spain, adopted Spanish styles. Those who condemned foreign fashions were probably more interested in satirizing the class who wore them; Dekker, of course, has it both ways by mocking the mockers.
41. Bakhtin, *Rabelais*, p. 320.
42. Peter Stallybrass and Allon White, *The Politics and Poetics of Transgression* (London, 1986) p. 21.
43. Inigo Jones was, perhaps, the most influential designer of masques employing the motifs of classical antiquity. He developed the Palladian style as part of a move towards a pure classical style.
44. Norbert Elias, *The Civilizing Process*, trans. by Edmund Jephcott, 2 vols: vol. I, *Power and Civility*; vol. II, The *History of Manners*, first published 1939 (New York, 1978), II, p. 249. For Elias,

> This conception of the individual as homo clausus, a little world in himself who ultimately exists quite independently of the great world outside, determines the image of man in general. Every other human being is likewise seen as a homo clausus; his core, his being,

his true self appears likewise as something divided within him by an invisible wall from everything outside, including every other human being. (p. 249)

Within this framework it is easy to imagine, therefore, that clothing symbolizes that barrier between self and world, and other people.

45. In *Father Hubbard's Tales*, Middleton makes fun of the limited proportions of Puritan neckwear: 'as little and diminutive as a puritan's ruff' (Bullen, vol. VIII, 69). Bullen's footnote embellishes Middleton's assessment by recounting a ditty describing a 'Puritan preacher'; 'With pate cut shorter than the brow, / With little ruff starch'd you know how'.
46. Breward, *The Culture of Fashion*, p. 50.
47. Definitions of the effeminacy or otherwise of men's fashion and identity was not confined to the conflict between Court and City. According to Breward, 'Male favourites at the court of James I took Elizabethan notions of effeminacy to ostentatious extremes.' Yet the 'epicene delicacy' which marked some factions within the Jacobean court was contrasted by a cult of 'ascetic chivalric masculinity' which developed around Henry, Prince of Wales, who appeared to be at odds with his father (Breward, *The Culture of Fashion*, pp. 78–9).
48. William Prynne, *The Unlovelinesse of Lovelockes*, The English Experience, its Record in Early Printed Books in Facsimile; no. 825, photoprint of 1628 edition, S.T.C. no. 20477 (Amsterdam: Norwood, 1976).
49. Bakhtin, *Rabelais*, p. 320.
50. See the portrait of Edward Alleyn in Aileen Reid and Robert Maniura (eds), *Edward Alleyn: Elizabethan actor, Jacobean gentleman* (London: Dulwich Picture Gallery, 1994) p. 10. As the title suggests, socially Alleyn was as much a metropolitan hybrid as the theatre which he supervised. His wife, Joan, also fashioned herself across class lines by wearing both a ruff and a copotain; the latter being a sign of the City's upper bourgeois.
51. After the political settlement which accrued around the Restoration aristocratic and bourgeois styles merged in some respects. The adoption of wigs, for example, went some way to bridging the round-head/cavalier conflict. Although there were still extremes at the fringes of both social groups producing some outlandish styles, the established centre, especially concerning the boundaries of the body, became more homogenized. As the eighteenth century progressed, a style of classicism developed through the extraordinary design of a skin-tight, skin-coloured waistcoat which merged into an almost seamless bodysuit. The effect gave the appearance of being naked, or literally like a statue, under the frock coat. This took the metaphors, concepts, and opaque body aesthetics of classicism straight into fashion.
52. Stallybrass and White, *The Politics and Poetics of Transgression*, p. 22.
53. de Marly, *Fashion for Men*, p. 50.
54. It's worth noting here that sometime in the latter sixteenth century the City Fathers insisted upon shaving the heads of prostitutes. Women punished in this way were called punks. Some prostitutes who were

not officially punished still shaved their heads, perhaps because it so signified their trade and appealed to their clients.

55. Harrison, in *Chronicles*, I, p. 289.
56. Ibid.
57. Richard Corson, *Fashions in Hair* (New York, 1969, first published 1965) p. 206.
58. Ibid.
59. A 'tollerable beard' here means one not too large so that it may not be confused with a citizen's beard.
60. Prynne's main line of attack was simultaneously to impugn the moral integrity and masculinity of those who wore long hair.
61. Jonathan Raban, *Soft City* (London: Fontana, 1984, first published 1974) p. 64.
62. See Jean-Christophe Agnew, *Worlds Apart: The Market and the Theater in Anglo-American Thought 1550–1750* (Cambridge, 1986) pp. 101–48.
63. In *Twelfth Night*, for example, Malvolio's attempt at social advancement, through what he thinks would be a beneficial marriage, involves him dressing up in a ridiculously out-of-date and inappropriate fashion.
64. See A. L. Beier, *Masterless Men: The Vagrancy Problem in England 1560–1640*, especially ch. 2 and 3, pp. 14–47.
65. Robert Greene, *The Life and Complete Works in Prose and Verse of Robert Greene*, edited by A. B. Grosart, The Huth Library, 15 vols (London, 1881–6) vol. X, p. 204.
66. Stallybrass and White, *The Politics and Poetics of Transgression*, p. 76.
67. Emrys Jones, 'London in the Early Seventeenth Century: An Ecological Approach', *The London Journal*, vol. 6, no. 2 (1980) pp. 123–33 (p. 129).

## 4  BREAKING LOOSE FROM HELL

1. Thomas Nashe, *The Unfortunate Traveller and Other Works* ed. by J. B. Steane (Harmondsworth, 1972), pp. 54–5 (Hereinafter 'Nashe.')
2. Few writers wrote as much popular literature about Hell as Thomas Dekker.
3. Nashe., p. 72.
4. Ibid., p. 56.
5. Ibid.
6. Ibid., p. 54.
7. In 'A private Epistle of the Author to the Printer, wherein his full meaning and purpose in publishing this book is set forth' Nashe makes a disclaimer, which is, of course, also a mock-disclaimer:

Faith, I am very sorry, sir, I am thus unawares betrayed to infamy. You write to me my book is hasting to the second impression: he that hath once broke the ice of impudence need not care how deep he wade in discredit. I confess it to be a mere toy, not deserving any judicial man's view. If it have found any friends, so it is; you know very well that it was abroad a fortnight ere I knew of it, and uncorrected and unfinished it hath offered itself to the open scorn of the world. Had you not been so forward in the publishing of it, you should have certain epistles to orators and poets to insert to the latter end ... (*Nashe*, p. 49)

Ironic, perhaps, but we sense the extent of the publishers' control and Nashe's unease at the commercialization of writing, though not enough to stop him suggesting a better addendum if he had been consulted. The insertion of 'poets' at the latter end, to give it a literary gloss which the market place cannot, is recognized somewhat ironically by Dekker in *A Knight's Conjuring* where Nashe newly joins a variety of deceased Poets in Elysium.

8. For different views on Nashe's rhetorical style see Neil Rhodes, 'Nashe, Rhetoric and Satire', in Clive Bloom (ed.), *Jacobean Poetry and Prose: Rhetoric, Representation, and the Popular Imagination* (New York, 1988) pp. 25–43; and Jonathan V. Crewe, *Unredeemed Rhetoric: Thomas Nashe and the Scandal of Authorship* (Baltimore, 1982).
9. *Nashe*, p. 53.
10. Ibid.
11. Ibid.
12. Ibid.
13. Ibid., p. 76.
14. Ibid.
15. Ibid., p. 57.
16. Dekker aligns failed patrons with Catholicism, an insult which operates as both a cultural and social treason.
17. Sandra Clark, *The Elizabethan Pamphleteers: Popular Moralist Pamphlets 1580–1640* (Rutherford, 1985), p. 30. Alexander B. Grosart did not include *Newes from Graves-ende* in his collection of Dekker's *Non-Dramatic Works*, but F. P. Wilson's argument that the work is Dekker's appears convincing. For the analysis see *The Plague Pamphlets of Thomas Dekker*, ed. F. P. Wilson (Oxford, 1925) pp. xi–xvi.
18. John Feather, *A History of British Publishing* (London, 1988) p. 25.
19. Ibid., p. 27.
20. Ibid., pp. 7–50.
21. Ibid., p. 27.
22. Clark, *The Elizabethan Pamphleteers*, p. 30.
23. For the relationship between Nashe's 'Herring' and satire see Lorna Hutson, *Thomas Nashe In Context* (Oxford, 1989); especially ch. 12, 'Patronage as the Red Herring of Lenten Stuffe', pp. 245–68, and Jonathan Crewe, *Unredeemed Rhetoric*, pp. 91–2.
24. See Raymond Williams, *The Country and the City* (London, 1973) p. 22.
25. See n. 16.
26. Allon White, *Carnival , Hysteria, and Writing* (Oxford, 1993) p. 134.
27. G. W. Bernard, 'The Church of England c.1529–c.1642' in *History*, vol. 75, no. 244 (June 1990) pp. 183–206 (p. 191).

28. Ibid., p. 202.
29. See White, especially ch. 6, '"The Dismal Sacred Word": Academic Language and the Social Reproduction of Seriousness', pp. 122–34.
30. John Stachniewski, *The Persecutory Imagination: English Puritanism and the Literature of Religious Despair* (Oxford, 1991) p. 3.
31. Ibid., p. 1.
32. Ibid., p. 7.
33. From 'The Book of Common Prayer', in *Sixteenth-Century English Prose* ed. Karl J. Holzknecht (New York: The Harper English Literature Series, 1954) p. 151.
34. D. P. Walker, *The Decline of Hell: Seventeenth-Century Discussions of Eternal Torment* (Chicago, 1964).
35. Stachniewski, *The Persecutory Imagination*, pp. 23–4.
36. Ibid., p. 49.
37. *Thomas Dekker's A Knight's Conjuring (1607): A Critical Edition*, ed. by Larry M. Robbins (The Hague, 1974), p. 45.
38. Stachniewski, *The Persecutory Imagination*, p. 80.
39. Those easily discernible are the Gunpowder Plot, the Battle for Calais, Elizabeth's death, and the figure of Tamburlaine.
40. Christopher Marlowe, *Tamburlaine The Great, part II* (V.iii.48); see also Alan Sinfield, *Literature in Protestant England 1560–1660* (London, 1983) p. 83.
41. Sinfield, *Literature in Protestant England*, p. 84.
42. Julia Gasper, *The Dragon and the Dove: The Plays of Thomas Dekker* (Oxford, 1990) p. 3. For Gasper, militant Protestants were those who were determined to defend the Reformation and made this their highest political priority. They regarded the Reformed Church as the only true Church, and conceived of it as a single, international body. They emphasized its common beliefs, whether Lutheran or Calvinist, and thought that a unified, active defence was necessary in order to survive in the struggle against their great adversary, Rome (p. 2).
43. Stachniewski, *The Persecutory Imagination*, p. 331.
44. Ibid.
45. Lois G. Schwoerer, *'No Standing Armies' The Antiarmy Ideology in Seventeenth-Century England* (Baltimore, 1974) p. 11. See also C. G. Cruickshank, *Elizabeth's Army* (London, 1946).
46. By echoing the practice and language of espionage, Dekker mocks the extensive spy network set up by Elizabeth's Controller of Intelligence, Francis Walsingham.
47. Gasper, *The Dragon and the Dove*, p. 109.
48. See Chapter 3, n. 6 above.
49. Cited in Walter W. Greg, *Henslowe's Diary*, part II: *Commentary* (London, 1908) p. 260.
50. Stachniewski, *The Persecutory Imagination*, p. 319.
51. Ibid.
52. Again Dekker uses a military metaphor to criticize the empty purses of patrons. Here he alludes to the fact that many soldiers were improperly paid, or not paid at all, for their service to queen and country.

53. Lorna Hutson, *Thomas Nashe in Context* (Oxford and New York, 1989) p. 198.
54. Ibid., pp. 198–9.
55. Ibid., p. 201.
56. Ibid.
57. Cited in ibid., p. 203.
58. Ibid., p. 203.
59. Jerusalem, 57: 8–9, from *The Complete Poetry and Prose of William Blake*, ed. by David V. Erdman (New York, 1982 revd edn) p. 207.
60. Thomas Dekker (Wilson, p. 82).
61. According to Andrew Gurr, 'the City's "Remedyes" over playing concluded that playhouses should not be open until the weekly bill of plague victims had been less than fifty for three weeks ... [though] the limits were not always exactly enforced', in *The Shakespearean Stage 1574–1642* (Cambridge, 1970) p. 56.
62. The City began using the plague against the theatre at least by the late 1560s. The corruption of seriousness and the ensuing disorder was a prime source of anxiety as this 1569 report reveals:

> Forasmuch as thoroughe the great resort, accesse and assembles of great multitudes of people unto diverse and severall Innes and other places of this Citie, and the liberties & suburbes of the same, to thentent to here and see certayne stage playes, enterludes, and other disguisinges, on the saboth dayes and other solemne feastes commaunded by the church to be kept holy, and there being close pestered together in small romes, specially in this tyme of sommer, all not being and voyd of infeccions and diseases, whereby great infeccion with the plague, or some other infeccious diseases, may rise and growe, to the great hynderaunce of the comon wealth of this citty, and perill and daunger of the quenes majesties people, the inhabitantes thereof, and all others repayring thether, about there necessary affares

(cited in E. K. Chambers, *The Elizabethan Stage*, 4 vols [Oxford: Clarendon Press, 1923] vol. IV, p. 267).

63. Leeds Barroll, *Politics, Plague, and Shakespeare's Theatre: The Stuart Years* (Ithaca, 1991) p. 173.
64. *Thomas Dekker*, ed. by E. D. Pendry, The Stratford-Upon-Avon Library (London, 1967) p. 5 (hereinafter 'Pendry').
65. Dekker puns on the town of Gravesend located on the Kentish side of the Thames estuary. Any ships coming into the port of London from the sea would have to pass this town.
66. Pendry , p. 13.
67. Barroll, *Politics, Plague, and Shakespeare's Theatre*, p. 94.
68. Ibid., see appendices, pp. 211–32.
69. Ibid., pp. 95–6.
70. Ibid.
71. Gasper, *The Dragon and the Dove*, p. 2.
72. See Paul Slack, *The Impact of Plague in Tudor and Stuart England* (London, 1985) pp. 144–72.

73. 'Thespian Bowle' is most likely a synecdoche for the Theatre. It could also be a more specific reference to one of the Elizabethan-style public theatres, like the Swan, Hope, or Globe. For a description of theatre types and function see Andrew Gurr, *The Shakespearean Stage* pp. 82–111.

74. Sinfield, *Literature in Protestant England*, p. 8.

75. Thomas White, *A Sermon Preached at Pawles Crosse* (1578), cited in John Dover Wilson, *Life in Shakespeare's England* (London, 1954; first pub 1944) p. 228.

76. See Gasper, *The Dragon and the Dove*, esp. p. 7.

77. From Article 17 of *The 39 Articles drawn up by the Elizabethan Church in 1562*.

78. From the prologue of *If This be not a Good Play, the Divell is in It*.

79. Sinfield, *Literature in Protestant England*, p. 11.

80. Ibid., p. 9.

81. Ibid.

82. Ibid., p. 81.

83. Cited in G. E. Bentley, *The Seventeenth Century Stage* (Chicago, 1968) pp. 15–16.

84. Heywood's tract, along with others including Nashe in *Pierce Pennilesse*, was most likely written to counter City-inspired anti-theatre sermons from preachers like Thomas White and John Stockwood, as well as pamphlets by Philip Stubbes and Stephen Gosson.

85. For Puritans, bell-ringing was both distasteful and anti-God; as Ananias (a Puritan) says in Jonson's *The Alchemist*, 'Bells are profane' (III.ii.61).

86. Yoshiko Kawachi, *Calendar of English Renaissance Drama, 1558–1642* (New York, 1986)

87. The 'three' devils, of course, are a dark echo of the Holy Trinity; and in this period appear as a parodic allusion to Catholicism.

88. Mary Leland Hunt, *Thomas Dekker, a Study* (New York, 1911) p. 153.

89. Larry S. Champion, *Thomas Dekker and the Traditions of English Drama*, American University Studies, Series IV, English Language and Literature, vol. 27 (New York, 1985) p. 97.

90. Ibid., p. 96.

91. Ibid.

92. Ibid.

93. See Sinfield, *Literature in Protestant England*, ch. 2.

94. Raymond Williams, *Marxism and Literature* (Oxford, 1977). 'Dominant, Residual, and Emergent': these are the terms which Raymond Williams uses to describe the historical process in the 'dynamic inter-relations' of a culture as a way of accounting for the various elements within it. He developed these formulations in order to talk more adequately and flexibly about the social transitions which inform Marxism; like that from feudalism to capitalism (*Marxism and Literature*, pp. 121–36).

95. Howard Dobin, *Merlin's Disciples: Prophecy, Poetry, and Power in Renaissance England* (Stanford, 1990) p. 47.

96. Gasper, *The Dragon and the Dove*, p. 121.

97. Champion, *Thomas Dekker*, p. 93 and Gasper, *The Dragon and the Dove*, p. 110.

98. Gasper, *The Dragon and the Dove*, p. 126.
99. Ibid.
100. *The Cobler of Caunterburie and Tarltons Newes out of Purgatorie*, ed. Geoffrey Creigh and Jane Belfield, *Medieval and Renaissance Texts*, vol. 3 (Leiden, 1987) pp. 146–7.
101. *The Wyll of the Devyll. And Last Testament* in *Illustrations of Early English Popular Literature*, ed. J. Payne Collier, vol. 1 (New York: Benjamin Blom, 1966) intro., p. i.
102. Collier, *Wyll*, pp. 6–7.
103. Peter Womack, *Ben Jonson* (Oxford, 1986) p. 45.
104. In many ways the scene takes off where *Dr Faustus* finishes. Marlowe exposes the apparatus of terror which the unknowing horror of Hell structures, whereas Dekker gives us a parodic glimpse into that 'unknowable' realm of terror.
105. According to English (Protestant) history, an insurgent Catholic revolt led by Guy Fawkes attempted to blow up the Houses of Parliament along with King James in November 1605. 'The Gunpowder Plot' failed when the 'conspirators' were discovered. The image of Guy Fawkes suffering the torments of Hell is thoroughly ritualized in English culture as an his effigy is burnt on a bonfire upon each 5 November, often to the chant 'remember, remember, the fifth of November'.
106. Michel Foucault, *Discipline and Punishment: The Birth of the Prison*, trans. by Alan Sheridan (New York, 1st US edn 1977) p. 60.
107. Roger Sales, *Christopher Marlowe* (New York, 1991) p. 25.
108. Foucault, *Discipline and Punishment*, p. 61.
109. Sales, *Christopher Marlowe* , p. 25.
110. Hunt, *Thomas Dekker*, p. 165.
111. In Elizabeth's time, the pressing need for troops meant that the gaols were raided by the forces of the muster and convicts conscripted. Many, including Barnaby Rich, condemned such practices: 'in England when service happeneth we disburseth the prisons of thieves', cited in Cruickshank, *Elizabeth's Army*, p. 10. Yet the practice remained one of the main recruiting planks of the Elizabethan period: in 1598, the Privy Council reported that conscripts 'were taken out of gaoles', cited in Paul A. Jorgensen, *Shakespeare's Military World* (Los Angeles: Berkeley, 1956) p. 143. Just how lucky Dekker was to be incarcerated during the period in which James was de-escalating foreign military campaigns – and so to miss being conscripted – is difficult to say, but it certainly contributed to his lengthy imprisonment.
112. Philip Shaw, 'The Position of Thomas Dekker in Jacobean Prison Literature', *Papers of the Modern Language Association*, vol. 62 (1947) pp. 366–91 (p. 373).
113. I say 'himself' here not because women never fell into debt (though they were rarely considered 'citizens' – Free of the City) nor because they fell outside the apparatus of self-policing, but because the consequence of the citizens' self-discipline had such a disastrous effect on their relations with women, as I explain in Chapter 2.
114. Shaw, 'The Position of Thomas Dekker', p. 374.

# Notes

115. Pendry, *Thomas Dekker*, p. 13.
116. For a sample of the considerable legislative activity upon the question of prison abuse see E. D. Pendry, *Elizabethan Prisons and Prison Scenes*, 2 vols., vol. 1, in Dr James Hogg (ed.), *Elizabethan & Renaissance Studies*, Salzburg Studies in English Literature, 17 (Salzburg, 1974) pp. 320–62.
117. Pendry, *Elizabethan Prisons*, p. 36.
118. Ibid.
119. Ibid., p. 34.
120. Sales, *Christopher Marlowe*, p. 24.
121. Ibid., p. 25.
122. Christopher Hill, *The Century of Revolution 1603–1714* (Wokingham, 1980; 1st pubd 1961) p. 146.
123. Roger Manning, *Village Revolts: Social Protest and Popular Disturbances in England, 1509–1640* (Oxford, 1988).
124. Faustus in *Dr Faustus* (Scene ɪv, 127).
125. Northrop Frye, 'Varieties of Literary Utopias', in Frank E. Manuel (ed.), *Utopias and Utopian Thought*, The Dædalus Library (Boston: Cambridge, 1966) pp. 25–49 (p. 34).
126. Keith Thomas, 'The Utopian Impulse in Seventeenth-Century England', in Dominic Baker-Smith and C. C. Barfoot (eds), *Between Dream and Nature: Essays on Utopia and Dystopia*, DQR Studies in Literature 2 (Amsterdam, 1987), pp. 20–46 (p. 20).
127. In many ways Bakhtin's theory of Carnival is predicated upon this function, rather than an unattainable Utopia for which he has been overly criticized.
128. Jonathan Dollimore, *Radical Tragedy: Religion, Ideology and Power in the Drama of Shakespeare and his Contemporaries* (Brighton, 1984) p. 119.
129. Samuel Hartlib, cited in Thomas, 'The Utopian Impulse', p. 45.
130. Here I mean revolution in its late medieval or early modern sense: 'The return or recurrence of a point or period of time ' (*OED*).
131. London's Lord Mayors came from the twelve premier companies; significantly Dekker chose a minor guild from which to draw the civic hero Simon Eyre.
132. Cited in Cruickshank, *Elizabeth's Army*, p. 128. The plight of the loyal soldier scorned and neglected upon his return seemed both a common and not so common thought in this period: in *Shakespeare's Military World*, Jorgensen writes

> And no less an authority than Queen Elizabeth acknowledged to the emissary De Maisse her opinion of English soldiers in France: 'She said ... that they were but thieves and ought to hang, and other words between her teeth which I did not well understand. Also it seemed as if she had put herself in choler about it, for which cause I forebore to discuss the matter further'. (p. 145)

For many, especially those in authority, the perception that conscripts were social 'riff-raff' altered little after their service.

133. Once again Dekker inverts the authorities' view that closing the theatres (under the pretext of plague) would reduce dissent and disorder.
134. Clark, *Elizabethan Pamphleteers*, p. 127.
135. J. R. Hale, *War and Society in Renaissance Europe 1450–1620* (New York, 1985) p. 44.
136. Ibid., p. 88. Large numbers of unruly discharged troops remained a problem in the city through this period; 'when in 1589 troops were returning from the expedition to Portugal, a mob of 500 of them were only prevented from looting Bartholomew Fair by the call-up of 2000 of the London militia' (p. 88).
137. Neil Rhodes, 'Nashe, Rhetoric and Satire', p. 31.
138. See Jonathan Crewe, *Unredeemed Rhetoric*.

# Bibliography

## PRIMARY TEXTS AND COLLECTIONS

Adams, Thomas, *Mystical Bedlam, or The World of Mad-Men* (London, 1615).
William Averell, *A mervailous combat of contrarieties* (London, 1588).
*The Complete Poetry and Prose of William Blake*, ed. David V. Erdman, revd edn (New York, 1982).
Brant, Sebastian, *The Ship of Fools*, trans. Edwin H. Zeydel (New York, 1944).
Bright, Timothy, *A Treatise on Melancholie* (London, 1586).
Chambers, E. K., *The Elizabethan Stage*, 4 vols (Oxford, 1923).
*John Clare*, ed. Eric Robinson and David Powell, The Oxford Authors (New York, 1984).
*The cobler of Caunterburie, and Tarlton's Newes out of Purgatorie*, ed. Geoffrey Creigh and Jane Belfield (Leiden, 1987).
Collier, John Payne, *Illustrations of Early English Popular Literature* (London, 1863; reissued, New York, 1966).
*The Costlie Whore, A Comicall Historie* (London, 1633).
Dekker, Thomas, *The Dead Tearme Or, Westminsters Complaint for long Vacations and Short Termes* (London, 1608).
*The Dramatic Works of Thomas Dekker*, ed. Fredson Bowers, 4 vols (Cambridge, 1953–61).
*Thomas Dekker's A Knights Conjuring (1607): A Critical Edition*, ed. Larry M. Robbins (The Hague, 1974).
*The Non-Dramatic Works of Thomas Dekker*, ed. A. B. Grosart, 5 vols (London, 1885; reissued, New York, 1963).
*The Plague Pamphlets of Thomas Dekker*, ed. F. P. Wilson (Oxford, 1925).
*Thomas Dekker, Selected Writings*, ed. E. D. Pendry, The Stratford-Upon-Avon Library no. 4 (London, 1967).
*Four Tudor Comedies*, ed. William Tydeman (Harmondsworth, 1984).
*The Life and Complete Works in Prose and Verse of Robert Greene*, ed. A. B. Grosart, The Huth Library, 15 vols (London, 1881–6).
*Greevous Grones for the Poore* (London, 1621).
*Grobianus; or, The compleat booby, an ironical poem. In three books. Done into English from the original Latin of Frederick Dedekindus by Roger Bull* (London, Printed for T. Cooper 1739).
Hall, Thomas, *The Loathsomnesse of Long Haire: or A Treatise Wherein you have the Question stated, many Arguments against it produc'd, and most materiall Arguments for it repelled and answer'd, with the concurrent judgement of Divines both old and new against it* (London, 1653).
*Hæc-Vir: Or The Womanish-Man: Being and Answer to a late Booke intituled Hic-Mulier* (London, 1620).
*The Works of Gabriel Harvey*, ed. A. B. Grosart, The Huth Library, 3 vols (London, 1869).
*Hic Mulier: Or, The Man-Woman: Being a Medicine to cure the Coltish Disease of the Staggers in the Masculine–Feminines of our Times* (London, 1620).

239

Holzknecht, Karl J. (ed.), *Sixteenth-Century English Prose*, The Harper English Literature Series (New York, 1954).

Howell, James, *Londonopolis* (London, 1657).

*John Howes MS., 1582*, intro. and notes by William Lempriere (London, 1904).

*Ben Jonson*, ed. Ian Donaldson (Oxford and New York, 1985).

Jonson, Ben, *The Alchemist*, ed. Douglas Brown (London, 1966).

*Bartholomew Fair by Ben Jonson*, ed. C. S. Alden, Yale Studies in English, XXV (New York, 1904).

Jonson, Ben, *Bartholomew Fair*, ed. E. A. Horsman, The Revels Plays (Manchester, 1960).

Jorden, Edward, *A Briefe Discourse of a Disease Called the Suffocation of the Mother* (London, 1603., STC 14790, G3).

Judges, A. V. (ed.) *The Elizabethan Underworld: A Collection of Tudor and Early Stuart Tracts and Ballads* (London, 1930).

Knappen, M. M. (ed.) *Two Elizabethan Puritan Diaries by Richard Rogers and Samuel Ward* (Chicago, 1933).

*The Ladies Remonstrance; or A Declaration of the Waiting-Gentlewomen, Chamber-Maids, and Servant-Maids, of the City of London ....* (London, 1659).

Lenton, Francis, *Characterismi: Or, Lentons Leasures* (London, 1631).

*The Life and Pranks of Long Meg of Westminster* (London, 1582).

Lupton, Donald, *London and the Countrey Carbonadoed and Quartred into Severall Characters* (London, 1622).

Markham, Garvis, *The Famous Whore, or Noble Curtizan* (London, 1609).

Marlowe, Christopher, *Tamburlaine the Great*, ed. J. S. Cunningham (The Revels Plays. Manchester, 1981).

*The Works of Thomas Middleton*, ed. A. H. Bullen, 8 vols (London, 1885–6).

*Middleton, Thomas, and Thomas Dekker, The Roaring Girl*, ed. Andor Gomme (London, 1976).

*Thomas Nashe: The Unfortunate Traveller and other Works*, ed. J. B. Steane (London, 1987; 1st publ. 1972).

*Pasquils Jests: With The Merriments of Mother Bunch, Wittie, pleasant, and delightfull* (London, 1629).

*Pasquils Palinoda and His Progress to the Taverne* (London, 1629).

*Thomas Platters's Travels in England, 1599*, trans. Clare Williams (London, 1937).

Prynne, William, *The Unlovelinesse of Lovelockes*, The English Experience, its Record in Early Printed Books Published in Facsimile; no. 825, photoprint of 1628 edition, S.T.C. no. 20477 (Amsterdam: Norwood, 1976).

*The Return of the Knight of the Poste from Hell, with the Divels aunswere to the Supplication of Pierce Pennilesse, withsome Relation of the Last Treasons* (London, 1606).

Salgado, Gamini (ed.) *Coney Catchers and Bawdy Baskets: An Anthology of Elizabethan Low Life* (Harmondsworth, 1972).

Stow, John, *A Survey of London*, ed. Charles Lethbridge Kingsford, repr. from the text of 1603, 1st publ. 1908, 2 vols (Oxford, 1971).

Taylor, John, *8 Satyres of Characterisation* (London, n. d.).

Tourneur, Cyril, *The Revenger's Tragedy*, ed. Brian Gibbons (London, 1985; 1st publ. 1967).

White, Thomas, *A Sermon Preached at Pawles Crosse on Sunday the Thirde of November 1577 in Time of Plague* (London, 1578).

Morgan, E. S. (ed.), *The Diary of Michael Wigglesworth 1653–1657* (New York, 1965).

*Wits Bedlam, Where is had, Whipping-cheer, to cure the Mad* (London, 1617).

*Witts Tearme: a Satyre on London Characters* (London, 1610).


SECONDARY READING


Agnew, Jean-Christophe, *Worlds Apart: The Market and the Theater in Anglo-American Thought 1550–1750* (Cambridge, 1986).

Akrigg, G. P. V., *Jacobean Pageant or The Court of King James I* (Cambridge, 1962).

Allderidge, Patricia, 'Management and Mismanagement at Bedlam 1547–1633', in Charles Webster (ed.) *Health, Medicine and Mortality in the Sixteenth Century* (Cambridge, 1986).

Althusser, Louis, 'The "Piccolo Theatre": Bertolazzi and Brecht: notes on a Materialist Theatre', in *For Marx*, trans. Ben Brewster, pp. 131–51 (New York, 1969).

Anderson, Perry, *Lineages of the Absolutist State* (London, 1974).

Andrews, Kenneth R., *Trade, Plunder and Settlement: Maritime enterprise and the genesis of the British Empire, 1480–1630* (Cambridge, 1984).

Armstrong, Nancy, and Leonard Tennenhouse (eds), *The Ideology of Conduct: Essays on Literature and the History of Sexuality* (New York, 1987).

Archer, Ian W., *The Pursuit of Stability: Social Relations in Elizabethan London* (Cambridge and New York, 1991).

Ashton, Robert, *The City and the Court, 1603–1643* (Cambridge and New York, 1979).

——, *The English Civil War: Conservatism and Revolution 1603–1649* (London, 1978).

——, 'Popular Entertainment and Social Control In Later Elizabethan and Early Stuart London', *London Journal*, vol. 9, no. 1 (1983) pp. 3–19.

Atkinson, David, 'Marriage Under Compulsion in English Renaissance Drama', *English Studies*, vol. 6 (1986) 483–504.

Aydelotte, F. R., *Elizabethan Rogues and Vagabonds*, Oxford Historical and Literary Studies, vol. I (Oxford, 1913).

Baker-Smith, Dominic and C. C. Barfoot (eds), *Between Dream and Nature: Essays on Utopia and Dystopia*, DQR Studies in Literature, no. 2 (Amsterdam, 1987).

Bakhtin, Mikhail, *Rabelais and His World*, trans. Hélène Iswolsky (Boston, 1968; Indiana, 1984).

Barker, Francis, *The Tremulous Private Body: Essays on Subjection* (London and New York, 1984).

Barroll, J. Leeds, *Politics, Plague, and Shakespeare's Theater: The Stuart Years* (Ithaca and London, 1991).

Barton, Anne, 'London Comedy and the Ethos of the City', *The London Journal*, vol. 4, no. 2 (1978) pp. 158–80.

Bauman, Zygmunt, *Legislators and Interpreters: On Modernity, Post-modernity, and Intellectuals* (Ithaca, 1987).

Baumeister, Roy, *Identity: Cultural Change and the Struggle for Self* (New York, 1986).

Beaven, Revd Alfred B., *The Aldermen of the City of London, Henry VIII–1908*, 2 vols (London, 1908–13).

Beier, A. L., *Masterless Men: The Vagrancy Problem in England 1560–1640* (London and New York, 1985).

——, 'Vagrants and Social Order in Elizabethan England', *Past & Present*, no. 64 (August 1974) pp. 3–29.

——, 'Social Problems in Elizabethan London', *Journal of Interdisciplinary History*, vol. 9 (1978–9) pp. 203–22.

—— and Roger Finlay (eds), *London 1500–1700: The Making of the Metropolis* (London and New York, 1986).

Berger, John, *A Seventh Man: Migrant Workers in Europe* photos by Jean Mohr (New York, 1975).

——, *Ways of Seeing* (London, 1972).

Bergeron, David, *English Civic Pageantry 1558–1642* (London and Columbia SC, 1971).

Berlin, Normand, 'Thomas Dekker: A Partial Reappraisal', *Studies in English Literature 1500–1900*, vol. 6, no. 2 (Spring 1966) pp. 263–77.

——, *The Base String; the Underworld in Elizabethan Drama* (Rutherford, 1968).

Bernard, G. W., 'The Church of England c. 1529–c. 1642', *History: the Journal of the Historical Association*, vol. 75, no. 244 (June 1990) pp. 183–207.

Best, Joel, 'Careers in Brothel Prostitution: St. Paul, 1853–1883', *Journal of Interdisciplinary History*, vol. 12, no. 4 (Spring 1982) pp. 597–610.

Boulton, Jeremy, *Neighbourhood and Society: a London Suburb in the Seventeenth Century* (Cambridge and New York, 1987).

Bowen, Thomas, *An Historical Account of the Origen, Progress, and Present State of Bethlehem Hospital, Founded by Henry the Eighth, for the Cure of Lunatics, and Enlarged by Subsequent Benefactors, for the Reception and Maintenance of Incurables* (London, 1783).

Bouwsma, William J., 'Anxiety and the Formation of Early Modern Culture', in Barbara C. Malament (ed.), *After the Reformation: Essays in Honour of J. H. Hexter* (Philadelphia, 1980) pp. 215–46.

——, 'Intellectual History in the 1980s; From History of Ideas to History of Meaning', *Journal of Interdisciplinary History*, vol. 12, no. 2 (Autumn 1981) pp. 279–91.

Braudel, Fernand, *The Structures of Everyday Life: The Limits of the Possible*, vol. I of *Civilization Capitalism, 15th-18th Century*, 2 vols, revd trans by Siân Reynolds (New York, 1981).

Brett-James, Norman G., *The Growth of Stuart London* (London, 1935).

Breward, Christopher, *The Culture of Fashion: A New History of Fashionable Dress* (Manchester, 1995).

Bristol, Michael D., *Carnival and Theatre: Plebeian Culture and the Structure of Authority in Renaissance England* (New York, 1985).

Brustein, Robert, '"The Monstrous Regiment of Women"; Sources for the Satiric View of the Court Lady in English Drama', in G. R. Hibbard (ed.), *Renaissance and Modern Essays* (London, 1966).

Brundage, James A., 'Prostitution in Medieval Canon Law', *Signs: Journal of Women in Culture and Society*, vol. 1, no. 4 (1976) pp. 825–45.

Burford, E. J., *Wits, Wenchers and Wantons: London's Low Life: Covent Garden in the Eighteenth Century* (London, 1986).

——, *Bawds and Lodgings: A History of the Bankside Brothels, c. 100–1675* (London, 1976).

——, *The Orryble Synne: A Look at Lechery from Roman to Cromwellian Times* (London, 1973).

Burke, Peter, *Popular Culture in Early Modern Europe* (New York, 1978).

Butler, Martin, *Theatre and Crisis, 1632–1642* (Cambridge and New York, 1984).

Carlson, Susan, '"Fond fathers" and Sweet Sisters: Alternative Sexualities' in *Measure for Measure, Essays in Literature*, vol. 16, no. 1 (Spring 1989) pp. 13–32.

Champion, Larry, 'The Malcontent and the Shape of Elizabethan–Jacobean Comedy', *Studies in English Literature 1500–1900*, no. 25 (1986) 361–79.

——, *Thomas Dekker and the Traditions of English Drama*, American University Studies, Series IV, English Language and Literature, vol. 27 (New York, 1985).

Chandler, Frank Wadleigh, *The Literature of Roguery*, 2 vols (New York, 1958).

Cheney, Patrick, 'Moll Cutpurse as Hermaphrodite in Dekker and Middleton's *The Roaring Girl*', *Renaissance and Reformation*, new series, vol. 7, no. 2 (May 1983) pp. 120–35.

Clark, Alice, *Working Life of Women in the Seventeenth Century* (New York, 1968).

Clark, Fiona, *Hats* (London and New York, 1982).

Clark, Peter, and Paul Slack (eds), *Crisis and Order in English Towns, 1500–1700: Essays in Urban History* (London, 1972).

Clark, Sandra, 'Hic Mulier, Haec Vir, and the Controversy over Masculine Women', *Studies in Philology*, vol. 82, no. 2 (Spring pp. 1985) 157–83.

——, *The Elizabethan Pamphleteers: Popular Moralist Pamphlets, 1580–1640* (Rutherford, 1983).

Clay, C. G. A., *Economic Expansion and Social Change: England 1500–1700* (Cambridge and New York, 1984).

Clode, Charles, M. (ed.), *The Early History of the Guild of Merchants Taylors*, 2 vols: I, *The History*, II, *The Lives* (London, 1888).

Collins, Stephen L., *From Divine Cosmos to Sovereign State: An Intellectual History of Consciousness and the Idea of Order in Renaissance England* (New York, 1989).

Collinson, Patrick, *The Puritan Character: Polemics and Polarities in Early Seventeenth-Century English Culture*, a paper presented at a Clark Library Seminar, 25 April 1987 (Los Angeles, 1989).

Comensoli, Viviana, 'Play-making, Domestic Conduct, and the Multiple Plot in The Roaring Girl', *Studies in English Literature 1500–1900*, vol. 27, no. 2 (Spring 1987) pp. 249–66.

——, 'Refashioning the Marriage Code: The Patient Grissel of Dekker, Chettle and Haughton', *Renaissance and Reformation*, new series, vol. 13, no. 2 (Summer 1989) pp. 199–214.

Conover, James Harrington, *Thomas Dekker, an Analysis of Dramatic Structure* (The Hague, 1969).

Copeland, A. J., *Bridewell Royal Hospital* (London, 1888).

Corson, Richard, *Fashions in Hair; The First Five Thousand Years* (New York, 1969; 1st published 1965).

Cruickshank, C. G., *Elizabeth's Army* (London, 1946).

Cumming, Valerie, *A Visual History of Costume: The Seventeenth Century* (New York, 1983).

Cressy, David, 'Foucault, Stone, Shakespeare and Social History', *English Literary Renaissance*, vol. 21, no. 2 (Spring 1991) pp. 121–33.

Crewe, Jonathan V., *Unredeemed Rhetoric: Thomas Nashe and the Scandal of Authorship* (Baltimore and London, 1982).

Darnton, Robert, *The Great Cat Massacre and Other Episodes in French Cultural History* (New York, 1985).

Davidson, Clifford, C. J. Giankaris and John H. Stroupe (eds), *Drama in the Renaissance: Comparative and Critical Essays*, preface by C. J. Giankaris (New York, 1986).

Davis, Mike, *City of Quartz: Evacuating the Future in Los Angeles* (London:, 1990; New York, 1992).

de Bruyn, Jan, 'The Ideal Lady and the Rise of Feminism in Seventeenth Century England', *Mosaic*, 17, part I (Winter 1984) pp. 19–28.

Dekker, Rudolfe M., and Lotte C. van de Pol, *The Tradition of Female Transvestism in Early Modern Europe*, trans. Judy Macure and Lotte C. van de Pol, foreword by Peter Burke (Basingstoke, 1989).

Deloney, Thomas, *The Works of Thomas Deloney*, ed. Francis Oscar Mann (Oxford, 1912).

de Marly, Diana, *Fashion for Men: An Illustrated History* (New York, 1985).

de Welles, Theodore, 'Sex and Sexual Attitudes in Seventeenth-Century England: The Evidence from Puritan Diaries', *Renaissance and Reformation*, vol. 24, no. 1 (Winter 1988) pp. 45–64.

Dobin, Howard, *Merlin's Disciples: Prophecy, Poetry, and Power in Renaissance England* (Stanford, 1990).

Dollimore, Jonathan, *Radical Tragedy: Religion, Ideology and Power in the Drama of Shakespeare and his Contemporaries* (Brighton, 1984).

——, *Sexual Dissidence: Augustine to Wilde, Freud to Foucault* (Oxford, 1991).

——, 'Subjectivity, Sexuality, and Transgression: The Jacobean Connection', *Renaissance Drama*, new series, vol. 17 (1986) pp. 53–81.

——, 'Shakespeare, Cultural Materialism, Feminism and Marxist Humanism', *New Literary History*, vol. 21, no. 3 (Spring 1990) pp. 471–93.

——, 'The Dominant and the Deviant: a Violent Dialectic', *Critical Quarterly*, vol. 28, nos 1 and 2 (1986) pp. 179–92.

—— and Alan Sinfield (eds), *Political Shakespeare: New Essays in Cultural Materialism* (Ithaca, 1985).

Douglas, Mary, *Purity and Danger: An Analysis of the Concepts of Pollution and Taboo* (London and Boston, 1984).

Dubrow, Heather and Richard Strier (eds), *The Historical Renaissance: New Essays on Tudor and Stuart Literature and Culture* (Chicago, 1988).

Eagleton, Terry, *Ideology: An Introduction* (London and New York, 1991).

Earle, Peter, 'The Female Labour Market in London in the Late Seventeenth and Eighteenth Centuries', *Economic History Review*, second series, vol. 42, no. 3 (1989) pp. 328–53.

——, *The Making of the English Middle Class: Business, Society, and Family Life in London, 1660–1730* (Berkeley, 1989).

Edwards, Christopher, *The London Theatre Guide 1576–1642* (London, 1979).

Elias, Norbert, *The Civilizing Process*, trans. Edmund Jephcott, 2 vols: I, *Power and Civility*; II, *The History of Manners* (New York, 1978; 1st publ. 1939).

Elliott, V. B., 'Single Women in the London Marriage Market: Age, Status and Mobility 1598–1619', in R. B. Outhwaite (ed.), *Marriage and Society: Studies in the Social History of Marriage* (New York, 1981).

Ellis-Fermor, Una Mary, *The Jacobean Drama: An Interpretation*, with additions by M. Cardwell, 4th edn (London, 1973).

Feather, John, *A History of British Publishing* (London and New York, 1988).

Ferguson, Margaret J., Maureen Quilligan and Nancy J. Vickers (eds), *Rewriting the Renaissance: The Discourses of Sexual Difference in Early Modern Europe* (Chicago, 1986).

Finlay, Roger, *Population and Metropolis: The Demography of London, 1580–1650* (Cambridge and New York, 1981).

Fletcher, Anthony, 'The First Century of Protestantism and the Growth of National Identity', in Stuart Mews (ed.), *Religion and National Identity* (Oxford 1982) pp. 309–17.

—— and John Stevenson, *Order and Disorder in Early Modern England* (Cambridge and New York, 1985).

Foucault, Michel, *Discipline and Punish: The Birth of the Prison*, trans. Alan Sheridan (New York, 1977; 1st US edn).

——, *The History of Sexuality*, trans. Robert Hurley. (New York, 1978).

——, *Madness and Civilization: A History of Insanity in the Age of Reason*, trans. Richard Howard (New York, 1965).

Gadd, Derek and Alan Thompson, 'Bridewell Palace', *London Archæologist*, vol. 3, no. 10 (Spring 1979) pp. 255–60.

Galford, Ellen, *Moll Cutpurse, Her True History* (Edinburgh, 1984).

Gartenberg, Patricia, 'An Elizabethan Wonder Woman: The Life and Fortunes of Long Meg of Westminster', *Journal of Popular Culture*, vol. 17, no. 3 (Winter 1983) pp. 49–59.

Gasper, Julia, *The Dragon and the Dove: The Plays of Thomas Dekker* (Oxford and New York, 1990).

Gentili, Vanna, 'Madmen and Fools are a Staple Commodity: On Madness as a System in Elizabethan and Jacobean Plays', *Cahiers Elisabethains*, no. 34 (October 1988) pp. 11–24.

George, Margaret, 'From "Goodwife" to "Mistress": The Transformation of the Female in Bourgeois Culture', *Science and Society*, vol. 37 (1973) pp. 152–77.

Gibbons, Brian, *Jacobean City Comedy*, 2nd edn (London, 1980).

Gilbert, Sandra M. and Susan Gubar, *The Madwoman in the Attic: The Woman Writer and the Nineteenth-Century* (New Haven, 1979).

Goldberg, Jonathan, *James I and the Politics of Literature: Jonson, Donne and their Contemporaries* (Baltimore, 1983).

Goldberg, P. J. P., 'Women in Fifteenth-Century Town Life', in John A. F. Thomson (ed.), *Towns and Townspeople in the Fifteenth Century* (Sutton, 1988).

Gottfried, Robert S., *The Black Death: Natural and Human Disaster in Medieval Europe* (New York, 1983).

Gramsci, Antonio, *A Gramsci Reader; Selected Writings 1916–1935*, ed. David Forgacs (London, 1988).
——, *Antonio Gramsci, Selections from the Prison Notebooks*, ed. Quintin Hoare and Geoffrey Nowell Smith (New York, 1971).
Greenblatt, Stephen, *Renaissance Self-fashioning: From More to Shakespeare* (Chicago, 1980).
—— (ed.), *The Power of Forms in the English Renaissance* (Norman, 1982).
Gregg, K. L., *Thomas Dekker; a Study in Economic and Social Backgrounds* (Folcroft, 1974, repr. of 1924 edn).
Griswold, Wendy, *Renaissance Revivals: City Comedy and Revenge Tragedy in the London Theatre, 1576–1980* (Chicago, 1986).
Gurr, Andrew, *Playgoing in Shakespeare's London* (Cambridge and New York, 1987).
——, *The Shakespearean Stage, 1574–1642* (Cambridge, 1970).
Hale, J. R., *War and Society in Renaissance Europe 1450–1620* (New York, 1985).
Hamilton, Roberta, *The Liberation of Women: A Study of Patriarchy and Capitalism* (London and Boston, 1978).
Harvey, Gabriel, *The Works of Gabriel Harvey*, ed. Alexander B. Grosart, 3 vols (London, 1884–5).
Haselkorn, Anne M., *Prostitution in Elizabethan and Jacobean Comedy* (Troy, 1983).
Hazlitt, William, *The Complete Works of William Hazlitt*, ed. P. P. Howe, after the edition of A. R. Waller and Arnold Glover, 21 vols, VI, 'Lecture III, On Marston, Chapman, Deckar, and Webster', pp. 223–248 (New York 1930–67).
Heinemann, Margot, *Puritanism and Theatre: Thomas Middleton and Opposition Drama Under the Early Stuarts* (Cambridge and New York, 1980).
Hendricks, Margo, 'A Painter's Eye: Gender and Middleton and Dekker's The Roaring Girl', *Women's Studies*, vol. 18 (1990) pp. 191–203.
Henke, James T., *Courtesans and Cuckolds: A Glossary of Renaissance Dramatic Bawdy exclusive of Shakespeare* (New York, 1979).
Henriques, Fernando, *Prostitution in Europe and the Americas*, Vol. II of *Prostitution and Society* (New York, 1965).
Hill, Christopher, *The Century of Revolution, 1603–1714*, 2nd edn (Wokingham, 1980).
——, *Intellectual Origins of the English Revolution* (Oxford, 1965).
——, *Society and Puritanism in Pre-Revolutionary England* (Harmondsworth, 1964).
Horwich, Richard, 'Wives, Courtesans, and the Economics of Love in Jacobean Comedy', in Clifford Davidson, C. J. Giankaris, John H. Stroupe, *Drama in the Renaissance*, pp. 255–73 (New York, 1986).
Howard, Jean E., 'Crossdressing, the Theatre, and Gender Struggle in Early Modern England', *Shakespeare Quarterly*, vol. 39, no. 4 (Winter 1988) pp. 418–40.
Howell, Martha C., 'A Feminist Historian Looks at the New Historicism: What's So Historical About It?', *Women's Studies*, vol. 19 (1991) pp. 139–47.
——, *Women, Production, and Patriarchy in Late Medieval Cities* (Chicago, 1986).
Hoy, Cyrus, *Introduction, Notes, and Commentaries to texts in 'The Dramatic Works of Thomas Dekker' Edited by Fredson Bowers*, 4 vols (Cambridge; London; New York, 1980).

Hughes, Geoffrey, *Swearing: A Social History of Foul Language, Oaths, and Profanity in English* (Oxford and Cambridge, Mass., 1991).
——, *Words in Time: A Social History of the English Vocabulary* (New York, 1988).
Hughes, Paul L. and James F. Larkin (eds), *Tudor Royal Proclamations, Volume III The Later Tudors 1588–1603* (New Haven and London, 1969).
Hunt, Mary Leland, *Thomas Dekker, a Study* (New York, 1911).
Hutson, Lorna, 'The Displacement of the Market in Jacobean City Comedy', *The London Journal*, vol. 14, no. 1 (1989) pp. 3–16.
——, *Thomas Nashe in Context* (Oxford and New York, 1989).
Jardine, Lisa, *Still Harping on Daughters: Women and Drama in the Age of Shakespeare* (Brighton, 1983).
Jones, Emrys, 'London in the Early Seventeenth Century: An Ecological Approach', *The London Journal*, vol. 6, no. 2 (1980) pp. 123–33.
Jones-Davies, Marie Thérèse, *Un Peintre de la Vie Londonienne: Thomas Dekker circa 1572–1632*, 2 vols (Paris, 1958).
Kahn, Coppélia, *Man's Estate: Masculine Identity in Shakespeare* (Berkeley, 1981).
——, 'Whores and Wives in Jacobean Drama', in Dorothea Kehler and Susan Baker (eds), *In Another Country: Feminist Perspectives on Renaissance Drama* (London, 1991) pp. 246–60.
Karras, Ruth Mazzeo, 'The Regulation of Brothels in Later Medieval England', *Signs: Journal of Women in Culture and Society*, vol. 14, no. 2 (1989) pp. 399–433.
Kastan, David Scott, 'Workshop and/as Playhouse: Comedy and Commerce in The Shoemaker's Holiday', *Studies in Philology*, vol. 84, no. 3 (Summer 1987) pp. 324–37.
Kawachi, Yoshiko, *Calendar of English Renaissance Drama, 1558–1642* (New York, 1986).
Kehler, Dorothea and Susan Baker (eds), *In Another Country: Feminist Perspectives on Renaissance Drama* (London, 1991).
Knights, L. C., *Drama and Society in the Age of Jonson* (London, 1968).
LaCapra, Dominick, *History and Criticism* (Ithaca, 1985).
Lang, R. G., 'Social Origins and Social Aspirations of Jacobean London Merchants', *Economic History Review*, second series, vol. 27, no. 1 (1974) pp. 28–47.
Larkin, James F. and Paul L. Hughes (eds), *Royal Proclamations of King James I, 1603–1625* (New Haven and London, 1969).
Leder, Drew, *The Absent Body* (Chicago, 1990).
Leggatt, Alexander, *Citizen Comedy in the Age of Shakespeare* (Toronto and Buffalo, 1973).
——, *English Drama: Shakespeare to the Restoration, 1590–1660* (London and New York, 1988).
Leinwand, Theodore, 'Negotiation and New Historicism', *Papers of the Modern Language Association*, vol. 105, no. 3 May (1990) pp. 477–91.
——, *The City Staged: Jacobean Comedy, 1603–1613* (Madison, 1986).
Levine, Laura, 'Men in Women's Clothing: Anti-theatricality and Effeminization from 1579 to 1642', *Criticism*, vol. 28, no. 2 (Spring 1986) pp. 121–43.

248 *Bibliography*

Liu, Alan, 'The Power of Formalism: The New Historicism', *English Literary History*, vol. 56, no. 4 (Winter 1989) pp. 721–72.

Lucas, Valerie R., 'Hic Mulier: The Female Transvestite in Early Modern England', *Renaissance and Reformation*, vol. 24, no. 1 (Winter 1988) pp. 65–84.

MacCabe, Colin, 'Abusing Self and Others: Puritan Accounts of the Shakespearean Stage', *Critical Quarterly*, vol. 30, no. 3 (Autumn 1988) pp. 3–17.

MacDonald, Michael, 'Popular Beliefs About Mental Disorder in Early Modern England', im *Heilberufe und Kranke im 17. und 18. Jahrhundert Die Quellen – und Forschungssituation*, Müstersche Beiträge zur Geschichte und Theorie der Medizin, nr. 18, herausgegeben von K. E. Rothschuh und R. Toellner, pp. 148–73 (Münster, 1982).

——, *Mystical Bedlam: Madness, Anxiety, and Healing in Seventeenth-Century England* (Cambridge and New York, 1981).

——, *Sleepless Souls: Suicide in Early Modern England* (Oxford and New York, 1990).

Macfarlane, Alan, *The Origins of English Individualism: The Family, Property, and Social Transition* (New York, 1979).

Maclean, Ian, *The Renaissance Notion of Woman: A Study in the Fortunes of Scholasticism and Medical Science in European Intellectual Life* (Cambridge and New York, 1980).

Malamet, Barbara (ed.), *After the Reformation: Essays in Honour of J. H. Hexter* (Philadelphia and Manchester, 1980).

Manley, Lawrence, 'From Matron to Monster: Tudor–Stuart London and the Languages of Urban Description', in Heather Dubrow and Richard Strier (eds) *The Historical Renaissance* (Chicago, 1988).

—— (ed.), *London in the Age of Shakespeare: An Anthology* (London, 1986).

Manning, Roger B., *Village Revolts: Social and Popular Disturbances in England, 1509–1640* (Oxford and New York, 1988).

Manuel, Frank E. and Fritzie P. Manuel, *Utopian Thought in the Western World* (Cambridge, 1979).

Marcus, Leah, *Puzzling Shakespeare: Local Reading and its Discontents* (Berkeley, 1988).

Marcuse, Herbert, *The Aesthetic Dimension: Towards a Critique of Marxist Aesthetics* (Boston, 1978).

Marotti, Arthur F., '"Love is Not Love": Elizabethan Sonnet Sequences and the Social Order', in *English Literary History*, vol. 49, no. 2 (Summer 1982) pp. 396–428.

Martines, Lauro, *Society and History in English Renaissance Verse* (Oxford and New York, 1985).

Maus, Katherine Eisaman, 'Horns of a Dilemma: Jealousy, Gender, and Spectatorship in English Renaissance Drama', *English Literary History*, vol. 54, no. 3 (Fall 1987) pp. 561–83.

McKerrow, E. B. (ed.) *Analytical Index to the Series of Records known as the Remembrancia preserved among the Archives of the City of London A.D. 1579–1664* (London, 1878).

McLuskie, Kate, *Renaissance Dramatists* (Atlantic Highlands, 1989).

McMullan, John L., *The Canting Crew: London's Criminal Underworld, 1550–1700* (New Brunswick, 1984).

Midelfort, H. C. Erik, 'Madness and Civilization in Early Modern Europe: A Reappraisal of Michel Foucault', in Barbara C. Malament (ed.), *After the Reformation, Essays in Honour of J. H. Hexter* (Philadelphia and Manchester, 1980).

Miles, Rosalind, *The Problem of Measure for Measure: A Historical Investigation* (New York, 1976).

Miller, Jo E., 'Women and the Market in The Roaring Girl', *Renaissance and Reformation*, vol. 26, no. 1 (1990) pp. 11–23.

Morse, David, *England's Time of Crisis: From Shakespeare to Milton: A Cultural History* (Basingstoke, 1989).

Mullaney, Steven, *The Place of the Stage: License, Play, and Power in Renaissance England* (Chicago, 1988).

Mumford, Lewis, *The City in History: Its Origins, its Transformations, and its Prospects* (New York, 1961).

Mylne, Revd R. S., 'Old Bridewell', *Transactions of the London and Middlesex Archæological Society*, vol. 2, part 1 (1910) pp. 84–110.

Neely, Carol Thomas, '"Documents of Madness": Reading Madness and Gender in Shakespeare's Tragedies and Early Modern Culture', in *Shakespeare Quarterly*, vol. 42, no. 3 (Fall 1991) pp. 315–39.

Newman, Karen, 'City Talk: Women and Commodification in Jonson's Epicoene', *English Literary History*, vol. 56, no. 3 (Fall 1989) pp. 503–19.

Norbrook, David, 'Life and Death of Renaissance Man', *Raritan*, vol. 8, no. 4 (Spring 1989) pp. 89–111.

O'Conell, Laura Stevenson, 'The Elizabethan Bourgeois Hero-Tale: Aspects of an Adolescent Consciousness', in Barbara C. Malament (ed.), *After the Reformation Essays in Honour of J. H. Hexter* (Philadelphia and Manchester, 1980).

O'Donoghue, Edward Geoffrey, *The Story of Bethlehem Hospital From its Foundation in 1247* (London, 1914).

——, *Bridewell Hospital, Palace, Prisons, Schools: From the Earliest Times to the End of the Reign of Elizabeth* (London, 1923).

——, *Bridewell Hospital, Palace, Prison, Schools: From the Death of Elizabeth to Modern Times 1603–1929* (London, 1929).

Otis, Leah Lydia, *Prostitution in Medieval Society: The History of an Urban Institution in Languedoc* (Chicago, 1985).

Owen, D. D. R., *The Vision of Hell: Infernal Journeys in Medieval French Literature* (Edinburgh, 1970).

Pahl, R. E., *Divisions of Labour* (Oxford and New York, 1984).

Palmer, Alan and Veronica, *Who's Who in Shakespeare's England* (Brighton, 1981).

Parten, Anne, 'Masculine Adultery and Feminine Rejoinders in Shakespeare, Dekker and Sharpham', *Mosaic*, vol. 17, part 1 (1984) pp. 9–18.

Paster, Gail Kern, *The Idea of the City in the Age of Shakespeare* (Athens, 1985).

——, 'Leaky Vessels: The Incontinent Women of City Comedy', *Renaissance Drama*, new series, vol. 18 (1987) pp. 43–67.

Patterson, Annabel, *Shakespeare and the Popular Voice* (Oxford and New York, 1989).

Pawling, Christopher, *Popular Fiction and Social Change* (New York, 1984).

Peake, Richard H., *The Stage Prostitute in the English Dramatic Tradition from 1558–1625*, PhD thesis (Athens, University of Georgia, 1966).

Pearl, Valerie, 'Social Policy in Early Modern London', in *History and Imagination: Essays in Honour of H. R. Trevor-Roper* (Oxford and New York, 1980).

——, 'Change and Stability in Seventeenth Century London', *The London Journal*, vol. 5, no. 1 (1979) pp. 3–34.

Pechter, Edward, 'The New Historicism and its Discontents: Politicizing Renaissance Drama', *Papers of the Modern Language Association*, vol. 102, no. 3 (May 1987) pp. 292–303.

Pelling, Margaret, 'Appearance and Reality: barber-surgeons, the body and disease', in A. L. Beier and Roger Finlay (eds), *London 1500–1700: The Making of the Metropolis* (London and New York, 1986) pp. 82–112.

Pendry, E. D., 'Thomas Dekker in the Magistrates Court', *English Literary Renaissance*, vol. 3 (1973) pp. 53–9.

——, *Elizabethan Prisons and Prison Scenes*, 2 vols (Salzburg, 1974).

Porter, Carolyn, 'History and Literature: "After the New Historicism"', *New Literary History*, vol. 21, no. 2 (Winter 1990) pp. 253–72.

Porter, Roy, *A Social History of Madness: The World Through the Eyes of the Insane* (New York, 1988, 1st US edn).

Price, George, *Thomas Dekker* (New York, 1969).

Quaife, G. R., *Wanton Wenches and Wayward Wives: Peasants and Illicit Sex in Early Seventeenth Century England* (New Brunswick, 1979).

Raban, Jonathan, *Soft City* (London, 1984).

Rappaport, Steven, *Worlds Within Worlds: Structures of Life in Sixteenth-Century London* (Cambridge and New York, 1989).

Reed, Robert Rentoul, *Bedlam on the Jacobean Stage* (New York, 1970).

Reid, Aileen and Maniura, Robert (eds) *Edward Alleyn: Elizabethan actor, Jacobean gentleman* (London, 1994).

Reynolds, Helen, *The Economics of Prostitution* (Springfield, 1986).

Rhodes, Neil, *Elizabethan Grotesque* (London and Boston, 1980).

Rhodes, Neil, 'Nashe, Rhetoric and Satire', in Clive Bloom (ed.), *Jacobean Poetry and Prose: Rhetoric, Representation, and the Popular Imagination* (New York, 1988).

Roll, Eric, *A History of Economic Thought* (London, 1973).

Roper, Lyndal, 'Discipline and Respectability: Prostitution and the Reformation in Augsburg', *History Workshop*, vol. 19 (1985) pp. 3–28.

Rosen, George, *Madness in Society: Chapters in the Historical Sociology of Mental Illness* (London, 1968).

Rose, Mary Beth, *The Expense of Spirit: Love and Sexuality in English Renaissance Drama* (Ithaca, 1988).

——, 'Women in Men's Clothing: Apparel and Social Stability in *The Roaring Girl*', in *English Literary Renaissance*, vol. 14, no. 3 (Autumn 1984) pp. 367–91.

Rosenthal, Margaret F., 'Veronica Franco's Terze Rime: the Venetian Courtesan's Defense', *Renaissance Quarterly*, vol. 17, no. 2 (Summer 1989) pp. 227–57.

Ross, Cheryl Lynn, 'The Plague of *The Alchemist*', *Renaissance Quarterly*, vol. 41, no. 3 (Autumn 1988) pp. 439–58.

——, *The Plague and the Figures of Power: Authority and Subversion in English Renaissance Drama*, PhD Dissertation. Stanford University, 1985.

Rosser, Gervase, 'London and Westminster: The Suburb in the Urban Economy in the Later Middle Ages', in John A. F. Thomson (ed.), *Towns and Townspeople in the Fifteenth Century* (Sutton, 1988).

Rossiaud, Jacques, *Medieval Prostitution*, trans. Lydia G. Cochrane (New York, 1988).

Russell, Conrad, 'Puritanism and Fashion 1570–1640', ch. 4, in *The Crisis of Parliaments: English History 1509–1660*, pp. 162–217 (Oxford, 1971).

Sales, Roger, *Christopher Marlowe* (New York, 1991).

Salgado, Gamini, *The Elizabethan Underworld* (London and Totowa, 1977).

Seaver, Paul S., *Wallington's World: A Puritan Artisan in Seventeenth-Century London* (Stanford, 1985).

Shapiro, Susan C., 'Sex, Gender, and Fashion in Medieval and Early Modern Britain', *Journal of Popular Culture*, vol. 20, no. 4 (Spring 1987) pp. 113–28.

Sharpe, J. A., *Crime in Early Modern England, 1550–1750* (London and New York, 1984).

Shaw, Philip, 'The Position of Thomas Dekker in Jacobean Prison Literature', *Papers of the Modern Language Association*, vol. 62 (1947) pp. 366–91.

Shepherd, Simon, *Amazons and Warrior Women: Varieties of Feminism in Seventeenth-Century Drama* (New York, 1981).

Shugg, Wallace, 'Prostitution in Shakespeare's London', *Shakespeare Studies*, vol. 10 (1977) pp. 291–313.

Sinfield, Alan, *Literature in Protestant England, 1560–1660* (London and Totowa, 1983).

Simmel, Georg, *The Philosophy of Money*, trans. Tom Bottomore and David Frisby (London and Boston, 1978).

Slade, Giles, 'The City as an Image of Social Dialogue in Jacobean Comedy', *Essays in Theatre*, vol. 8, no. 1 (November 1989) pp. 61–7.

Skultans, Vieda, *English Madness: Ideas on Insanity, 1580–1890* (London and Boston, 1979).

Slack, Paul *The Impact of Plague in Tudor and Stuart England* (London, Boston, Melbourne, 1985).

——, *Poverty and Policy in Tudor and Stuart England* (London and New York, 1988).

Slater, Victor L., 'The Lord Lieutenancy on the Eve of the Civil Wars: The Impressment of George Plowwright', *The Historical Journal*, vol. 29, no. 2 (1986) pp. 279–96.

Smith, Alan G. R., *The Emergence of a Nation State: The Commonwealth of England 1529–1660* (London and New York, 1984).

Smith, Steven R., 'London Apprentices as Seventeenth Century Adolescents', *Past and Present*, no. 61 (November 1973) pp. 149–61.

Sontag, Susan, *Illness as Metaphor* (New York, 1978).

Stachniewski, John, *The Persecutory Imagination: English Puritanism and the Literature of Religious Despair* (Oxford and New York, 1991).

Stallybrass, Peter and White, Allon, *The Politics and Poetics of Transgression* (Ithaca, 1986).

Stone, Lawrence, *Family, Sex and Marriage in England 1500–1800* (New York, 1977).

——, *The Crisis of the Aristocracy, 1558–1641*, abridged edition (London and New York, 1967).

Tawney, R. H., *Religion and the Rise of Capitalism* (London, 1926).

Taylor, Barry, *Vagrant Writing: Social and Semiotic Disorders in the English Renaissance* (Hemel Hempstead, 1991).

Tennenhouse, Leonard, *Power on Display: The Politics of Shakespeare's Genres* (New York, 1986).

Tennenhouse, Leonard, 'Representing Power: *Measure for Measure* in its Time', in Stephen Greenblatt (ed.), *The Power of Forms in the English Renaissance* (Norman, 1982) pp. 139–56.

Theweleit, Klaus, *Male Fantasies*, 2 vols: vol. I, *Women, Floods, Bodies, History*, translated by Stephen Conway in collaboration with Erica Carter and Chris Turner; vol. II, *Male Bodies: Psychoanalyzing the White Terror*, trans. Stephen Conway in collaboration with Erica Carter and Chris Turner (Minneapolis, 1987 and 1989).

Thomas, Keith, 'The Utopian Impulse in Seventeenth-Century England', in Dominic Baker-Smith and C. C. Barfoot (eds), *Between Dream and Nature: Essays on Utopia and Dystopia* DQR Studies in Literature 2, pp. 20–46 (Amsterdam, 1987).

Thomson, John A. F. (ed.), *Towns and Townspeople in the Fifteenth Century* (Gloucester, 1988).

Toews, John E., 'Intellectual History After the Linguistic Turn: The Autonomy of Meaning and the Irreducibility of Experience', *American Historical Review*, vol. 92, no. 4 (October 1987) pp. 879–907.

Tricomi, Albert H., *Anticourt Drama in England, 1603–1642* (Charlottesville, 1989).

Twigg, Graham, *The Black Death: a Biological Reappraisal* (London, 1984).

Tydeman, William, 'The Image of the City in English Renaissance Drama', *Essays and Studies*, new series, vol. 38 (1988) pp. 29–44.

Unwin, George, *The Gilds and Companies of London*, 2nd edn (London, 1925).

——, *Industrial Organization in the Sixteenth and Seventeenth Centuries* (Oxford, 1904).

Ure, Peter, 'Patient Madman and Honest Whore: the Middleton–Dekker Oxymoron', in R. M. Wilson (ed.), *Essays and Studies*, pp. 18–40 (London, 1966).

Veeser, H. Aram (ed.), *The New Historicism* (New York, 1989).

Venuti, Lawrence, *Our Halcyon Days: English Prerevolutionary Texts and Postmodern Culture* (Madison, 1989).

——, 'Transformations of City Comedy: A Symptomatic Reading', in Peggy A. Knapp (ed.), *Assays: Critical Approaches to Medieval and Renaissance Texts*, vol. 3 (Pittsburgh, 1985) pp. 99–134.

Volosinov, V. N., *Marxism and the Philosophy of Language*, trans. Latislav Matejka and I. R. Titunik (Cambridge, Mass. and London, 1973).

Waagé, Frederick O., *Thomas Dekker's Pamphlets, 1603–1609, and Jacobean Literature* (Salzburg, 1977).

——, 'Meg and Moll: Two Renaissance London Heroines', *Journal of Popular Culture*, vol. 20, no. 1 (Summer 1986) pp. 105–117.

Walker, D. P., *The Decline of Hell; Seventeenth-Century Discussions of Eternal Torment* (Chicago, London, Toronto, 1964).

Weber, Max, *The Protestant Ethic and the Spirit of Capitalism*, trans. Talcott Parsons (New York, 1958).

Webster, Charles (ed.), *Health, Medicine, and Mortality in the Sixteenth Century* (Cambridge and New York, 1979).

Wells, Susan, 'Jacobean City Comedy and the Ideology of the City', *English Literary History*, vol. 48 (1981) pp. 37–60.

White, Allon, *Carnival, Hysteria, and Writing* (Oxford, 1993).

Williams, Raymond, *The Country and the City* (London, 1973).

——, *Marxism and Literature* (Oxford and New York, 1977).

Wilson, Elizabeth, 'The Invisible Flâneur', *New Left Review*, no. 191 (Jan./Feb. 1992) pp. 90–110.

Wilson, John Dover, *Life in Shakespeare's England* (London, 1954).

Wiltenburg, Joy, 'Madness and Society in the Street Ballads of Early Modern England', *Journal of Popular Culture*, vol. 21, no. 4 (Spring 1988) pp. 101–27.

Womack, Peter, *Ben Jonson* (Oxford and New York, 1986).

Woodbridge, Linda, *Women in the English Renaissance: Literature and the Nature of Womankind, 1540 1620* (Urbana, 1984).

Louis B. Wright, *Middle-Class Culture in Elizabethan England* (Ithaca, 1935).

Wrigley, E. A., 'A Simple Model of London's Importance in Changing English Society and Economy 1650–1750', *Past and Present*, no. 37 (July 1967) pp. 44–70.

Yachnin, Paul, 'The Powerless Theater', *English Literary Renaissance*, vol. 21, no. 1 (Winter 1991) pp. 49–74.

# Index

absolutism, 44, 52, 150
Agnew, Jean-Christophe, 5, 50, 58
Alleyn, Edward, 115, 154, 156
Anglicanism, 142, 145
Archer, Ian W., 52, 54, 72, 73, 79, 82
Arminianism, 142–3, 167
Averell, William, 73

Bakhtin, Mikhail, 15, 31, 100, 102, 111–14
Barroll, Leeds, 160–2
Bedlam
    as asylum/institution, 10, 20–1, 30
    public scandal at, 27
    as site of metropolitan contention, 12, 20–2, 26, 28, 30–1, 33, 40, 46
    as social drama, 11, 22, 28–30, 32–3, 39, 42, 46, 51, 179
    see also madness; Bridewell
Beier, A. L., and Finlay, Roger, 1, 4
Bernard, G. W., 141–2
Blake, William, 158
body
    classical, 15, 33, 82, 110–15, 116
    diseased, 9, 77, 121
    disciplined, 77, 82, 114, 117, 183
    as encoder of urban anxiety, 15, 31–3, 57–8, 62, 68–75, 77–9, 103, 106
    in fashion, 15, 99, 102–3
    grotesque, 15, 32, 69, 86, 101–2, 105, 107–8, 119–21, 169–70, 196
    politic, 25, 26, 32, 36, 38, 85, 93, 101, 116, 113
Book of Common Prayer, 146
Breward, Christopher, 98–9, 101, 103–4, 106, 186
Bridewell
    as brothel, 26–7
    public scandal at, 25–6, 46
    as punitive institution, 2, 21, 24, 25, 28, 37, 73–4, 77

    as site of metropolitan contention, 10, 20–3, 28, 51–2
    as social drama, 23, 28, 36, 46, 52
    as workhouse, 10, 22–3
    see also Bedlam; prostitutes
brothels, 2, 27, 37–8, 52, 54, 57–8, 75, 82
Bankside, 3, 38, 57
Bunyan, John, 145
Burton, Robert, 145

Calvinism, 17, 141–55, 165, 167, 170, 174–8, 186, 189, 192–3
canting, 7, 13, 67, 88–90, 97
Castiglione, Baldassare, 115
Catholicism, 18–19, 21, 141–2, 167, 175–7, 179–80
Civil War, 117, 145
Charles I, 4, 142
Champion, Larry, 171–2
Chettle, Henry, 7
Clark, Sandra, 198
Collier, John Payne, 177
Collinson, Patrick, 17–18
conscription, 25–6
Corson, Richard, 122
Court, the
    as City's rival, 4, 10, 24, 26, 44–5, 48, 51, 108, 114, 127–8, 141, 197
    fashions of, 103, 105–6, 108–9, 122
    as object of satire, 11, 23, 48, 97, 138, 171, 174
    as part of metropolis, 1, 3–4, 34, 52
Cruickshank, C. G., 25

Day, John, 7
Darnton, Robert, 13
Dekker, Thomas
    Dekker his Dreame, 18, 182, 188–91
    The Guls Hornebooke, 15, 95, 98, 99, 100, 105–10, 118, 120–5, 127–8, 128, 134

254